PIKE

In Pursuit of *Esox lucius*

PIKE

In Pursuit of *Esox lucius*

·Martyn Page & Vic Bellars·

The Crowood Press

First published in 1990 by
The Crowood Press Ltd
Gipsy Lane, Swindon
Wiltshire SN2 6DQ

British Library Cataloguing in Publication Data

Page, Martyn
    Pike: in pursuit of Esox Lucius.
    1. Pike. Angling
    I. Title   II. Bellars, Vic
    799.1753

    ISBN 1 85223 068 1

Dedication
For Lynne and Lynne, our forbearing wives.

Acknowledgements
Line-drawings and colour painting by Vic Bellars. All black and white photographs
by Martyn Page except for those appearing on pages 66 (top), 154, 161, 164, 174,
175, 206, 213 (top), 235, 236, 239 (bottom), 244, 245, 246, 248, 249 (bottom) and
250 which are by Bert Rozemeijer and on pages 149, 150, 151, 260 and 261 which
are by John Stephenson. All colour photographs by Martyn Page and Vic Bellars
except for Plates 12, 13, 14, 21 and 27 which are courtesy of Bert Rozemeijer,
Plate 11 which is courtesy of Colin Dyson and Plate 24 which is courtesy of Max
Cottis.
    We wish to thank Ann and Claire for producing a model typescript. The credit is
theirs; any errors are ours.
    We particularly wish to thank those fine anglers and good companions Chris
Liebbrandt and Bert Rozemeijer for their valuable contributions to this book, on
lure fishing and piking in Dutch waters respectively.

Typeset by Inforum Typesetting, Portsmouth
Printed in Great Britain at The Bath Press

Contents

Foreword

What else can I call Vic Bellars? I have already dubbed him 'the Peter Pan of angling', and perhaps I was the one who christened him 'Vic the Rig'. There's not much left which is appropriate, except, perhaps, 'septuagenarian schoolboy'! He is one of the few pike fishing companions who happens to be older than I, but you would never know it if you saw us together. It's always Vic who grabs the oars and does all the work; it's always his brain which is still working overtime when mine has accepted the inevitability of defeat; it's always his enthusiasm which is still bubbling away long after mine has curdled.

Yes, 'septuagenarian schoolboy' will do nicely, I think. Most anglers of his age have lost all their boyish excitement, and would long ago have settled for one effective way of doing particular jobs. 'I've been fishing sixty years, my boy, and, believe me, this is the best way to . . .' You know the type, but it isn't Vic. He has moved with the times, searching relentlessly for better ways of doing things. In that he has succeeded, many times.

We fish together less often than I would like, but when we do there is always something fermenting away in the think-tank. The last time it was trolling with a deadbait with its nose stuffed into a purple muppet. We all laughed – until he caught on it. On the same trip it was 'attractor crimps' – coloured red to grab the attention of a passing pike. The time before it was the deepwater pin and a wonderful new deadbait wobbling hook, of which he will not wish to be reminded. But I will anyway.

We were in Holland at the time, and for several days Bert Rozemeijer and I had been regaled with the case for this wonderful prototype. It seemed almost inevitable that he should hook the first pike, a goodly fish which promptly broke the hook. I finger-tested the remaining supply, and three-quarters of them broke. The hook is now better tempered, and brazed where Vic had vainly insisted that it should be, but at the time he suffered a merciless ribbing. With good grace, I might add. He laughed as loud and as long as we did. Fishing with Vic is primarily what it should be – fun. But always one learns something.

Martyn Page I have yet to fish with. All I know about his expertise as an angler I have gained from what Vic has had to say, and from reading his contributions to this book. My puny contribution to the history of Norfolk pike fishing ended when I moved north in 1968, some months before prymnesium wiped out most of the upper Thurne system. Even though I was no longer directly affected, it was a dagger blow to my pike-angling heart, and it was some years before I regained my enthusiasm. To this day I have not wet another pike line in the upper Thurne area, and was not even tempted when the thirties and forties started to show again. The character of Norfolk angling, and of many Norfolk anglers, had changed irrevocably. I preferred to live with the memories of happier times and, I suspect, of happier men.

I catch many more good pike now than I did when I was learning with and from such great anglers as Dennis Pye, Frank Wright, Ken Smith, Edwin Vincent, Len Spencer, Bill Giles and several others. I wish I could go back in time, to impose present skill and knowledge upon that same wonderful wilderness of reed and water, but simply going back is a step I feel unable to take. That era is over, but another was in progress in Broadland, even as the prymnesium was going about its deadly business.

A young lad called Martyn Page was feeling his way into piking on the dykes running off the Bure at Wroxham, eventually finding his way on to the main river. There he discovered, by accident, he says, the merits of trolling. For me the development of Martyn Page into a thinking and accomplished angler was one of the most interesting parts of this book. He started fresh, and learned for himself. He discovered better ways to fish the Bure than we had, years before. For us it was an occasional diversion from Horsey, Hickling, Heigham and the rest. We just transplanted methods, spending too much time on Bridge Broad and Wroxham Broad, and not enough on the main river. We blew it; he didn't.

It's an object lesson for any pike angler. Master one water and you can adapt to all the rest, especially when there are books as good as this one to help you on the way. I am unsure when the paths of the joint authors finally crossed, but it was a happy encounter. Their skills and knowledge both match and overlap, and where they think someone knows more than they do they rope him in — Chris Liebbrandt on lures, for example, and Bert Rozemeijer on Dutch fishing.

They dumped their massive manuscript on me at Christmas, would you believe? Despite the necessary pauses to seek the cause and cure for hangovers it had been read by the New Year. It held me from the first page to the last of a somewhat curious epilogue, which still has me wondering. Is it Bellars, indicating a preferred method of departure from this life, I ask myself. No, it couldn't be. To manoeuvre a boat far from civilisation one first has to learn to untie the stern end from the dock (another incident he will not be allowed to forget). In any case, drowning seems an unlikely way to quieten such an active mind. Yet another idea for a new rig would surely flash into it. A great surge of adrenalin would generate survival. He would find himself on the bank, trying it out. Hours later he would come to wonder how he managed to get wet.

No, I know you don't know what on earth I'm talking about. But you will, when you have read the book. It is interesting, instructive, thought-provoking and maybe even a bit controversial in some areas — a welcome and valuable addition to pike angling literature.

COLIN DYSON
President
Pike Anglers' Club of Great Britain

Prologue

PIKE MEETS MAN, TWO HUNTERS TOGETHER

Through the crystal depths, the eyes of the hunters clashed and each hunter's gaze was momentarily fixed on the other. Water cascaded through the air as the trance broke. There was no evil contempt, and no malice in that cold and impersonal stare as the great hunter vanished into the murky depths.

In the jaws of the executioner death called to the roach but once. The cascade subsided. At that moment our hunter struck, with expertise and precision. The roach sank forgotten to its muddy grave and the pike, the hunter, found herself staring, once more, into the eyes of man, her hunter.

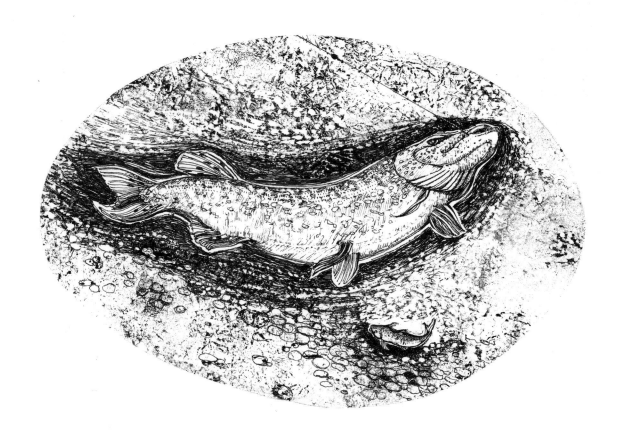

Introduction

When John Bailey and I compiled our book *Pike: The Predator Becomes the Prey* we made a conscious decision to produce a book which provided an insight into modern pike fishing as practised by selected anglers in specific types of water. In this way the resulting book effectively cut across the subject of pike fishing and, we hope, produced an informative and enjoyable read.

We recognised at the time, however, that more detailed information on the pike itself, many past and present pike-angling methods and much information which would be of use to the complete pike angler could not be contained within that format. A sister book would therefore be necessary. It is this sister, the bookshelf companion to *Predator*, that I was commissioned to produce.

An awesome task, to produce a book which would undoubtably be compared with *Predator* and classed in some ways as a follow-up or a sequel. But this is not our intention. I hope the reader will draw the same conclusion: that this is very much a companion, filling in more of the detail on this vast subject. This book is written to stand alone, but also together with *Predator*, in order to produce a greater understanding of pike and pike angling.

To undertake such a challenging yet enjoyable task and to create a book which would meet such exacting requirements it became obvious that two heads would be better than one. The obvious choice was Vic Bellars, my close friend and angling companion. Vic's wealth of experience over many years of pike angling (his first twenty came before I was born), his knowledge of rigs and his great inventiveness, with perhaps a touch of English eccentricity, lend much to the enrichment and enjoyment which I hope you will find in the ensuing chapters.

Throughout the book we have attempted to provide an insight into pike and pike angling in what we hope is a refreshing way. We make no apologies for raising topics and issues so often left unfaced, or for questioning generally accepted rigs and techniques. Our intention has been to make the reader question his choice of tactics, to think more about situations, to adapt, and not only to catch more pike but to find more enjoyment in each and every piking session.

Inevitably, we will have covered ground in this work which can be found in its sister or in other pike books. Where more detail on a subject can be found within *Predator* we mention this fact for the sake of completeness and in an attempt to achieve that balance whereby the two books stand as both separate and united reading.

Why another pike book? We hope these words of explanation provide some insight and as you, the reader, close the last page we will have succeeded in our objective if you have found each chapter informative, refreshing, at times controversial or questioning, and, above all, enjoyable.

MARTYN PAGE

1

A Lifetime of Dreams –
Martyn's Story

GENESIS

A pike angler's career, his whole way of thinking, revolves as much round dreams of uncaught fish, of monsters that one day will succumb to his wiles, as it does about actual captures. For him there will always be something to aim for, a dream to fulfil, an unrealised ambition. Perhaps pike more than any other fish capture the imagination of young lads, of the general public and the news media – this mysterious predator lurking unseen in the depths, which can grow to immense proportions, its huge jaw laced with crocodile teeth, the freshwater shark.

You may recall the days of your childhood, at school listening to a teacher rambling in some foreign language on a winter's afternoon. As boredom sets in your mind may have begun to wander. You know how it is: your attention dances out of the classroom and looks across the playing fields, first at the sixth-form girls playing hockey but then out, out and beyond until you arrive at the waterside. A magical lake, deep in a wood on a misty morning. Nothing would be moving to break the spell except the occasional bob of your float indicating that the livebait was sending out its signals. Then, suddenly, before your eyes the float is gone amidst a great swirl of water and line spills from your spool. You strike into this unseen adversary, larger than your greatest expectations, the ultimate dream fish – a thirty. Just as suddenly reality returns with a start as with a sharp rap on the knuckles from the teacher the mystical dream is broken.

Something triggers the first thoughts of pike and the conception of a pike angler, the genesis. And so it was with me. The pike on the wall of the biology lab at school and Mr Crabtree's exploits sparked my imagination. I began to plan the downfall of great pike; they constantly haunted my mind; I just wanted to catch one of these incredible beasts. Unfortunately it was to be a year or two before I was ready for the conquest. For a while I had to make do with my six-foot rod catching dace, roach and little gudgeon. But the seed was sown.

Line was pouring from the spool as I struck into my unseen leviathan. Something on the other end of my line resisted strongly. This time I would succeed. During the anxious minutes that followed we saw the fish several times. On one occasion it almost swam into the net; on another it came within inches of the submerged tree roots. Surely this magnificent fish was mine – but each time another run, another heart-stopping moment. Then suddenly the pike yielded, surfacing with great jaw uppermost, signalling its defeat. The battle was won. Slowly it was eased over the waiting net. Quickly the fish was brought to the bank and displayed for all to admire. I had succeeded. There it was, living proof for all to see. I had passed my entrance exam and here was my reward, my first pike, all of 1lb 9oz, completing the genesis – the birth of a pike angler.

Time passes. The value of an achievement fades in the memory, bigger goals and dreams supervene. That first double, 10lb, on a gudgeon livebait at Costessey Mill on the River Wensum. The second, caught at night

whilst eel fishing, just 2oz greater. And the third – now, how big was that one? I can't recall now without reference to my diary. But the first, they will always live on.

Then one day the first twenty fell to a trailed livebait on the Bure at Wroxham. It weighed 20lb 8oz. I can remember the second and third, but even twenties eventually became hard to recall as personal bests creep slowly upwards. The first 25lb-plus fish will always etch itself into one's memory. In my case it weighed 28lb 15oz and is captured in *Predator Becomes the Prey* for always. But other such fish, each magnificent at the time, can never hold the pride of place held by the first ones. The firsts always signify the achievement of ambition, and the knowledge that the goal-posts have been moved again.

Over the years, as each pike came my way I believe that they all gave me some satisfaction, some sense of achievement, but inevitably, as time passes and experience is gained, lesser fish do not receive quite the same reverence as their larger brethren. And as those years passed there still remained that ultimate dream, a legacy of schoolboy dreams, a thirty – not so much a driving ambition but something still to fill daydreams. With each successive year additional

knowledge and experience began to suggest that, with just a little extra luck, eventually the dream could become reality.

INTERLUDE

Bill was a loner by nature. He could never see the need or find the time for unnecessary socialising and certainly did not suffer fools gladly. Born to the land, he did things the way they should be done – no short cuts, no modern contraptions. At one with nature, he performed his tasks traditionally.

From generation to generation families such as Bill's had passed on their knowledge, not clouded or diminished by city comforts or made easier by electronic gadgetry. Bill could detect a change in the weather through instinct, without the need for weathermen and even before the barometer moved. He knew of the ways of the countryside animals and had witnessed sights in real life which others only see on wildlife programmes. Indeed, he was wise in all rural and natural things.

Bill loved to fish in *his* way. Only rarely would he venture into a tackle shop, and then perhaps only for a packet of hooks and some line, or a few peacock quills or weights. He would not stop to wonder at the new gimmicks and had no time for boilies, hair rigs and other such 'improvements', part of the modern angler's world.

As the years had passed Bill had seen the changes. More young men than ever before, armed with a battery of tackle and innovations, arrived on all his favourite haunts. He saw the tide turning from the natural methods in favour of modern technology, planned campaigns and sophistication. He saw the success of swimfeeder bashing, stumbled upon bivvy after bivvy and listened in despair to birds returning their mating calls to the bleeps of Optonics. None of this was for him; his was the way of watercraft, of knowledge of the true underwater environment. So Bill fished on, in his way, and because of his way he continued to capture great fish. Increasingly, however, he moved to new waters to avoid the onslaught, to fish in peace and quiet, man against fish, not angler versus angler. Bill was a realist and reluctantly he accepted the change: modern society was here to stay, like it or not. Naturally, he reflected on the good old days.

Bill had never really been a pike angler; to a degree, it was a fish that had always evaded him. Indeed, in all his years he had caught only a handful of twenties, but then pike had never really been his favourite fish and he had not devoted much time to the species. Nevertheless, he understood their habits and had watched huge fish spawning. He could even tell of the great Broadland days, before prymnesium, and of the enormous numbers of pike deaths on the Thurne system in the 1960s. It was while reflecting on these events and, perhaps, having caught wind of possibilities from a solitary, almost unbelievable report of a pike catch by a holidaymaker that he cast his mind back to the Thurne system. The report had not gone unnoticed; others too began to wonder.

The more Bill mulled things over in his mind the stronger the feeling and the urge became to catch a truly large pike, the one coarse fish swimming in local waters that he hadn't caught to great size. With those growing dreams the dormant pike angler in Bill was awakened.

The jigsaw did not take long to piece together. Since the prymnesium, local pike anglers had kept away from the Thurne system, but it was obvious that not all the fish had been killed. There were areas of sanctuary and, as with any fishery, it was inevitable that the pike would have thrived on neglect. His quest began.

It was later in the season, after recovering from a minor disappointment on finding the signs of one or two others already thinking along the same lines, that Bill came to terms with the system through his natural ability and watercraft. Within the last few weeks of that season he achieved his ambition, taking several 20lb-plus fish and one enormous monster, beyond all his dreams, just a few pounds short of forty. To even Bill this was an achievement worth mentioning to others, but he wisely kept the knowledge of this success within a small circle of friends. Fortunately, they were the ones who had already paid exploratory visits to the system and so the news was contained.

Despite all the secrecy, by the next season more and more anglers began to catch wind that something special was happening in Norfolk and with each passing month Bill saw new arrivals. Soon one or two tremendous catches broke the headlines and the system's secrets were revealed to all. Bill reflected gloomily on the storm clouds now massing on the horizon. But in this second season Bill had fished the waters hard. It was a rare day when he didn't fish and although he saw more and more new arrivals he would be away from the hotspots by the time they arrived. Bill would fish at night, in the early morning and most evenings. A simple method was all he needed – a herring gently wobbled, or left static on the bottom. Stealth and quietness were the essential ingredients in the shallow, clear waters. Fish after fish fell to his rods that season. Great numbers of twenty-pound pike, possibly as many as seven in a session, and a good sprinkling of thirties. Even

A simple method was all he needed – a herring gently wobbled, or left static on the bottom.

Dennis Pye would have raised his eyebrows at Bill's success. As the season closed Bill had boated an enormous tally of twenties. Perhaps the numbers will never be fully disclosed. Rumoured at fifty over this weight, it may have been a few more or a few less. That does not matter greatly now. For Bill had been the first to arrive on the neglected waters. He had reaped the rewards and now, with the ever-increasing numbers of anglers taking up the search, it was time for Bill to call it a day. He packed his rods away and left the pickings for everyone else.

The following few years on the upper Thurne are now history. The second helpings which were left behind produced some of the most incredible fish that had been seen from the Broads in years, but no one angler came even close to matching Bill's results and only one or two privileged friends know the full story. Where Bill fishes now one can only guess – perhaps at some as yet unknown Redmire, or another pike haven.

In March 1982, at the end of the season following his first successes, Bill wrote a letter in which he said:

That just leaves pike, and at last I can say I have finally made it with these fish, after many years of struggling. I started piking at the end of October and carried on until the end of the season, except for the freeze-up, when I didn't fish at all. I really got keen on pike and the more I fished for them the more interested I became and the more I wanted to catch. My total score was 69, including 33 doubles. These I will list.

Bill then listed the fish, which included five twenties and a thirty-seven. A magnificent season, but only an indication of what was to follow the next year.

In my diary I noted: 'Having fished a few times on the system over the last two seasons, I was becoming despondent. It's such a strange system, so shallow and clear and all the fish seem to weigh between seven and ten pounds. I know the big fish must be there. Now with Bill's letter he has proved we are right, that paradise must be just round the corner.'

Bill's story may be just a few paragraphs of literary licence, reflecting a dream we would all wish to come true – paradise found. On the other hand, it may be based on one angler's true adventures. That I leave to you, the reader, to decide. I would not wish to shatter anyone's dreams.

REVELATION

And so, as those early years of the 1980s passed, many large Thurne pike found their way into my net – including, on one balmy day in 1985, amongst a catch of three twenties, another first, my personal best, my first twenty-nine. During those years I saw several thirties, both in and out of water, and the dream of a thirty became a very positive ambition.

A year later, on a hot, still October morning, ideally suited to surface carp fishing, with temperatures approaching the seventies, I rounded the corner, once more, into a piker's paradise. This was not the classic textbook day so suited to good autumn piking and, predictably, as the morning passed such rules were reinforced. Only one low double had shown any interest,

falling to Steve in the other boat, fishing *the* known swim. As it happened, however, we did not lack confidence – quite the contrary. Experience had shown us that these conditions were ideal on this water for the big fish.

Dave and I moved swims. Perhaps that was the problem. The new swim was less of a swim exactly, more of a great weedbed. We thought there might just be a pike lurking in the dark tunnels underneath, away from the sun. Such thinking was quickly reinforced as, within minutes, there was a quick succession of runs to Dave's rods, resulting in three fish to seventeen pounds. Strange, I thought, at least one in three of the fish from this water are twenties, surely the next fish . . . I didn't have time to deliberate as the water confirmed its reputation and my first run of the day resulted in a superb fish, just over 26lb, which insisted on embedding itself immovably in the weed. In the end we had to up-anchor and drift out over the fish. We could see it lying passively on the surface with the line cobwebbing between numerous parts of the weedbed. As we approached it wasted no time in soaking us as it bolted back to its sanctuary. Eventually, however, it was subdued, netted, admired and returned. Having disturbed the area, we moved and settled in another weedbed on the other side of the broad. This particular swim produced one mid-double, on my first cast, but little else. All went quiet for the next hour.

Eventually Steve and Charlie decided to try our earlier productive swim and again, after a quick mid-double, they too settled into a long period of inactivity. During this time I began to experience a desire to move. I wanted to have a try at *the* swim, the swim which had produced my twenty-nine pound fish the previous year and numerous other twenties. I knew Steve and Charlie had been fishing it all morning but a feeling is, after all, a feeling and we firmly believe that it should always be followed up. Dave wasn't so sure: surely nothing was feeding in that swim; it hadn't produced a run for five hours. But Dave knew that my feelings often paid dividends and he agreed to a move.

It is quite well known that sometimes things you have always desired in life ultimately happen faster than expected or can be appreciated. After years of waiting suddenly there it is, that special something you have always wanted. Perhaps that day fate was to take a hand. I am not sure. When my first bait landed I knew it was right – the perfect cast. So it proved, for within seconds, and before I had chance to cast a second bait, the multiplier sang warnings of pike. An instantaneous take. The bait must have landed on the top of a pike's head, in a swim that had been fished all morning. Surely that was the hand of destiny.

I struck firmly into this unseen but obvious monster. As the hooks went home, with a degree of confidence which surprised even Dave I advised him that this was bigger than the twenty-six I had caught earlier. There was no doubt.

There was nothing spectacular about the actual fight. The pike kited purposely to the right, swimming past the boat and – alarmingly, perhaps, in other circumstances – towards a reedbed. Although the adrenalin was pumping fast, I was possessed with a cool confidence and experienced no fear or thought of losing my prize. It was as if I was a spectator to my own dream. Careful pressure turned the head and she came round, as I knew she would, and swam past the boat. In the clear, shallow water this huge fish swam by, with back

An ambition realised – Martyn's first thirty.

The final seconds of one battle.

breaking the surface, turning on a run away from the boat. We both marvelled at the size. This was one of *the* Thurne fish – large crocodile head, bream-shovelling jaws and a long, long body, a fish of great years, unquestionably within a fraction of four feet in length. Surely, this was my dream.

Eventually, after two or three more runs, the fish was subdued. Slowly, grudging every inch, it was eased across the weed and into the waiting net. It lay graceful, but defiant in defeat, at the bottom of the boat. Dave turned and confirmed to the world the knowledge in my mind, with the words 'It's a thirty, my son.' He was right. There could be no doubt and the scales finally proclaimed the expected.

It had all happened so fast. Time had stood suspended in the depths of my dream unwinding and it took some considerable time before I realised that this was not a dream. Then, like a flash flood, came the knowledge of my pike-angling ambition fulfilled and complete, the revelation of the dream, now a reality, a thirty at last, with ounces to spare.

With that complete knowledge came a sudden chilling and unwanted realisation. The childhood dreams of the unknown monster were, perhaps, gone for ever. What price now imagination, a pike angler's career complete? Where to now, and what next? But it takes perhaps seconds to reapparaise such revelations. A forty might be rather pleasant. Now, let me see – there are these waters in Holland one closer to home in Wales, or what about . . . ?

PART ONE

IN PURSUIT OF
ESOX LUCIUS

2

The Strange Things Pike Do

HOW LITTLE
DO WE KNOW?

In this chapter we propose to examine a few behaviour aspects of this unique fish and to illustrate how easy it is to become complacent by assuming that the pike must always conform to a particular pattern or routine. The pike, of course, are not bound by any such rules.

As pike are predators, so the obvious bait to catch them is some form of prey. But the pike's predatory function tells us more. First, it provides clues on location. 'Find the prey and then you find the pike' is often quoted and it can hold true. But not always. Seek good ambush-type swims from which the pike can attack its prey, or stimulate the fish into instinctive attacks at passing objects, such as lures. The exploitation of such knowledge is useful, for it enables the angler to fish a swim with purpose rather than selecting one by chance.

The pike is a long, lean killing machine with powerful muscles and a powerful tail, and is equipped with a capacity for incredibly fast and instant bursts of speed. It is this standing-start acceleration that makes for efficient predation. But, contrary to public opinion, it will not always be on the feed. Often it will lie for hours, even days in winter, with no apparent desire to eat. Prey fish sense this and will even swim near a dormant pike. However, a sudden stiffening of the dorsal is enough to send them fleeing, perhaps too late.

Sometimes a pike will approach a live fish yet show almost indifferent interest in its movements. Perhaps the erratic behaviour caused by the prey being tethered as a bait merely arouses the pike's inquisitive nature. It might even push the bait with its nose and may then swim away, coming back moments later but still with seeming indifference. Then, suddenly, like lightning it will strike. Indeed, it is possible to wind up such a docile pike, stimulating its natural instincts so as to invoke a strike. Trout livebaits are excellent for this. However, it is wrong to assume that pike will always strike at a bait and are always feeding. The pike's behaviour is not that predictable. We do not feed all the time, so why should pike? A pike eats to live and will, instinctive reaction aside, feed only when it needs to.

Perhaps it is true of all fishing. It certainly holds good in pike angling that the more you think you know, the less you really do. All too often pike defy all the rules, or at least seem to. You'll be sitting at the right place, at the right time, with what is obviously the right bait and rig, fished at the correct depth, yet the pike will not oblige. Then perhaps a young lad will arrive at the water, cast out the wrong bait, fished at some 'silly' depth on totally wrong tackle, only to catch a 20lb-plus fish within five minutes of starting. Rules, it seems, are made to be broken and, sure enough, pike angling can reinforce this belief. As soon as you begin to become blasé and overconfident the pike will change its habits completely, defying all logic, sending you firmly back to square one. But that is just part of the fun and challenge of the sport and at times it shows just how little we know.

As we emphasise many times in this book, pike must not be thought of as human beings. They are not guided by our complicated emotions. Theoretically, this should make it easier to predict their behaviour – we are a more intelligent life form. Unfortunately, we fall into the trap of attempting to predict such

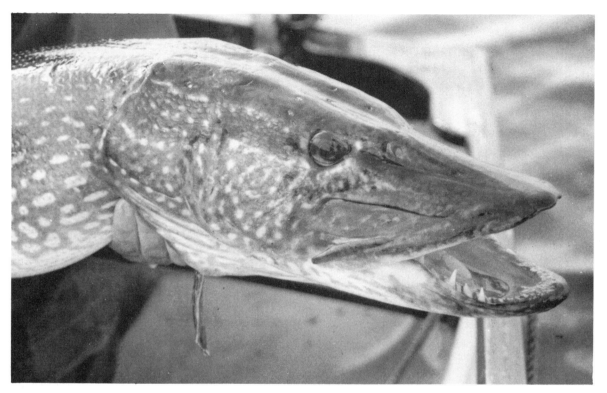

Esox lucius – *scavenger or hunter?*

behaviour on a human basis. It is necessary to look through the eyes of the pike, to think like a pike. If we do so some of their behaviour patterns begin to make sense. Others, however, will remain a mystery. Obviously, some reference to human behaviour can be relevant. For instance, since humans are all different, why should pike all react in the same way, eat the same baits or remain in the same places? Obviously they do not – but it is easy to forget this. Some pike may be roamers; others may prefer to stop at 'home'. Some may have a distinct preference for dead fish; others may be more cannibalistic in their feeding. Given a virtually unlimited environment (such as the Broads) it is possible that some fish will be encountered only very rarely, whilst others will become household names, constantly turning up in the same swim year in, year out. But even in relatively small lakes particular fish may be

very difficult to catch, even though their presence may be known. Perhaps they have some peculiar feeding habit and need a different approach from the norm.

Over the years we have seen some classic examples of extreme behaviour. For instance, on one local trout water all the fish are removed. Most of the big pike find their way into a small muddy pit close by. That little pit has received a stocking of large numbers of 20lb-plus fish and they are often seen on the move. Yet they can be extremely difficult to catch. Then, as if a switch has been turned, someone will fish the water and quickly catch a brace of twenties before it returns once more to its stubborn ways. How so many pike in such a small environment can defy capture is a mystery, but the fact that such behaviour occurs is well proven.

The River Thurne pike are another

example. Many of these upper Thurne fish are well known. Some twenties show themselves time and time again, coming from the same areas. Then suddenly for a space of a few weeks these fish are gone and a new batch of fish appear, often smaller, pristine fish which have obviously never seen a hook. Then as suddenly they are gone and the old residents return. Did they go away on holiday? What of the new fish? Where have they gone, perhaps not to be seen for several years? There is, of course, a sanctuary on the upper Thurne in the form of Somerton Broad, but we are not entirely convinced that this is their hide-out. However, seemingly out of the blue comes an exceptional fish which hasn't turned up for two or three years. Where had that been? Obviously not resident with its colleagues and obviously well away from other anglers' baits. A classic case, if it is true, is a more recent capture of Dora, the famous Thurne record breaker. Having appeared periodically for a number of years, growing from 33lb to her massive 42lb, she suddenly disappeared. However, in 1987 there was a report of a lure-caught, and witnessed, 40lb pike from Hickling Broad whose markings apparently matched those of Dora. Had she emigrated and is she now living happily in pike exile away from the Martham pressure? We are convinced that there is more than meets the eye in this story, but certainly pike movement does occur on a much larger scale than is often imagined. Repeated capture, for instance, can cause fish to move considerable distances and hotspots will change under pressure, even becoming devoid of fish for a considerable period.

As we mention in Chapter 3, understanding pike movement is crucial. Certainly the Broads pike-movement theories, although never scientificially proven, have much to be said for them. Generally it is considered that during the months of October and November the majority, but not all, of the pike begin to leave many of Norfolk's Broads and move into the rivers following the prey fish. It is then believed that the pike remain in the rivers until the spawning

instinct strengthens and they return to the shallower Broads. During the winter months they wander along the rivers, loosely following the prey fish and never far from available food sources. Certainly, our results on the Thurne suggest that this pattern of behaviour has merit. By the end of November, at Martham for instance, most of the pike appear to have left and are wandering in the river. But by the beginning of January, unless the winter is severe, the big fish are already on the move, slowly returning towards the Broad, and by late February the movement has accelerated and the fish will be near to or back in the Broad. It is often said that the smaller pike move first. Certainly there appears to be some truth in this and it will often be found that the smaller pike congregate first, though not necessarily actually on the spawning ground. Perhaps the small pike gather early, shoaling for protection, knowing that the big females will soon arrive and may fancy a small pike or two for a meal.

Other Broadland complexes may not conform so readily to this pattern and it is rare to find any broad entirely devoid of pike even in mid-winter. Nevertheless, with careful planning and local knowledge it is possible to keep in touch with the majority of the fish throughout much of the winter, moving with them as they wander the river and being ready for them as they return to the broads.

Other Broadland theories suggest that many of the big pike remain semi-dormant throughout the winter months in the shallowest water away from the rivers. On the vast Hickling and Heigham complexes there seems to be some merit in this theory, but, unfortunately, after the plague of prymnesium, it is now hard to draw any firm conclusions since the pike here are still very limited in numbers.

Such theories on movement or non-movement are not specific to the Broads only. Movement occurs on all pike waters and it is something which must be appreciated if a water is to yield results constantly.

ODD THOUGHTS ON WEIGHT GAINS AND FEEDING

Angling pressure affects pike feeding, perhaps by changing the times when they feed, where they feed and certainly the way in which they feed. But angling pressure may also affect the weight gain of pike. We are uncertain whether constant capture forces a check on growth but we consider it probable. If a pike is already large, at or near its maximum weight, repeated capture is unlikely to have a great effect, but during the growing years it is possible that constant capture restricts a fish's full potential. Certainly the golden rule of looking for neglected waters adds some support to this.

Pike occasionally make strange weight gains. A pike which has remained at a constant weight for several years may suddenly spurt forwards, gaining weight rapidly. Its length will not have changed; perhaps it is some form of middle-aged spread. As mentioned, Dora is a typical example. For several years she free-wheeled around 33–34lb and then disappeared for a while. When next reported she had put on over 6lb in weight, becoming the esteemed forty. Other pike may be caught year in, year out with only ounces of variation in their weight. It is often so easy to catch a large pike and to return her thinking, 'In one or two years time what size will she have grown to?' The truth is that she may not grow at all.

In recent years more and more large pike appear to have been caught throughout England. Thirties are certainly more numerous and the forty-pound barrier has been broken several times, and not only from one water. The Broads, Wales, Ardleigh and one or two other trout reservoirs and gravel pits have proved that they can produce fish of this calibre. Have there always been such pike? It is interesting to note that in the late 1970s tench suddenly appeared to get bigger. At one time 7lb fish were enormous; now it takes a nine,

even a double, to really make the headlines. Queenford did the same for bream. Is there some underlying reason why fish seem bigger nowadays? Possibly it is that more anglers are more specialised and prepared to tackle waters which have been neglected for years or which were inaccessible or just too daunting. This is probably the reason, but there may be a more ominous underlying cause. Ecologically the effects of chemical spraying, pollution and perhaps even the greenhouse effect may be showing through. Fewer fish in our waters, fewer surviving young fish, could be affecting the ecological balance, enabling those fish present to become larger. If there is any truth in this the final result will not be seen for several years, and it cannot be determined by just a few unique waters. It is necessary to look at more general fisheries and see what is happening to the average weight of the fish in those waters. For instance, locally, the Ormesby system has shown a marked change in pike weight over the last decade. At one time a 20lb fish from those waters was very big indeed. True, there were tales of odd bigger fish but they were few and far between. Nowadays, however, the various waters comprising the system have all produced 25lb-plus pike and, although we have yet to see an authenticated thirty, there have certainly been fish very close to that weight. Is it just a cycle or is this some evidence that there is a problem? We do not know the answer but we can all feel the change in the climate, the warmer winters, the strange summers – indeed, the lack of seasons. Is this the prelude to an ominous future of sparsely populated natural fisheries? Leaching of phosphates and nitrates into our waters enriches them, weed proliferates, algal blooms turn clear water into a fair imitation of pea soup. At first as the water becomes richer insect life increases dramatically and fish can feed with little effort – that is, those fewer surviving fish in a water where fry mortality is high. This may perhaps explain the current increase in sizes we have mentioned.

SPAWNING AND RELATED FEEDING

Pike weight varies through the year, not just by annual growth. If a fish is still growing, other factors also affect its weight. It has always been thought that a pike will put on weight as it nears the spawning period. Certainly, this weight gain can be observed in tench and therefore it makes sense to consider the theory as arguable. Captures of known fish tend to support this theory and the back end of the season is a time when it is theoretically possible to catch pike at their heaviest. We are not entirely convinced that in an ordinary winter the added weight is necessarily spawn at all. In a mild winter this maybe the case but we suspect that much of the weight increase due to spawn occurs only in the week or two before spawning and is the result of egg swell caused by water retention. We are not biologists and we draw our conclusions more from changes in tench weights both before and after spawning and from specific pike captures.

We would be quite prepared to admit that we are wrong, but our observations lead us to conclude that more often the added weight towards the back end of the season is caused through substantially increased feeding activity. Perhaps it is aimed at building up energy for spawning. Nevertheless, sport with pike can change quite dramatically some time during February, depending on the weather. It appears that when the pike start moving towards spawning grounds their metabolism accelerates and they are no longer docile winter feeders. Indeed, we have experienced times when fish become quite ravenous in this pre-spawning activity. Interestingly, we have also noticed this with tench, but only during a very limited period just before spawning, though the tench have been particularly finicky prior to that sudden feeding activity.

In February and the first two weeks of March 1989, following a particularly mild winter, Martyn witnessed this ravenous behaviour on several occasions. It occurred on the Thurne system in areas where not many fish were known to be present. However, the initial results suggested that large numbers of pike had been located. It soon became apparent that the same fish were appearing not only on successive occasions but in some cases several times in the same day. A noticeable example was a 16lb fish which Martyn caught, returned and then caught again. Interestingly, a fish of similar weight had been caught by an angler an hour previously not fifty yards away. Perhaps it was the same fish. On another occasion Steve Harper caught a 26lb fish and returned two days later to catch the same fish, albeit several hundred yards away. Then, in one mad ten-minute feeding spell, Steve boated three 20lb fish. The next day Martyn returned and in a nearby swim caught one of those fish, the day after Dave Humphries' son, Gary, caught another, and in the meantime a lesser fish of 17lb merrily kept showing itself. Those fish were totally preoccupied with feeding and could have led us to quite misleading conclusions about the numbers of pike in the areas involved.

ROLLING PIKE AT PLAY

Rolling pike are another phenomenon which we have experienced on occasions. We do not mean striking pike; we are talking of those slow rolls where you catch a glimpse of dorsal, a back, or indeed the snout of a pike, almost as though they are coming up for air, rolling gently, and then returning to their environment. On a few occasions we have experienced a period of perhaps an hour or two during which several pike have continued to roll around the boat and we have been frustrated in efforts to catch them. Martyn likens it in some ways to rolling tench, not only because of the quietness of the roll but also because in his experience when tench are rolling in the swim they are not necessarily feeding. It is often found that it is an angler in an adjacent swim

On occasions great pike can be seen swimming rapidly close to the surface . . .

with no rolling tench who meets with success. Perhaps the tench, and also in this case the pike, are rolling at play, or in some prelude to feeding, for as soon as the rolling stops action may start. We cannot give a precise answer, but merely outline our observations. Certainly, on such occasions when we have had several large

All pike have unique spot markings. This small-spotted fish will be easy to recognise again.

fish rolling in the area they have not been interested in our baits during that period.

Another observation concerning preoccupied pike has often been made on the shallow waters of the upper Thurne. On occasions great pike can be seen swimming rapidly close to the surface above the dense weed. The pike move with purpose and are obviously intent on covering a great distance. If such a fish passes close to a boat it is natural to expect some response, particularly to the action of a frantic livebait or a wobbled deadbait, but rarely have we managed to interest these moving pike. Vic has experienced the same problem with large rainbow trout. On the other hand, close observation can sometimes enable you to anticipate their destination and once they have exerted all that energy and come to rest then surely they must feed.

In this short chapter we have merely mentioned a few observations of pike behaviour from our encounters. Without a doubt it is aspects such as the unpredictable and seemingly erratic feeding patterns, the intriguing movements, and inexplicable weight changes and more, which add that extra dimension to pike fishing.

3

Location – To Be a Hunter or a Trapper?

Part of the satisfaction and excitement of pike fishing comes from the ability to catch pike in a great variety of ways and from many types of water. First however, the pike must be found. Clearly, it is impossible to catch them by fishing swims where they are not present or where they are unlikely to roam. Similarly, if your only ambition is to catch a 30lb pike you will not catch it fishing a small stream where a double-figure fish is considered a specimen.

We cannot stress too strongly that location is the single greatest factor in your success as a pike angler. Pike are relatively easy to catch in most circumstances, usually by quite simple methods. A variety of styles adds interest but not necessarily numbers of pike. If you have not located the pike, however, varying styles will serve no purpose whatsoever.

Throughout this book we emphasise location and moving when success is not forthcoming.

October, a month of furious action, with Vic footloose on Alderfen Broad.

Last-minute action with a double.

Similarly, we mention some of the stranger behaviour traits of pike, emphasising how little we all really know. In this short chapter we wish to put the question of location in perspective. Of course, the choice lies with you, the angler, and often the amount of time at your disposal will affect that choice. Large waters may require weeks, possibly seasons, of research to establish the most likely areas from which to take pike. Extremely large waters can be totally awe-inspiring but, fortunately, modern technology has provided a means of assistance with graph recorders, which not only help plot the bottom contours but which can locate the fish and identify the depth at which they are lying.

The majority of pike anglers will only have the usual weekend breaks and the occasional day's holiday. Clearly, at the outset it is necessary to decide exactly what is required from your pike fishing. For most anglers, we would recommend an overall approach of enjoying catching pike, whatever their size, balanced with campaigns on waters likely to produce larger fish. At the end of any season, this approach should produce a number of pike and with one or two better specimens will add peaks of excitement. Alternatively, you may prefer to seek super-large specimens week in, week out. On many waters this will mean fewer fish and less variety, and almost certainly the super-specimen will be caught (that is

Vic proudly displays the result.

almost inevitable with modern piking techniques). However, during the numerous blanks there will probably have been little satisfaction and, we feel, this does not add up to the total enjoyment that can be obtained from pike fishing.

Assuming, therefore, that you adopt an approach of pursuing any pike and not just pots of gold at the end of the rainbow, location becomes that much easier. Generally, you will be fishing waters where there is a good head of pike of all sizes. With each water you can follow the approach of the hunter, searching new areas, constantly changing swims, adapting and moving with the fish according to the times of the year and so on. You should be constantly

aware that a hotspot (and we use the term loosely) can quickly change as the pike move, possibly because of bait-fish movement or angling pressure itself. It is very important to realise that pike will respond to pressure and will move, not necessarily far, though on some occasions a 'shoal' of pike will move great distances away from angling disturbance.

On virtually all new waters the hunter's approach will produce greater returns. It will enable you to locate the pike sooner by covering more water, which gives a greater chance of finding feeding fish, or at least finding fish. Our approach would be to change swims every 45 minutes if no fish has been caught. If there has been activity in the swim we would delay this

A large fish powers away after seeing the net.

move for perhaps another 30 minutes and keep delaying it every time another pike is caught. Obviously, on some waters movement is restricted but, assuming it is possible, a hunting style will eventually succeed.

There are numerous hunting methods which can be used. Possibly the most neglected is wobbling, and we discuss it in great depth in Chapter 11. Similarly, trolling and trailing on rivers and very big waters are deadly methods of location. The use of a boat immediately provides greater chances of success by opening up the whole of a water to exploration.

However, the hunter style will not always produce the greatest returns. On some waters to sit and wait patiently with a baited trap in a specific area may produce greater rewards. The trapper waiting patiently on a known passing

point on a river, fen drain or known patrol route in a great lake already knows his water, and may almost be able to predict exactly when fish will pass through and when the trap will be sprung. The successful trapper, like the hunter, will have studied and learnt his water, he will understand why his bait is sitting waiting in one swim throughout the day and will be able to give you the reason when he is asked. He will not merely have cast out, sat back and hoped that this was the place. How will he have gained this knowledge? So often the productive areas have no obvious features. We have all seen those piky-looking spots which positively ooze pike only to find them unproductive while a totally uninteresting-looking swim has turned up trumps.

Almost certainly the trapper will have gained

Esox takes to the air in her bid for freedom.

his knowledge through hunting in the first instance and will have concluded that a certain area is by far the most productive but that it requires the long-wait approach. One day he may be a trapper but the next he may be back to hunting. Once again an understanding of the pike's habits influences the angler. Usually the hunter catches more pike, but the long vigils and campaigns in pursuit of the one monster sometimes require the patience of the trapper once an area considered to have great potential has been located. Our advice is to hunt first, to get to know your water, and then by all means to lay the trap and wait, if that is likely to produce the fish you require.

Location is so much a question of watercraft. There are always short cuts but these will not necessarily give the greatest rewards or greatest satisfaction. For instance, following other anglers, even well-known ones, into areas they are fishing does not guarantee success. They may be fishing blind or searching and if they are in the wrong area you will be too. The known productive spots may have already declined as the pike have moved away from the pressure. It is always the first angler in a new productive area who reaps the greatest rewards, for once a new area or water is found and is being fished it is already on a downhill slide. It is unfortunately a sad fact that angling pressure seriously affects results. The law of diminishing returns applies partly as a result of pike movement, partly as a result of the pike becoming more cautious. Also, pike losses will inevitably occur in any area under great pressure from numerous anglers. They may result from bad

Surface action — so often a feature of early-autumn fish.

Twenty pounds long – for in early autumn such fish are often very skinny and underweight.

A plump 21-pounder caught from a spawning area in the last days of the season.

handling, inexperience, deliberate killing, excessive retention (particularly in autumn) in sacks, and so on.

Short cuts are therefore all well and good provided they are actually productive. Following other anglers will not always provide a short cut to success. There are times when pike themselves give away their presence by striking near the surface. Obviously it would be foolish not to take advantage of such easy location when it is offered. In the depths of winter such a gift is rare and therefore a knowledge of the pike and its likely whereabouts is necessary. Watercraft and understanding the pike's environment become the keys to success. For instance, on the Norfolk Broads it would be wrong to assume that all the pike will be lying in the seductive reedy margins. Most of the Broads produce the majority of their large pike from the open water, with the reedy swims yielding only smaller fish, unless the pike have driven some prey fish into a reedy bay for a specific feeding spree. But this rule is not inviolate for each broad, and each water is different from another. It was for that reason that Martyn and John Bailey wrote their book *Predator*, in order to provide an insight into various water types and an understanding of pike location in each. In this chapter we wish to emphasise the importance of location and to distinguish between hunting and trapping techniques. If these are combined with an understanding of the pike's habits and habitat, greater success and enjoyment should be inevitable.

4

Ringing the Changes

Before we examine methods of both live- and deadbating we wish to discuss some aspects of the feeding habits of pike in order to provide an insight into the various times and waters most likely to bring success to either method.

At the outset we must stress that in our opinion there are no waters which will not respond at some time to both deadbait or livebait techniques. Pike in a particular water may be notoriously slow to respond to deadbaits for one reason or another but fish will ultimately be forthcoming. However, there are many times, on many waters, where livebaits will prove more effective than deads, and sometimes vice versa. Appreciation of this fact and the application of such understanding will result in more fish on the bank.

Waters vary from season to season and month to month. It is not uncommon to find that a water is transformed into a 'deadbait'

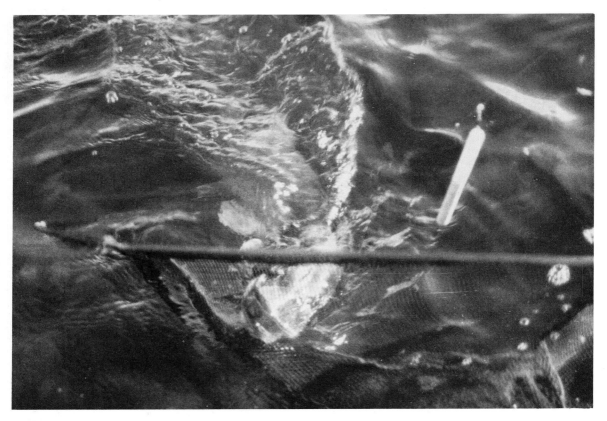

Safely into the net.

water from one season to the next. This may depend on a whole variety of factors. Large-scale deadbait introduction, such as we mention in Chapter 9, could affect the pike's habits, as could the long-term result of discarded baits being introduced to the water at the end of the day, eventually educating the pike. On the other hand, angling pressure can cause methods to switch on and off. So too can water clarity, fodder fish movement, and shoal density. It is important to be aware of such changes, and to endeavour to keep one step ahead of the pike's behaviour traits. There can be no substitute for knowing a water, appreciating its subtleties, and learning in part by ringing the changes with regard to baits where necessary. If you merely depend on one method throughout the year your chances of constant success are severely limited.

Behaviour fluctuations are not only seasonal; monthly variations also occur on most waters. It is not uncommon to find deadbaits producing a response in the early autumn months, but, as the frosts cause the water to clear, livebaits may become increasingly effective. Deadbaits may become totally ineffective, perhaps because of extreme water clarity. On some waters overfishing with deadbaits makes the pike wary of a particular variety, though with the vast range of bait variations now available, as well as a range of colours, allied to differing styles of presentation, this can usually be overcome.

Results on live- and deadbaits may vary not only from month to month but even from hour to hour. On most waters feeding times during the daylight hours will occur as flurries of activity over a limited period, whilst the rest of the day will result in only spasmodic activity. For instance, during the long daylight hours of early autumn most of the fish may take baits at first light, with action tapering off progressively, ceasing entirely during late morning and early afternoon. Then a minor period of feeding activity may coincide with the approach of dusk. Later in the year, however, late morning or dinner time is likely to be the key feeding period. Less common, but not to be neglected,

are those late-afternoon and evening waters where very little happens during the morning but the water really livens up as dusk approaches, with fish often feeding well past the onset of darkness. Very often a water which is responding in this way is one which has been very heavily fished in the past and the pike seem to become conditioned to the fact that the activities of pike anglers decrease in the late afternoon. Most anglers will have packed up as a result of the lack of success throughout the morning, having concluded that the pike were not on the feed that day. It is essential to get to know feeding times on a water and to be at the water at those times to get the maximum out of each swim. But it is necessary to adapt with the changes in the feeding patterns as the season progresses or as the habits of the pike change.

Not all waters conform to such a pattern. Some are random and erratic; others defy all rules. But, however erratic feeding may appear, some form of pattern will eventually emerge. Other factors, in particular the weather, may throw the whole feeding pattern off beat for a while. This is the great problem when attempting to predict one day's fishing. There are so many uncertainties! For instance, on some waters deadbaits will be most effective early in the day when light values are low but, later in the morning as light increases, success on deadbaits may diminish, whereas livebaits may suddenly be taken more readily.

The influence of the weather is probably the key disturbance factor to any established pattern. As a general rule, research such as that conducted by Barrie Rickards indicates that high pressure – associated with warm, settled weather and often producing bright sunny days – produces the days when pike usually respond best to livebaits. With the very warm bright sunny days in winter this response is often limited to early morning only. On the other hand, low pressure is associated with increased feeding on deadbaits.

There are, however, problems with such a generalisation. Some pike do not behave according to such established rules. Take the

Thurne, for instance, a classic example. Much of Martyn's success in recent years has been during extremely warm, still conditions in early autumn. The water at that time is clear and very shallow. With exceptionally bright sunshine, in this shallow water, one would usually expect to catch a few fish in the early hours but very little during the day. However, in contradiction to established theory, few fish have fallen at first light and most have been taken during the middle of the day, with the sun at its brightest. On these balmy, almost summer days, the fish have all taken deadbaits, often ignoring a seemingly more attractive live alternative fished nearby. Sometimes it doesn't make sense but that's part of the fun – adapting and changing, learning to expect the unexpected.

An interesting observation has emerged from our records concerning bright, sunny weather. This observation may be confined to the Broads, where most of our fishing is undertaken, but we suspect that it has greater applications. Although such days usually produce far fewer fish, and on most waters the sport will be confined to the early hours of the day, we consider that it is very significant that on several occasions the one run which has come on such a day, often about 10 a.m., has been from fish of more than 25lb. As we say, it may be that this is something associated only with the shallow Norfolk Broads, waters which are notorious for their lack of response during bright weather. We obviously consider that this reputation is unjustified, in view of our success with larger fish in these conditions and Martyn's experiences on the Thurne.

Similarly, there are days when everything seems ideal – dull and overcast – and yet nothing moves. You will know of such days. The atmosphere presses heavy and claustrophobic, enclosing the water in an envelope of almost menacing silence. On these days even the waterbirds feel the oppression and remain quiet. During such conditions we have rarely caught unless, quite suddenly, the spell is broken by a change of wind – a sudden breeze and the depressive weight of the atmosphere is lifted.

CLIMATIC CHANGES AND CONDITIONS

We all draw from each other's optimism or pessimism. You will know what we mean. If your companion on the way to the water mentions the sudden drop in temperature and the cold north-east wind, his depression and despondency affect you too. Alternatively, a sudden rise in temperature sees both of you hurrying keenly to the waterside. But such changes, in the short term, like attractive floats, may have more effect on the mind of the angler than on the fish themselves. We would not deny that possibly the best piking conditions are a fairly mild day in winter with frequent changes of light, the sun occasionally breaking through the clouds, the wind strong enough to ruffle the surface, preferably blowing from the south or west. On such days sport may be enjoyed throughout the day. However, those sudden climatic changes in weather conditions may not actually be as sudden as they at first appear. Pike are much more sensitive to coming changes and will often react well before we, protected by clothes and warm homes, with many of our original instincts virtually dormant, can detect that change is imminent. Pike will have known for several days before, even before the barometer has made its predictions. This uncanny reaction to forthcoming change can place us at a severe disadvantage unless we appreciate and predict the pike's reactions. For instance, if the pressure is about to change but we do not know, the pike may have already varied their preference between dead- and livebaits, and hence an apparent contradiction to the general rule may appear to prevail on a particular day. Actually, however, the pike may still be conforming to their inherent behavioural pattern.

It is a source of amazement how pike can detect a cold or warm spell well in advance of its occurrence. So often pike will switch on for a week of hectic feeding for no apparent reason. Usually, however, the weather will soon take a turn for the worse and a cold spell will be on its way. Initially there will have been no hint from the weatherman and the only indication to us will have been the sudden increase of pike activity. This makes it difficult to predict sport by the weather on the day. For instance, the coming of a warm spell is more often likely to be celebrated by anglers than by the pike. If it is only a very temporary mild spell there may be some reaction but this may have started even while the cold spell was still in evidence. On the other hand, if a long warm spell is in the offing, pike may be far more casual in their feeding attitude. So much depends on the length of the cold or warm spells. It is apparent, however, that the pike react far more to the threat of a cold spell than they do to the actual coming of a warm period. Obviously, given a few days of settled weather, cold or warm, pike actively settle down into a fairly regular pattern. We must emphasise, however, that these weather influences are most obvious in the middle of winter. In autumn, for example, the general feeding patterns will be more dominant, as the pike are actively feeding in advance of the onset of winter. In winter, with metabolism slowed, pike need to feed far less frequently.

It is interesting to note that pike behaviour

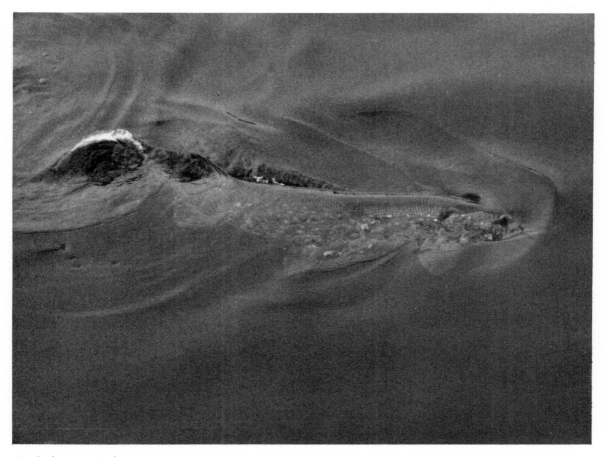

Nearly, but not quite, beaten.

varies in different geographical areas of the country and, while each water has its own characteristics, others elsewhere may respond better to entirely different conditions. Martyn remembers well the day, many years ago now, at an early Pike Anglers' Club fish-in on a Norfolk gravel pit, which Neville Fickling had agreed to attend. All the local Pike Anglers' Club members met at the water on the morning projecting an air of doom and despondency because of the overnight frost and the promise of a very bright, still, sunny day to come. On the other hand, Neville arrived full of confidence and expectancy on the grounds that frost and sun were ideal conditions. He was extremely surprised to see the look of despair on the locals' faces. We were both interested to exchange opinions about how conditions affect pike behaviour on particular waters. For instance, the fens that Neville fished were noted for fishing well in sunny conditions following an overnight frost, whereas on a Norfolk gravel pit these conditions were far from ideal. This appears to contradict slightly our subsequent findings regarding the behaviour of large fish in bright sunny conditions. We would add one caveat, therefore: overnight frost can affect waters. Broadland waters will often fish very well for a short space of time on frosty mornings, but if accompanied by bright sunshine this feeding spell is often very limited. We cannot recall any instances when we have had success with large pike in sunny conditions coupled with anything more than a mild frost during the night.

This whole theme of differing areas responding to certain conditions can be taken one stage further. You will often find that pike in an environment will not only respond to a certain weather condition but there will be periods when every other water appears to be fishing badly too. Similarly, the reverse can apply, where every water may be responding well. Certainly, on our local waters if one broad is not producing, very few in the vicinity will be fishing well. In these conditions we would usually move to the rivers, where pike can generally be expected to feed more frequently.

We have mentioned variations of time of year and time of day, the pike's preference for live- or deadbait on particular waters, and the variations between them. We have mentioned some of the effects of weather, water clarity, and so on, and how it is necessary to adapt to these differences. The thinking pike angler is one who is willing to adapt and experiment in order to obtain a sure knowledge of the waters he fishes. Only then will more constant success be achieved.

5

Night Pike

We have not undertaken a great deal of piking at night mainly on the grounds that daytime fishing is usually productive enough anyway and also because in midwinter it is just plain cold. Any serious night-piking foray in winter should not be attempted without many extra layers of thermal clothing, possibly a warm sleeping bag and adequate supplies of warm, non-alcoholic lubrication.

Our limited experiences at night are quite interesting, however. Martyn, for example, spent quite some time fishing the River Bure from a floodlit swim during the evening hours to midnight several years ago. His results

The stillness of the night was suddenly broken by the sound of a pike striking . . .

were encouraging in that following a spell of inactivity fish would often come between 10 p.m. and midnight. He did not catch any particularly large fish, though by the same token there were no jacks whatsoever in his catch. Most of the fish fell to livebaits, not deadbaits. Shortly after he ended his mini-campaign one of his companions, who had continued, caught a 20lb-plus fish just before midnight.

It does indeed appear that few very small pike are caught at night. This does not confirm the experience of Vic, who has had to suffer little pike when night fishing for zander. It may also be that some of the larger, more cautious pike may lose their caution after dark. On a water which has been very heavily fished more night feeding may be undertaken than is suspected. In addition, those pike which feed at night have no objection to taking livebaits, so do not be misled into thinking that only deadbaits work at night. Indeed, Martyn's largest night-caught pike fell to a livebait. On that occasion he arrived at his swim several hours before dusk, the baits were cast out and both he and Dave Humphries settled in the bottom of the boat, not expecting activity until the morning. They had arrived extremely early in order that the swim should not be disturbed in any way before dusk. As they both lay dozing, the stillness of the night was suddenly broken by the sound of a pike striking, followed by the clicker of a multiplier screaming. Minutes later a 23lb-plus pike lay in the bottom of the boat. It is at this stage that difficulties can arise with unhooking. Obviously a strong torch is needed, but even so you can expect more finger lacerations at night than is usual during the day. Certainly on that occasion, the pike managed to drive one of its more developed teeth into Martyn's thumb. Apparently Lord Nelson used to paint the decks of his ships red to prevent the sight of blood discouraging the sailors. On that occasion perhaps the bottom of their boat should have been painted red as well.

That fish was caught rather by accident than by design. The whole purpose of arriving so early was to avoid disturbance at dawn. The fact that as light comes the swim has not been disturbed by your arrival can be one of the added benefits of night fishing for pike.

Finally, it is worth bearing the state of the moon in mind. It is very likely that pike will feed much more avidly at night during those brighter periods of the full moon. Indeed, Martyn's second-ever double-figure pike came in exactly these conditions while he was eel fishing.

Without a doubt pike do feed at night, though we suspect that this may be on a more random and unpredictable basis than during daylight. The possible exceptions are on heavily pressurised waters and during the first or last hour of darkness.

PART TWO

THE VERSATILITY OF DEADBAITING

6

Dead-or-Alive Theories – I

Until comparatively recently deadbaiting has been a method unique to the British Isles. Elsewhere in the world, the majority of pike anglers rely on livebaiting or lure fishing. This is something we predict will change during the next few years, particularly in the case of neighbouring European countries. This will occur partly through a greater awareness of the methods pioneered in the United Kingdom but also, in some countries, partly through a misguided sense of conservation (see Chapter 14) resulting in a ban on the use of livebaits.

Why should the United Kingdom have developed this particular form of pike fishing? Why is deadbaiting more popular than any other method of pike fishing in England? Is it that we are lazy, do not wish to spend the time catching a few livebaits or cannot be bothered with the constant casting necessary to catch fish on lures. We wish merely to set up our rods, cast to the horizon and sit back and wait . . . and wait? Possibly there is some truth in this. Certainly, many anglers practise only this form of pike fishing, missing out on the delights of numerous other, more active methods. Yet do they miss out on fish? We believe that they miss out on numbers of fish if this is their only approach, not only because on many occasions a different method would prove better, but also because a more adventurous approach to deadbaiting could result in more fish. It is all too easy to become set in one's ways and rely on one particular method alone.

Laziness, however, is not the reason why deadbaiting has become our number one method. There is more to it than that to British anglers. Deadbaiting is not new. There are references to its use in books written in the 1700s and even in the Boke of St Albans published in the fifteenth century. The effectiveness of herring was well known even in those days. Deadbaiting did not become a generally practised method, however, until centuries later, and it was the middle of the twentieth century before it began to become popular with pike anglers. This may be because declining fish numbers made the catching of livebaits less easy, but frankly we doubt it. There is a more likely reason for its rapid increase in popularity in the last decade. Some thirty or forty years ago it became a method popularised by people such as Bill Giles, Reg Sandys, Fred J. Taylor and other great innovators of that age. Vic, of course, featured amongst those happily catching great pike on deadbaits in the 1950s and 1960s. As more people tried the method so more pike were caught. The wheel kept turning and accelerating as it became apparent that deadbaiting, although on average it produced fewer fish, seemed to single out the larger specimens. It became clear, and remains so, that deadbaiting is an extremely effective method for catching larger pike. It is perhaps singly the most efficient long-term method available to the modern pike angler fishing British waters. But you will of course realise from that very statement that it is not necessarily the most efficient method on a particular day, at a particular time or on a particular water. Do not get caught in the trap of being a one-method pike angler. Do not pretend that deadbaiting will always result in bigger fish on the bank. Stay adaptable, but by all means practise deadbaiting in the knowledge that it is a great method.

As deadbaiting grew in popularity – and at times through necessity, for even then a number of water owners did not allow the use of live fish as bait – a popular concept began to develop that large pike skulked along the lake bed, only occasionally striking at live fish, preferring to scavenge on dead fish lying on the bottom. The reasoning behind this was that the pike was rewarded with maximum energy and growth potential for little effort. Such a concept initially makes good sense but, like many aspects of pike angling, its logic is now being questioned.

Let us just think for a minute about a new water. All things being equal, in a *healthy* water a pike will not come across numbers of dead fish. Occasionally the odd juicy morsel will be found lying on the bottom, and who could blame the pike for taking advantage of an easy meal. Usually, however, it will need to hunt live fish for its food. It might have a preference for sick or dying fish, since these are easier to catch, and our predator plays an important role as nature's means of stock control helping eliminate overcrowding and the spread of disease. This surely indicates that livebaiting must be the best method by which to catch large pike. Nature designed this beautiful creature to eat live fish; unlike a catfish, it is not primarily designed to search the bottom as a scavenger. It follows therefore that there are serious flaws within the argument that pike prefer deadbaits. Another comes from the pike's inability to reason. We can quite happily sit here writing theoretically about such concepts, but the pike does not have this power; he or she merely swims in the water, a supreme predator acting instinctively as nature intended.

Why then do deadbaits produce larger pike? Quite simply they don't. Both live- and deadbaits produce the same size of pike over a period of time, provided each method is practised equally. If one examines Steve Harper's and Martyn's records over the course of the last two decades, it can be seen clearly that in years when they practised livebaiting more than deadbaiting that method produced more of the bigger fish, and vice versa. Over recent years Martyn has developed a preference for active deadbaiting, whereas Steve is perhaps one of

the great livebait anglers of our time. A comparison of their records indicates that Steve has caught more big pike on livebaits whereas Martyn has had more of his big fish on deads. These records cover a number of waters and number of years fishing together. Some waters respond consistently better to deads than others and some hardly respond at all – a case of getting to know the peculiarities of each water.

Whilst it is true that one can catch as many big pike on live- as one can on deadbaits, the average size of fish caught on deadbait does appear larger. Quite simply, young pike are far more active than their adults, in much the same way as are our young children. They are growing, and require more food. They are also learning their trade, which is as a hunter of live fish. They take these with greater frequency because their growth and survival depend on their growing too big for other pike to eat. Nature hasn't told them that pike anglers would come along and provide them with quantities of dead fish to feed on. In addition, their eyes are not usually bigger than their stomach. We have all seen examples which attempt to prove otherwise but these are the exception. Usually a whole herring or mackerel left on the bottom will be ignored by jack pike, and a small live roach is likely to provide a more acceptable meal. To a degree this accounts for why a smaller bait such as smelt, sardine or sprat seems to produce more fish but of a lower average size than a whole herring or mackerel or offerings of a similar size.

Livebaiting usually catches more pike as well as a sprinkling of larger fish. With deadbaiting not so many smaller fish are caught and because the average size appears larger anglers tend to consider that deadbaits attract more large fish than livebaits. We must stress, however, that this example is based on all things being equal, with a variety of waters being fished and on each occasion an equal number of livebait rods and deadbait rods in use for comparison. If, for example, you are allowed to use three rods and two are fished with deadbaits and one with livebaits the results will be inaccurate. Simi-

A 21-pounder caught on pilchard in a flat calm.

larly, a false assumption as to the merits of either bait could arise when one particular water is fished. Take Filby Broad in Norfolk, which seems to respond very well to deadbaits in early winter. If you fish only at that time you will catch very few big pike on livebaits. Deadbaiting will reign supreme. But try that water later in the year when the water has cleared, let's say in late December and on towards the end of the season. The deadbait rods would then remain static for most of the day while, at times, livebaits would provide hectic sport. A totally different picture!

Returning to the theme, we have our new healthy water which has never seen a pike angler's deadbait. Initially we would expect to find deadbaits very slow and livebaits producing most of the fish (although we are very much aware that there are exceptions to all concepts and rules). But man can exert an influence and we are certain that the continuing use of deadbaits in waters over the last few

decades has materially affected the feeding habits of those pike. With our new water, as more and more deadbaits are thrown away at the end of the day it becomes more usual for the pike to encounter these free meals. After a time fish become accustomed to expect these offerings and, being opportunists, are effectively weaned on to this diet. The water becomes a deadbait fishery, so more and more anglers use deadbaits, which reinforces its reputation.

An analogy of this weaning process can easily be made with the use of boilies by carp anglers. In such cases a large input will produce results relatively quickly. Similarly, on a new water a few weeks of dead prebaiting could make deadbaits acceptable to the pike that much sooner. Finally, we would again qualify our theory as a generalisation. On some waters the pike will respond to deadbaits instantly. Often these are those more coloured waters, or waters where there is an abundance of prey fish. In the latter case the reason may be that the pike are more

An estate lake pike fishery in winter.

used to finding sick, dying and dead fish, and have already been weaned on to them. It could be that because the deadbaits look different and are different they stand out like a signal beacon, whereas our little livebait fishing amongst a horde of other fish may not be singled out so easily. It is only one of the many available, like the needle in the proverbial haystack. Alternatively, in coloured water the deadbait may be found by smell whereas the pike may find it harder to home in on a livebait.

Returning once more to the original question, why have we in the United Kingdom developed deadbaiting to such a fine degree and left the rest of the world standing? It is not that we are better anglers. That would be conceited. We believe that it is because there is more competition. This little island of ours supports a large number of anglers with limited access to water. Inevitably, this results in a competitive spirit, a search for virgin territory or a search for a better method, a more sophisticated method that will result in more fish. People such as the great Dick Walker turned a

key which unlocked a growing desire to catch bigger fish because he proved that it was possible. Since then the rapid development, through specimen groups to specialists, has resulted in more and more competition and the pursuit of larger and larger fish. This has resulted in English angling methods becoming far more sophisticated than those used in other parts of the world. Arguably, some things have been lost on the way – including, for many, we believe, the ability to really enjoy fishing, something which the rest of the world has not lost. But the English are notorious for leadership and invention and in angling we have certainly upheld our reputation. Quite simply competition was the spur which led to the deadbait revolution. The same competitive urge has led to the constant search for a better method, a better bait and a bigger fish. At the beginning of Part Three we compare deadbaits to sweets, the abnormal but preferred titbit. Once the pike is aware of their availability, its lazy nature and 'sweet tooth' does the rest.

7

A Multiplicity of Choice

The versatility of deadbaiting lies not only with the large choice of baits available but also with the large number of variations and presentations which can be achieved with all these baits. With livebaiting it is relatively straightforward; there are a limited number of effective rigs and a limited number of live species. For instance, it is not possible to present an artificially coloured livebait or a half or sectioned livebait. Similarly, it is not practical to continually cast and retrieve a livebait as one would in wobbling, unless one has an enormous supply, for very soon the live fish would become very dead indeed.

Deadbaiting is made easy because the baits are readily available from fishmongers and, more recently, from most good tackle shops.

There is an enormous choice, from the all-time favourite herring to the exotics such as bonkers, red gurnard, and so on. Let us look at some of them.

HERRINGS

If we were limited to just one deadbait this would probably be our choice. Herrings are probably the most versatile and, initially, the most effective deadbait available. They were, of course, also one of the first to be recognised as an effective bait for catching pike. There is no question that an enormous number of the large pike caught in Great Britain in the last few

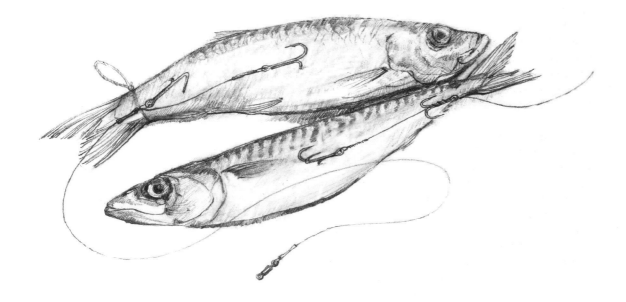

decades have fallen to herring. Why are they so effective? There are probably several answers to this question. One is that they are often one of the first deadbaits to be used on a water. Always readily available, they are the cheapest choice offered by the fishmonger, so quite naturally they became the most commonly used deadbait. However, ignoring this, the herring has much to offer in itself.

A herring has high attraction qualities. Its silver-blue colour, so akin to a roach, the pike's natural prey, is highly visible in or on the bottom of most waters. In addition, a fresh herring – and more on this point later – has masses of tiny scales which not only find their way onto reels and rod handles and into the sandwich box but also come adrift on impact with the water, leaving a cascade of silver homing beacons slowly sinking through the water ages after the bait has settled on the bottom. This must surely enhance the bait's effectiveness.

Another point in favour of the herring is the oils which are also released on splashdown. It is easy to tell a fresh from an old herring, not only from the scales and the lively silver-blue sheen of the bait, but also by the large oil slick which causes an expanding calm area to drift slowly downwind from the point where the bait enters the water. Much has been said in the past about oils and their effectiveness. The inability of some oils to diffuse in water has been put forward as a counter-argument to any suggestion that the oils attract pike. However, it is surprising how many times a fresh oily herring will score over an old manky offering. In very coloured water it is doubtful whether it is the bright colour so much as the scent being released from the bait which attracts a pike.

Vic says that the properties of a bait which stimulate pike are, in order of importance, sight, vibration and smell. The latter sense is the least developed in the pike but he agrees that they can detect scent and can find food using this sense alone.

Martyn believes that the weaning process can result in an increased use of this sense over the course of time.

Having established that the herring attracts by both appearance and smell, and that the first of these, sight is the more important, we can consider some of its other positive attractions. One of these is the general size. We have all searched the fishmonger's for small herrings – not the huge specimens that are so often caught off the Scottish coast but ideally fish of such size that four or five of them weigh a pound. It is the 3–4oz size which makes such an ideal bait for double-figure and even larger pike. They

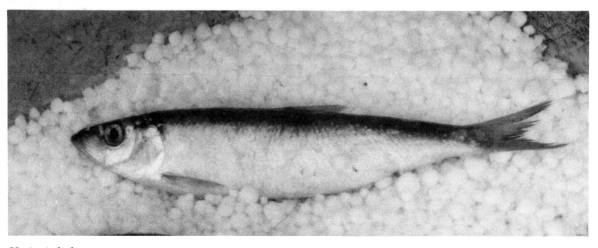

Herring in hailstones.

are relatively easy to cast with an adequate pike rod and, most important, they provide a good square meal for the pike. A herring is also a relatively soft bait – not so soft that it falls apart after the first cast but soft enough for the hooks to break clear of the flesh on striking, so ensuring positive hooking. The herring really has so much else going for it. It can easily be dyed to any colour, it is not a difficult bait to fish suspended (more on these two methods later), it is durable enough to fish as a large wobbled bait, and it is ideal as a trolled deadbait.

There are one or two disadvantages with a herring. The biggest, strangely enough, is that it is so effective and easy to obtain. This means that it will almost certainly have been used quite extensively on any water you intend to fish which has already received attention from pike anglers. On any new water it pays to research as much as possible what baits have been used and when. Pike do have a form of memory – not in the same calibre as carp, but they do go off baits after they have been caught on them. Fortunately, if you ring the changes the herring has a very extended life. A change from fishing a whole herring to the tail half (an exceptionally deadly bait) can bring life back into the bait. If action tails off again the head section may become favourite, and then perhaps a coloured herring. Eventually, all these choices will decline in effectiveness, but it is very rare for them to become totally ineffective. In addition, a pike's memory is not that long and a bait which seems to have 'blown' may well come back to life the next season or later in the same season. It does mean, however, that on a popular heavily fished water the herring may not be the ultimate bait. We use the word 'ultimate' with extreme caution since we really believe that there is no such thing. We will discuss this further when talking about our next bait, the smelt.

Before leaving herrings it is worth mentioning again the question of fresh baits. These comments apply to most deadbaits but certainly to some more than others – herrings and smelt are perhaps prime examples. Pike are easy to catch; they will take anything which provides them with a satisfactory meal. It does not matter to a hungry feeding pike that the meal in front of her is a manky old herring with its guts hanging out which has been refrozen six or seven times and is over a year old. She is hungry, she wants a meal and there it is. But then she actually happened across the bait, by accident. But what of the pike which is yards away, swimming positively but not particularly worried whether a meal comes now or in an hour's time. The old herring lies on the bottom. It has losts its bright silver sheen and has a sort of old yellow look about it, certainly not bright and attractive, and it is unlikely to catch our pike's eye. Then there is the smell. Gone is that sea-fresh 'please eat me' attractive aroma. It has been replaced by a high 'I belong in the dustbin' pungent odour, not exactly an irresistible invitation. Unquestionably the fresh deadbait has more attractive qualities and our results over the years support the conclusion that there is a very significant difference in the effectiveness and hence the results obtained between fresh and not-so-fresh deadbaits. We like to meet the fishmonger when he receives his delivery of fresh-caught baits. The fresher the better, which leads us to digress slightly into the question of bait storage.

We live now in the day of the freezer. It is easy simply to buy a few baits already frozen from the tackle shop or directly from the fishmonger, throw them in the freezer and only think about them when it comes to the day's piking. You will catch plenty of pike this way, in the course of time, and pike fishing is all about catching pike. We believe, however, that you can catch more with a little bit of thought when the baits are first bought, and a little more care to ensure that when you first cast the bait out it is the most effective offering that can be obtained.

Let's say you have just bought several pounds of herrings from the fishmonger. He will probably have wrapped them all together in newspaper. If they are merely chucked in the freezer in this state not only will they form a solid mass but the paper will absorb much of the surface slime. When you come to use a bait it will not have that pristine sheen referred to earlier. As soon as possible after the baits are acquired they should be removed from the paper and ideally individually wrapped in cling film. This stops any further contact with the air and preserves that attractive sheen and as many scales as possible. In addition, there is no difficulty in breaking one herring away from the frozen block, which inevitably ruptures the skin and causes the fish to fall apart very quickly. Immediately all the baits are wrapped in cling film they should be frozen as quickly as possible to preserve their freshness. If you do not use cling film they should be wrapped in polythene (lunch bags for example), in such a way that each bait is kept separate. The bags should then be sealed so that they are airtight. We usually wrap baits in batches. First wrap them in the cling film and then place enough of these wrapped baits for a day's piking into a sealed polythene bag. The individual packages can be labelled as to their contents, which makes recognition easier. Obviously, you need an understanding partner or preferably an independent bait freezer in order to build up a good supply of well prepared deadbaits.

We have found that herrings are even more effective if they are bought fresh the day before they are to be used and not placed in the freezer at all, but are wrapped as described and kept cool overnight in the fridge. Every time a bait is frozen it seems to lose a little of its effectiveness and the pure non-frozen fresh herring seems to be the most deadly of all.

Ensuring that baits are fresh at all times can prove costly in money terms but we believe that this cost is outweighed by more fish on the bank. To help save some cost baits can be taken on the day in a cool box or bag, which will ensure that they remain virtually frozen throughout the day. Those unused can then be replaced in the freezer when you return home. We do not refreeze a bait that has been used, even if only for a few minutes, on the grounds that much of the freshness will have been lost

by the time it is refrozen. After two or three outings baits need a careful inspection. Almost certainly one or two will have suffered from refreezing, their fresh look will have disappeared, and they are discarded. So many anglers refreeze used baits, and continue to refreeze time and time again those baits which have lost that fresh smell and appearance, which diminishes with each sojourn in the freezer.

As with every theory, it doesn't always pay to be too set in one's ways and on one occasion Martyn had this fresh-bait fanaticism nearly rebound on him. He was fishing a gravel pit which had suffered some fairly extensive piking and returns had really dropped off, with virtually no runs coming to herrings. This was many years ago and there were very few change baits available at the time. On one particular outing, because of bad weather the fishmongers had not managed to obtain any herrings that week. All Martyn had for the weekend's pike trip was one or two very old herrings. With very little confidence these were cast into the pit and he sat back for a long unexpectant wait. Several pike later it appeared that the pike were back on herrings. However, the following weekend, armed with fresh herrings, he had no runs. Fortunately, Martyn realised that the only difference was the use of old baits and for the next few weeks he enjoyed good sport using extremely old baits while others blanked. The theory was that the pike had become very wary of fresh baits during the period of intensive fishing, and so avoided them. Instead they were picking up the old baits as these were 'safe', being similar to the ones thrown away at the end of the day's fishing. This did not last long, however, and – interestingly – very fresh sprats became the effective bait within a matter of weeks.

That is probably a good illustration of why generalisation is dangerous. But we are still very firm advocates of paying just that little bit more attention to detail with regard to our baits. We believe it can only result in better catches.

SMELTS

This bait rose to number one place in popularity a few years ago. At that time smelts were extremely difficult to obtain and a few lucky anglers who managed to secure a supply began reporting enviable catches. Soon the 'cucumber fish' began to gain a reputation as the ultimate pike bait. This is of course a nonsense as there is no such thing. The smelt is just another very effective bait, especially on waters where it has not previously been used.

As the popularity of smelt increased, so too did the publicity and with this came the anglers' demand which was eventually supplied by the enterprising. Most tackle shops now stock smelts and recently fishmongers, having come to realise the size of the angling market, have begun to stock fish specifically for anglers. There has of course always been a limited

When the deadbait starts feeding things must be getting tough – a smelt.

supply of smelts since they are regarded as a delicacy by some.

Obviously the smelt has gained popularity because it catches pike. But why is it so effective? The size is nothing special; the average smelt falls somewhere between a sprat and a herring, though it is much more slender. It is not highly visible. Indeed, the sandy colour can impair its visibility in coloured water. Fresh smelts are quite tough and durable but once the freshness is lost the belly become very soft and prone to split on casting. The attributes of the smelt seem to rest on two factors: first, smell and, second, buoyancy. We believe that the first is the main reason for its effectiveness and the second can be used to advantage in certain circumstances – a point which reaffirms Martyn's conviction that smell is a very important factor in deadbaiting.

The smelt isn't naturally buoyant, but as the freshness decreases it appears to achieve a form of neutral buoyancy. This means that a frozen smelt which is not extremely fresh often fails to sink, which can prove extremely frustrating at times. A very fresh smelt is therefore fairly light and the insertion of a short section of deadbait foam or a deadbait floater stick results in an even more buoyant bait, which can prove particularly effective on silty bottoms.

The smell, however, seems to be the key to this bait's effectiveness. It smells unmistakably of cucumber, whence its nickname, and, being so unique, seems to offer the pike something completely different. Fortunately, that smell is to the pike's liking. This brings us back once more to the question of fresh baits. We are of the opinion that an old smelt which does not give off a strong cucumber smell is a relatively ineffective deadbait. It has lost its main attribute. It is not highly visible, so it really offers little inducement to the pike. It still catches occasionally, but a comparison between anglers using very fresh and not so fresh smelts has proved to us fairly conclusively that this smell factor is of the utmost importance. On several occasions a change to a new bait after a couple of hours has brought an instant response in the

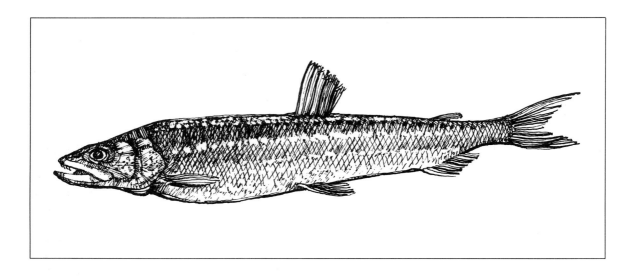

same swim. Time and time again the fresh smelts have produced all the takes whereas more ancient smelts have been left untouched. We cannot emphasise this point too strongly. We firmly believe that unless these baits are fresh results will actually be worse than would be achieved by using others.

There is currently a trend for the use of super-smelts. Anglers search for the biggest possible smelt because it is believed that these will produce bigger pike. It is akin to the notion that the grass is always greener . . . The problem with big smelts is that very often they turn out to be much softer and less 'cucumbery' than their smaller brethren. Perhaps they have been subject to selection and refreezing, which means that they are not as fresh. We are not convinced that these super-smelts, unless they are also super-fresh and super-smelly, are as magic as some believe. Smelts are usually sold in packs in tackle shops whilst the super-large ones have usually been sorted and are sold in packs of just one or two. Our greatest success has come with the larger ones found in the pound packs (middle-sized smelts). What else can be said about smelts? Apart from having an amazing mouthful of fang-like teeth, they undoubtedly rank amongst our top three choices of deadbaits, along with herrings and mackerel,

but they have not fulfilled some people's original contention that they are the ultimate bait.

MACKEREL

A strange one, this! So many pike anglers consider mackerel a slow bait but a great selector for giant pike. Martyn's first thirty came on mackerel and Vic has caught two thirties on very large whole mackerel. One fish took a huge mackerel that had not been moved all day. They certainly seem to attract very big pike and all pike anglers will experience at some time that heart-stopping realisation that the mackerel has at last been taken after hours of waiting. Surely this is *the fish*!

This bait is rarely the first deadbait to prove very effective on a water, but after a while, when returns on a herring, smelt and the rest start to diminish, mackerel sometimes comes into its own in a quite incredible fashion. It seems almost as though the pike become wary of high-visibility baits rather than being attracted to them, or perhaps they just get bored with the flavour, and then the uniqueness of mackerel takes effect. Often this bait will have an extremely long life.

We have described the bait as unique and we

say this for several reasons. First, its barred coloration is unlike most of the other baits we use. It is extremely oily and goes on emitting its oil hour after hour. It doesn't seem as susceptible to the fresh-bait concept mentioned earlier. Mackerel seems effective even after several re-freezings, the oily aroma retaining its own unique smell. Possibly in some ways a mackerel lying on the bottom looks like a small dead pike; it is streamlined like a pike and it has the barred coloration and, although admittably the wrong colour, such a subtle distinction between blues and greens may not be particularly noticeable to a pike underwater. Perhaps the mackerel's reputation for attracting giant pike rests partially on the fact that the bait appeals to their cannibalistic instinct.

The ideal mackerel bait is an unusual concept. Martyn remembers hearing of the occasion when a young pike angler was told to try 'a good-sized mackerel' on one of the Norfolk Broads where he was meeting with little success. The lad went to the fishmonger's and bought a 'good-sized' one and, fishing according to instructions, he caught a 21lb pike. He was over the moon about his largest pike, but explained that he had difficulty in casting and thought the bait too expensive to use very often. On further inquisition it transpired that when asking the fishmonger for a good sized mackerel he was given a bait which weighed over 2lb. A good-sized bait indeed!

Generally, at the beginning of the pike season the mackerel in the fishmongers' are far too big, most weighing over a pound. As the winter progresses smaller mackerel begin to appear on the slab. Mackerel are not fat fish but are long and oval-shaped and an 8oz one is quite a mouthful for a pike and weighs rather more than many pike rods can safely handle. To overcome these deficiencies mackerel are seldom fished whole, unless some small joey mackerel can be obtained. These often appear in the shops around January and February and although they can prove an extremely effective bait it is sometimes found that they are not as effective as a half-bait.

We believe that this is because one of the mackerel's greatest attributes is its smell. This strong aroma is fully released only when the bait is cut. When using a whole mackerel we usually puncture the skin in several places, which we are sure improves its attractiveness. The half-bait gives off an even more powerful scent.

There is often discussion among pike anglers about whether the tail half or the head half of a mackerel is the most effective. Quite honestly, we haven't noticed any difference either way. Martyn compares this with herring, of which he believes that the tail half is much more effective. Vic doesn't entirely agree, he thinks that the red colouring round the eye makes the head half of a herring even more attractive than the tail.

The mackerel has another considerable advantage over many baits. With a streamlined shape and composed of very dense flesh, it can be cast like a rocket, especially when frozen. This can be extremely useful where distance fishing is necessary.

The mackerel's tough skin is this bait's only disadvantage. Great care must be taken when inserting hooks in a mackerel otherwise a number of pike could be lost because the tough skin and flesh can prevent the hooks pulling free before lodging in a pike's mouth. If the hooks are deeply embedded the bait may act as a lever, enabling the pike to eject the bait when head-shaking. A few anglers aware of these problems have been known to leave a run for rather longer than is wise. This practice should be discouraged at all costs. There are effective rigs for overcoming the problem of hooking tough baits for long-range casting, such as the flick-off ring illustrated on page 70, and for closer range the problem can be overcome if the bait-holding hook is nicked lightly under the skin of the mackerel but not into the flesh itself. The VB and recently introduced SD double hooks can be used with the flick-off casting link and are particularly efficient in this respect.

We have mentioned that it takes pike rather

more time to accept mackerel than herring. As with so many aspects of piking such bold statements do not always hold true. For instance, in strong tidal waters mackerel are often one of the first deadbaits to produce a good response. Possibly this is due to the oil filtering downstream, its scent drawing pike to the bait. If this is the case it must discount the theory that if the oil does not diffuse but emulsifies in cold water it cannot be attractive to the pike.

If we were limited to a choice of only three types of deadbaits there would be no hesitation in choosing herrings, for their visibility and versatility, smelts, for their exotic smell, and mackerel for their many unique characteristics (not necessarily in that order).

SARDINES AND PILCHARDS

Sardines, in larger sizes called pilchards, are another extremely effective bait. They have the disadvantage of being very soft-fleshed so it is often necessary to secure them to hooks with weak cotton in order that they are not lost on the cast. Tail-looped sardines used with a flick-off casting link offer another solution to this problem. It is unlikely that there is any such thing as a fresh sardine available in this country since they are imported frozen. However, they are another bait whose effectiveness does not appear to diminish noticeably with refreezing.

Possibly, if we could obtain really fresh sardines they would make superb baits.

The sardine is another extremely oily bait. This oil is readily exuded from the fragile skin. Martyn has used these baits quite extensively over the years and has noticed that the smaller baits produce a considerable number of takes from smaller-size fish compared with most other baits of similar proportions. A few years ago he managed to obtain some colossal pilchards and used them with devastating effect. One catch included three 20lb-plus fish, with the largest over 29lb, whilst others around him struggled to catch on other live- and deadbaits.

In summary, we have concluded that in general the small-sized sardines are a very good pike bait and they do of course catch large pike. But it seems that a far better bait for a big pike is a large pilchard.

SPRATS

Most pike anglers will have used sprats at some time during their angling careers. This small silvery version of the herring is often the first deadbait used by anglers new to pike fishing. They are not generally an effective big-pike bait, possibly because their size makes them less appealing to larger pike, but they are, unquestionably, a very good bait for smaller ones. There are exceptions: Vic knows of three thirties that fell to sprats.

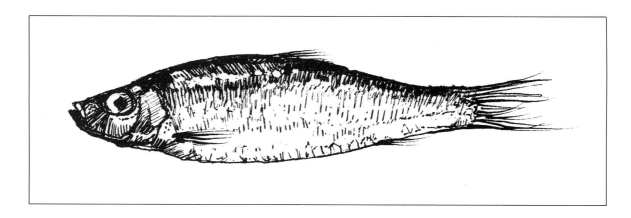

A buoyant sprat fished amongst fry-feeding pike can attract the larger fish. As the pike lunge in for a kill and the smaller fish scatter, the bright sprat remains to become a target. This tactic works best where the fry shoal is not too dense, or if the sprat can be fished at the edge of the fry concentration.

The sprat really comes into its own as a wobbled bait, particularly on rivers. It can also prove useful for very long-range fishing, where, if it is used with a very heavy lead, extreme distances can be obtained, which may not always be possible with some of the larger deadbaits, whose greater surface area is more affected by air resistance. (The exception is a mackerel tail, which is not only dense-fleshed and relatively heavy but aerodynamic in shape as well.)

COARSE FISH

Fresh coarse fish such as roach, dace, bream and others are often neglected by pike anglers. We do not fully understand why this should be the case, except that sea baits are easier to obtain, and on many waters will prove to be just as effective most of the time. This is not always the case, however, and occasionally fresh coarse fish will outfish all other forms of deadbait. A good example is one of our local waters once again, Filby Broad. This water receives a considerable amount of attention from local pike anglers and the pike have seen most standard, and indeed most exotic, sea baits. For years, however, a very effective method has been to fish a paternostered coarse deadbait suspended about 2 feet off the bottom. Martyn recalls John Harwood demonstrating how well the Filby pike respond to this style on one occasion when John took eight pike, including five doubles, in a morning session, compared with Martyn's one caught on sea baits.

Apart from their use as suspended baits they can also prove fairly effective on the bottom, with results often improving if they are stabbed several times so that their natural juices are released more freely. Incidentally, the use of a very fresh natural deadbait (by this we mean one killed on the day) which is freshly stabbed can prove extremely effective for zander and perch. With these predators it seems much more essential that the bait is exceedingly fresh.

Perhaps the greatest use of natural deadbaits is for wobbling and sink-and-draw fishing. Bream, with their flat shape, are not quite so effective for this but roach and dace are ideally suited. Coarse fish are fairly durable and will withstand much more casting than most sea baits – an important attribute.

GAME FISH

Dead trout, salmon parr, and the like are an interesting choice of deadbaits. They do not seem to have many outstanding characteristics except perhaps where pike and game fish share the same environment. We have occasionally experienced reasonable success but have never been convinced that game fish are as effective as most other deadbaits. They are tough and durable and make quite a good wobbled bait, but they are not highly visible and on most waters we have not found that they are particularly effective. The possible exception, of course, is a trout water and even here success has usually been more noticeable with a suspended trout rather than one fished hard on the bottom. They do not come high on our list of deadbaits, though no doubt some pike anglers will think otherwise. However, as a livebait they are something else!

EEL SECTIONS AND SANDEELS

Quite why any self-respecting pike should wish to eat a chunk of eel lying on the bottom in preference to a more fish-shaped offering can cause much astonishment to some pike anglers. On some waters eel sections may prove to be a very attractive bait and one with an extremely long effective life. There are numerous theories why this should be so. It is often said that since eels are not active in winter pike should not be accustomed to finding them and therefore there is little reason why the bait should be effective.

Current thinking seems to indicate that eels may be much more active in winter than suspected. Another suggestion which has been put forward is that eels lie virtually buried in bottom silt with just their heads protruding and the pike take great delight in ferreting the eel from its sanctuary. There maybe some merit in this supposition. There has for many years been considerable speculation as to what food forms the main diet of those pike which remain on some of the Norfolk Broads throughout the winter months, even though most of the roach have migrated into the rivers. Current theory is now suggesting that eels become a staple diet. We are not entirely convinced. Certainly, the theories on pike and fish movement on the Broads need far more research before such speculation is proved. In addition, if this was the only reason why pike enjoyed eels with such relish one would not expect the eel to be such a killing bait on harder bottoms. However, research on some of our larger tidal and hard-bottomed river systems, the Waveney being one example, suggests that eels can form a greater proportion of the pike's winter diet.

Why then should eels prove such an effective bait on so many waters? Quite simply we believe that, unlike some deadbaits, eels are not only the natural food of the pike but, where they are present, they form a significant part of their preferred diet if they are present in quantity. In other words, the pike enjoy their taste. In addition, it may well be that pike find eels easy to catch. This may be hard to accept for anyone who has handled the things, but to a sharp-toothed pike eels could form an easy prey.

Sandeels make a change bait from freshwater eels and can prove very effective in their own right. Perhaps they are regarded by the pike as an exotic eel dish similar to our concept of a Foo Yung as an exotic omelette.

Other points to remember with regard to eels are that they are very tough-skinned, so do not embed the bait-holding hook deeply in the flesh. Vic cuts away a small section of skin so that the bait-holding hook can be inserted into the flesh. It holds well during casting yet pulls away from the bait when the strike is made. A long eel section or a sandeel can make an extremely effective bait for wobbling.

OTHER EXOTICS

Virtually any dead fish can be used as a deadbait. We have outlined above most of the more common baits but English pike waters will in the course of time see even more unusual varieties, from flying fish and travelly to horse mackerel and bonkers. Generally such exotics are an expensive luxury rarely needed, but in heavily fished waters where the pike have become wary of the more usual baits there is this vast array of different exotics available to try, and like any other deadbait they can be fished in many different ways as well as dyed strange colours. The pike angler can vary his baits, their colour and flavour much as the carp angler doctors his boilies. It is these almost unlimited variations which give contemporary pike anglers such versatility.

8

Dyed Deadbaits – Colouring Your Approach

Vic has undertaken extensive research in past years into the use of coloured baits, the results of which he outlines in this chapter.

I cannot imagine that I was the first to experiment with coloured pike baits, but it must have been at least twenty-five years ago that I tried wobbling sprats dyed a deep yellow. After some initial success, I soon began to dye herrings and mackerel for use as bottom-fished baits as well. I do not claim that using dyed baits was a sudden flash of inspiration, but because I am an all-round angler, and having practised my share of game fishing, I was well aware that spinning a golden sprat was, in certain conditions, a most effective way of taking salmon. If salmon liked golden sprats it seemed probable that pike would also take kindly to them, and so it proved.

I searched round for a suitable dye and after some trial and error found that Dylon cold-water dyes used double-strength produced deep colour. In dying natural baits, such as roach, the mucus had to be removed and the fish wiped dry before immersion in the dye bath. The same procedure applied for sea baits. Normally, immersion for 15–20 minutes is sufficient to produce strong colour. I wondered if the dye would taint the bait and mask its natural scent, so at first I used to brush the dyed baits with pilchard oil. I suppose it was quite a good idea, but hardly necessary for baits which were to be wobbled. For static baits anointing with oil seemed sensible at the time, but having caught numerous pike on plain dyed baits I cannot prove that a coating of pilchard oil made all that difference. Perhaps essence of

smelt and similar contemporary concoctions may enhance a bait's attractions. I keep an open mind on the subject.

With fish the dye cannot be fixed as it can with fabric, so it tends to wash off in water, particularly when continuously cast and retrieved in deadbait spinning or wobbling. But by the time the colour has weakened the bait needs renewing so it is of no importance. Static baits retain their colour for much longer. Nowadays blast-frozen dyed baits are available from tackle shops, so the tedium of home dying is no longer necessary, unless of course, you wish to experiment with colours not normally available.

In imitation of a golden sprat I experimented at first with deep-yellow baits, and shortly afterwards with a few dyed a rich orange. Strangely, these colours have proved to be better than all the others I have tried. When wobbling, and I used mainly sprats and small herrings in those days, I took no account of light values and just tried out a coloured bait for no particular reason, except that I thought a change might interest any pike that had ignored a naturally coloured one. Not surprisingly, this haphazard approach produced little conclusive evidence that dyed baits were any better than those in their natural state. However, I was encouraged because I caught pike on both yellow and orange wobbled baits, though during the early part of that season I caught as many on undyed ones. As far as I was concerned dyed baits were no better or worse than normal ones but useful as a change bait when the fishing was slow.

My opinion soon changed and I came to realise the value and potential of coloured baits one November day which I spent wobbling sprats on a Norfolk Broad. At that time I used to fish wobbled baits as a relief from the boring tedium of sitting by a couple of rods waiting for a pike to happen along and pick up a deadbait – not just for an hour or so but for a whole day's fishing. I caught more fish, too, even though the larger pike were usually taken by the more static approach. This may have been because I generally tended to use sprat-sized baits for wobbling. Now, with specially designed rigs which can accommodate more substantial baits, wobbling techniques will account for any pike that swims.

I suppose the reason I chose to use wobbled baits on that particular day was that I had selected some extra-large sprats at the fishmonger's, the first to be landed that year. They were fresh, firm and ideal for mounting on a wobbling rig. I dyed half of the sprats yellow.

By mid-morning it had become unseasonably warm, a butterfly day, the blue sky patterned by cumulus clouds for all the world like small puffs of cotton wool, hanging motionless, hardly moving or changing shape by the hour. Blue sky reflected from the surface of the Broad as a deeper rich blue, which was further reflected on to the white undersides of the ever-restless gulls. Occasionally a slight breeze, a mere cat's-paw, ruffled the surface in the centre of the Broad, but the water remained oily calm by the reed-fringed edges. Feathery reed tops hung motionless.

Because it was a weekend other boats with two anglers apiece lay anchored by mud weights and surrounded by orange-tipped floats which patterned the water round them. As far as I could ascertain only one pike had been caught and as I rowed past that boat, just within hailing distance, I learnt that it had been caught on a livebait. All those floats, no doubt indicating where herring or mackerel deadbaits were lying on the bottom, remained motionless.

Two stalwarts, like me, were wobbling sprats. One changed to a silver spoon which, as it hung suspended from the rod tip, twisted and

flashed in the sunlight as though adorned with diamonds. In answer to my query they told me that they had put in a great deal of effort for no reward. I knew just how they felt for I too had been wobbling my blue-and-silver sprats along the reed edges, then casting progressively further out into the Broad, each cast covering new ground. I had not had a response from any pike, nor even one of the smaller jacks which usually were suckers for a wobbled bait.

I decided to stop fishing, have a cup of coffee, munch a sandwich and sunbathe a little as I watched the other anglers lazing in their boats, no doubt half-heartedly watching their floats.

I let the boat drift against the reeds. By now I knew that it was going to be one of those bright, warm days full of sunshine, which always seemed to make the pike in that particular broad difficult to catch. I had suffered similar conditions before, having fished all day in a desultory manner and only reawakening my full interest when the light began to fade as evening approached. I considered that the only chance of a fish would perhaps come with a livebait and I was singularly lacking in those. Remembering the sage remark made to me by an ancient angler when I was a small boy – 'You won't catch a fish with your bait out of the water' – I bestirred myself and set about fishing with rather more ardour than before. I cannot imagine why I had not tried out one of the yellow baits, but perhaps I had decided to save them as a last resort. The decison to change was inevitable, as I only had a couple of natural baits left and I thought it best to save them until the sun was setting.

The yellow sprat shone golden in the water as it was drawn towards the surface close by the side of the boat. To me it looked most attractive and I hoped any pike that it passed by would think likewise. I tried some longer casts, watching the bait's parabolic trajectory before it splashed down on the surface to sink slowly, leaving an ever-widening circle of ripples which disturbed the mirror-calm water. After perhaps half a dozen casts, always watching for the bait as it neared the boat, I caught a glimpse of a long green shape which, for a fleeting second, materialised by the bait, then as quickly disappeared. I had moved a fish, at long last, and I started wobbling with renewed enthusiasm. Whether it was the same fish I shall never know, but shortly after a cast or two the line tightened and I felt a solid tug which bent the rod tip. Taken unawares, I reacted hurriedly. It was a natural instinctive response which made me strike back. For hardly a second I remained in contact with the fish, then the line slackened, and disconsolate, I retrieved a sorry-looking tooth-marked bait. That fish would have none of my further offerings, so I moved to pastures new and fished on, determined to react to any further takes in a more proficient manner. I was ready for the slight tightening of the line, followed this time by a gentle delicate pluck. I swung the rod tip back towards the bait, allowing the line to slacken, at the same time opening the bail arm. A couple of feet of line was drawn off the reel spool, so with a turn of the reel handle the bail arm snapped down, two or three further turns tightened the line and the rod was swept back sideways, tip low down over the water. The rod bent gracefully as the pike shaking its head, sought the sanctuary of deeper water. It was only a moderate-sized fish, possibly weighing 6 or 7lb, and after a final lunge by the boat side it was lifted out by hand, unhooked and returned.

I let the boat drift slowly on and cast a fresh yellow bait. Within minutes I was playing a better fish, which powered away strongly, making it necessary to yield line. I cannot remember its exact weight but I do know it was a nicely conditioned 15lb-plus fish. I was now thoroughly enjoying my fishing, oblivious of my surroundings, casting and retrieving with growing confidence, only standing up when it was time to wield the net. During a lull I noticed that my antics were being noted, as one angler had his binoculars trained in my direction. Shortly afterwards I landed a second double-figure pike, followed by another that didn't quite weigh 10lb.

By the end of the day I had boated seven fish, failed to hook a couple more, and had run out of yellow baits. I tried the last two natural sprats, wobbling one and conserving the last by suspending it under a float. Both these baits were ignored, as similar baits had been, as well as bottom-fished deadbaits used by others. Only odd pike had been caught on livebaits.

I did not immediately assume − which would have been understandable − that the colour of the baits had accounted for my success. It might have, but because I was moving around the Broad I was bound to come across pockets of pike grouped together, attracted into certain areas by a concentration of prey fish. I pondered the reason for some time and tried to find a logical answer. I never have, but I am inclined to think that a combination of very high light values and clear, shallow water made the more natural blue-and-silver sprats emit so much flash that they were inclined to scare or put off, rather than attract, pike.

Many anglers will agree that a dull-coloured, even black lure, spoon or spinner is more effective in clear water and strong sunlight. Bright, shiny lures are near-useless. I think that the same criterion applies with spun or wobbled baits. No doubt the dyed baits eliminated excessive flash, but the colour may also have added to their attraction. The pike on that Broad have been fished for for centuries; only in the last couple of decades have they been caught and returned. It takes only a few years for them to recognise that herrings, for example, which they like, are not always what they seem. I and others proved that dyed herrings were not treated with the same suspicion. I am pretty sure that the pike had not encountered yellow or orange sprats before and that may in part have accounted for their attraction. I am far from convinced that this was the case. All too easily anglers are inclined to credit fish with human reactions to any given situation, which implies some degree of conscious thought. Fish react instinctively; their thought processes, if they possess any, must be of the most rudimentary kind. By far the most important instinct, which is highly developed in fish, is the instinct to survive. Some pike, in some waters, have become instinctively wary of herrings, probably of sprats and the ever-popular smelt as well. If these baits are coloured they are no longer recognised as dangerous. The fear instinct is not triggered, so a pike will pick up a coloured bait but instinctively leave a natural one alone. Not always, but sometimes. There are no hard-and-fast rules in angling. A factor or a set of factors of which we may be totally unaware can cause fish to behave so unpredictably as to be bewildering. Therein lies the fascination of angling. The more years an angler fishes the more he comes to rely on a set of rules gained from experience. For instance, he may be convinced that tench are more likely to feed in the early morning or late evening, that heavy continuous rain puts fish off the feed, as does the first day or two of a cold north-east wind. Such beliefs are more often true than not, but at times these rules are blown sky high because the fish do not abide by them. Some unknown factors cause changes in more normal fish behaviour – possibly an instinctive awareness of impending climatic variations. But who knows?

So it is virtually impossible to explain why the pike in the Broad, on that day, would take coloured baits avidly but not natural ones. I tend to the theory that it was solely due to a combination of four factors: very bright sunlight, shallow water, water clarity, and, by sheer coincidence, the colour and tones of the dyed baits which exactly neutralised the effect of the first three so that when a bait entered the pike's zone of vision it induced a feeding response.

Whatever the reason I have since proved many times that dyed baits will catch pike in similar or near-similar climatic conditions.

Of course, to confound the issue I have caught pike on dull days and in murky water, but rarely wobbling. In nearly all cases the dyed baits have been static or buoyant, lying on or suspended just off the bottom.

I can see little point in using coloured baits in water over 25 feet deep. Less light penetrates the deeper the water becomes and colours change tone and saturation the deeper they are submerged. Orange and red change to brown and eventually black; yellow baits appear more green then grey and they too become blackened. Naturally, the clearer the water the deeper a coloured bait can sink before its colour is neutralised.

I have experimented with a number of colours, two-toned baits, and baits striped vertically, like a perch, in one or two contrasting colours. Generally, in brighter conditions and clearer water, colour of a deeper tone seems best. Bright-red baits, one would think, should drive pike crazy but, except on the brightest of days, I have found them no better than the other colours and generally less effective. Wobbled or moved red baits seem to have the edge over static ones. The two colours that seem to

The eyes of two hunters clash as Esox is returned to her home.

be most attractive to pike are the very first I tried, deep yellow and orange.

Light-green baits have taken a fish or two; dark-green baits have led to indifferent results. Two-toned baits – half yellow, half red or orange – are as effective as yellow or orange baits, but no better. As for striped baits, I have caught pike on them, but baits dyed just one colour have done as well on the day. Because blue is the last colour to neutralise in deep water I have tried electric-blue and turquoise bottom-fished deadbaits in deep water. I cannot say if such colouring improves their attraction for I have not used them alongside undyed

baits for long enough for a conclusion to be reached.

Dyed baits are just another weapon in the angler's armoury. Used in the right conditions they can be devastatingly efficient, but even when conditions have seemed perfect they have occasionally proved no better than natural ones. That is an enigma which defies any rational explanation. Sometimes, even on the same water a yellow bait has accounted for fish and other colours have been ignored. On another day, when conditions were similar, yellow has not been nearly so effective as orange. Certain colours work well on one

A 23-pounder is returned to a weedy Thurne backwater.

water but do not seem to do so well on another. Then again, on a particular day one colour will take pike anywhere in preference to others yet, within a few hours, the pattern changes and the successful colour no longer works as well. Or a killing colour can be deadly on just one water but not on any of the others, even though conditions appear to be identical.

I cannot even attempt to explain such intriguing behaviour traits, which seem inherent in pike as a species, but I suspect that their reaction is due to an ever-changing combination of climatic conditions, water clarity and light values at different depths. How these factors enhance or inhibit a particular coloured bait's effectiveness cannot even be guessed at. The key to this fascinating mystery has yet to be found. The Americans, for instance, use electronic meters to advise on choice of lure colour (as discussed by Chris Liebbrandt in Chapter 21). Perhaps they have unlocked some of the answers?

One can only attempt to solve the problem partially by using baits of differing type, size and colour as well as undyed ones. By ringing the changes, action, size and method, eventually a combination, arrived at as much by chance as by design, succeeds. Such experimentation is bound to work sometimes, but not necessarily in what appears to us to be identically similar conditions on another occasion.

What has become apparent over the years is that in clear water and bright sunshine coloured baits are sometimes more attractive to pike than naturally coloured ones, even more so on hard-fished waters. I say 'sometimes' rather than 'often' because the more I fish the more I have learnt never to say 'always' about fish behaviour. As quickly as one problem seems to have been solved I have been all too quickly disillusioned. I would not have it any other way. It is such intriguing and seemingly insoluble problems which make the art of angling so absorbing.

9

Attractors and Baiting

Relatively little has been written about the use of attractors, prebaiting and actual groundbaiting in pike fishing, possibly because very few people have thoroughly researched these subjects. Most anglers, including ourselves, have only toyed with the subject on occasions. Generally, the approach has not been conducted with the necessary depth or in a specific scientific or analytical form in order to obtain meaningful results. This is strange, really, considering that most pike anglers spend considerable time in spring and summer on long and expensive prebaiting campaigns and in researching more attractive baits for other fish such as carp and tench. We are no exception.

At times we have conducted some limited experiments but rarely have they been extensive enough to enable anything but sketchy conclusions to be drawn. We will, however, discuss some of our observations and thoughts on the matter in the hope that some anglers will experiment further.

PREBAITING CAMPAIGNS

It may be that prebaiting campaigns are so often neglected because of the very nature of pike angling. Deadbaits are more likely to be used in the depths of winter, when fishing from dawn to dusk in single sessions. Carp-fishing sessions, on the other hand, may consist of several days' fishing at one particular water. Additionally, few anglers seem prepared to travel daily to a pike water to prebait prior to the start of a week's campaign, as carp anglers do on theirs.

So many factors inhibit a baiting campaign for pike. The vagaries of winter weather can deter all but those impervious to its rigours. Perhaps pike fishing does not lend itself to prebaiting in quite the same way as carp angling, but at the same time, if the effort is made, we consider that intelligent prebaiting could yield some interesting results.

It would be wise to examine the purpose of prebaiting before conducting a campaign. This could be threefold. The first purpose, and one which unquestionably succeeds, is the intention to educate and convert pike to feed on a particular deadbait. This is really an extension of our thoughts a few chapters earlier concerning the weaning of pike on to deadbaits in the first place. On a new water pike may be slow to take deadbaits in the first instance but so often anglers discard their used and leftover baits at the end of the day, and over the course of time pike become accustomed to finding these baits and begin to take them more readily. Hence anglers use deadbaits more often, and so more and more baits are discarded, until the water eventually becomes known as a deadbait fishery.

Accustoming pike to the sight and scent of dead fish or a particular type of dead fish on the bottom seems a sensible strategy. The second purpose of prebaiting is to concentrate pike into a particular feeding zone and encourage them to stay there. We consider that this has little chance of success unless undertaken with great thought and care as to where the baits are placed, how many are introduced, and how often. For instance, if bait is placed on a pike patrol route, it may well help in stopping a number of pike for a while, and may be a useful exercise if a baiting campaign is conducted for several days. Beware of overbaiting, however.

If, instead, the bait is placed in a definite

holding area – a hotspot, for want of a better description – does it really achieve anything? The pike are already there and if they are already accustomed to deadbaits prebaiting may prove a total waste of time and effort – as well as providing them with so much food they might not be overkeen on taking an angler's bait.

Finally, the baits may be placed where few pike ever venture. Although pike often congregate together they are not shoal fish by instinct and hence one pike wandering over this new spot, recently prebaited with juicy morsels, is unlikely to dash off to find its mates – unlike seagulls, which seem to sense what every other gull is up to a mile away. It is much more likely to eat one or two pieces and then move on. We consider that in most cases such prebaiting is unlikely to succeed in establishing a new hotspot. One exception to this may be where there is a known holding area very close by and it is thought worth while to move the pike a few yards. This may be possible. The only reason for moving fish from one hotspot to another is to make the pike shift away from the angling pressure exerted on them by others.

Apart from education and congregation (encouraging a number of fish into a small area), the final reason for prebaiting is to acheive results over a much longer period, with the objective of attempting to make the pike gain weight. In small waters, with enough bait being used, this might possibly work. If you intend to fish the water beware of just how much bait is introduced. In the depths of winter the pike's metabolism will have slowed down and pike are not insatiable. It would be quite frustrating to have fished, and blanked, for a whole day, only to realise that because of your hard work the pike already have extremely full bellies.

An interesting example concerning overfeeding probably used to occur on Ranworth Inner Broad, which was famous for its opening-day catches many years ago. The Broad would open on 1 March and inevitably on that day several large pike would be caught.

However very few were caught in the few days before the season closed. Possibly there were only a few pike present, but even then one would expect the pike caught on the opening day to turn up consistently during the remaining days. Another, plausible explanation is that since so many people fished this popular broad on opening day there is every likelihood that many baits were dumped at the end that day, which would keep the pike busy for quite some time. Such a habit needs considering. This point is worth thinking about for if you are going to fish the water the next day it may not be sensible to throw away baits which might be taken in preference to your own the very next morning. Similarly, during a spell of very cold weather, when the pike are hardly feeding, a bait thrown away one weekend may form a midweek meal for a pike, satisfying her right through the next weekend, whilst your baits remain untouched.

It follows that prebaiting with whole fish could result in negative returns. It would seem sensible, therefore, to undertake any prebaiting with diced or sliced baits so that each offering is merely an appetiser as opposed to a substantial meal. It is possible that the pike would develop a liking for a particular shape, such as a mackerel disc, if enough were introduced to the water. Barry Rickards and Hugh Reynolds have experimented along these lines with some success and this further indicates yet again the full versatility of deadbaiting methods.

GROUNDBAITING

We turn now to the use of groundbait during fishing in an attempt to bring fish into the swim or possibly to arouse resident lethargic fish into feeding. This means the use of attractors and stimulators – in sharking terms, rubby-dubby, or, as the Americans call it, chumming. We consider it essential that the offerings are kept chopped small so as not to offer a full meal to any pike. Either one is offering lots of fishy lumps spread over the fishing area to encourage the pike to search and track down a scent source or alternatively one is concentrating groundbait into a central area, hoping that pike will congregate there. This concentration of fish pieces and oozing oils will spread a scent trail with the current or wind undertow.

The first approach is fairly easy. Several chopped-up deadbait sections are catapulted round the target area. The second either employs a mesh bag containing mashed fish which is lowered to the bottom and occasionally lifted and shaken, or the mashed fish may be made into balls of groundbait stiffened with breadcrumbs or the like. All sorts of additives can be tried. Virtually anything fishy, meaty and oily is likely to have the power of attraction.

This brings us to another form of groundbaiting, which is almost totally neglected by pike anglers, yet we are sure that if you asked most matchmen they would suggest this technique immediately. The idea is to use normal cereal-based crumb baits not to attract the pike but to attract the fodder fish. We have all heard of numerous occasions when match and pleasure anglers bring in small fish and a pike whips their catch from the hook. Why not apply the same groundbaiting method to draw the small fish into the area you are fishing, with the knowledge that any pike nearby are sure to follow? This concept, of course, applies equally to livebaiting as to deadbaiting.

ATTRACTORS

We have mentioned elsewhere the question of oils and their diffusion in the water. We are of the opinion that there is merit in the use of oils and this opens up further scope by the use of attractors. Oils can be injected into deadbaits to increase the subsequent emissions. For instance, pilchard oil, smelt extract and similar products are all readily available and may help in the catch of one or two extra pike. At the very least, experimenting with these enhancers adds to the fun of pike fishing.

How many pike anglers make use of Alka-Seltzer tablets? These can be added to rubby-dubby bags or swimfeeders, a topic we will discuss shortly, and they do assist in the break-up and emission of oils and fish particles as they fizz away on the bottom, giving off clouds of bubbles which rise to the surface. In fact Vic was one day using Alka-Seltzer for this purpose when a passing pleasure angler happened to remark that the bream appeared to be bubbling well in his swim. Vic did not have the heart to explain to the angler that it was his Alka-Seltzer tablets bubbling away merrily.

Martyn's first experience with Alka-Seltzer was perhaps even stranger. It was suggested to him that several Alka-Seltzers pushed down the throat of a dead fish would allow it to lie on the bottom while the Alka-Seltzer slowly dissolved, when the accumulated gas would lift it off the bottom until the air managed to escape from mouth, vent and skin. Then the bait would start sinking again until more gas accumulated. Effectively, this would cause the bait to flutter, rise and fall, giving the deadbait an action which would, with luck, prove irresistible to a pike. When first told of this Martyn checked the calendar to make sure it was not 1 April. Later he secretly disappeared to fill the bath tub to conduct experiments. His conclusions were that it was possible to achieve this action with smaller deadbaits in 'laboratory' (bath tub) conditions, but that the effect was uncertain in practice. Still, it may be worth trying.

SWIMFEEDERS

Swimfeeders have a well proven track record in most forms of fishing, so logically it is worth experimenting with feeders packed with chopped fish in pike fishing. This produces a rubby-dubby effect very close to the bait and could assist in attracting pike. Adding an Alka-Seltzer produces extra effervescence. Perhaps cold winter days with fingers already numbed are not the time for piling mashed fish into a feeder and then plugging the ends with groundbait, and presumably this is why they are not often used. Martyn has experimented with the method in the past and his largest zander was caught while he was using very fresh chopped and mashed deadbait in a feeder, with a small dead roach as bait (in spite of or because of, one wonders). On one lake he and a piking companion, Kevin, actually conducted an experiment over ten sessions when they fished the same swim alternating the position of their rods, with Martyn exclusively using feeder and Kevin without. The result was that only one fish fell to the rods without a feeder,

A pike powers across the surface in its bid for freedom.

whilst the feeder rods produced nine fish. At least on that swim, in that gravel pit, the findings seem conclusive enough. Vic often uses a weighted closed-end feeder instead of a bomb on the paternoster link. It seems to work likewise, even when fishing deadbaits lying on or suspended off the bottom.

In conclusion, the whole subject of baiting for pike is still very much in its infancy. To draw any conclusions will require considerable effort by numbers of pike anglers. Unquestionably, in the current search for more efficient ways of catching pike, and spurred by increased pressure and competition on our waters, this is an area where significant developments will take place in future years. The findings will certainly make interesting reading. We suspect, however, that the majority of pike anglers will only occasionally delve into this fascinating area of our sport.

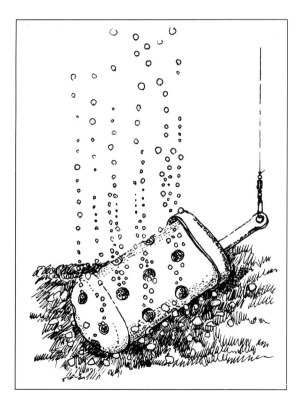

10

Styles and Methods

All too often deadbaiting is classified as a 'chuck it out and chance it' method. This label is unjustified, but unfortunately it is probably still the belief most commonly held by deadbaiting anglers. Possibly some of the blame lies with the carp angler, or, more correctly, the modern bivvy-style approach to long-stay angling. We do not overcriticise this approach as such, since it can certainly pay dividends on many carp waters. Long-stay pike fishing also produces results, for eventually a feeding pike is bound to come across the baits. But there is more to deadbaiting than long waits combined with this 'chuck and chance it' attitude.

In this chapter we will analyse the more common deadbait practices and give our own comments and thoughts on their application. It should always be remembered that we consider that pike fishing is fun. At times we may seem critical of a method because it does not necessarily provide us with the same satisfaction as other styles. For this we apologise in advance as, of course, one man's meat may be another's poison. We may find long-wait static deadbaiting less rewarding mentally (not necessarily less successful) than more active styles whilst others may prefer such techniques. In some cases, of course, such a method is the only practical one. Our intention is to show which other methods are available and when they might succeed, and strongly urge you to try all methods. In this way not only will you gain more piking experience but, we believe, your pike fishing will be far more rewarding.

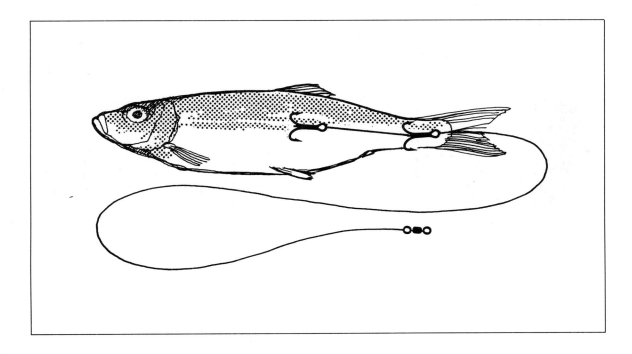

THE STATIC APPROACH

Let us start with the static approach, the one most associated with the use of deadbaits. In simple terms this involves merely casting the bait into a pike water and then sitting back to watch a float, or waiting for a drop-off indicator to signal a take. This is the way deadbaiting is practised on countless occasions and in this crudest form it is no wonder that the method is associated with spells of inactivity. Its only justification is that such a technique may produce a better than average fish.

In this simplest form, all that is needed for terminal tackle is a lead and a trace, or sometimes a lead and sliding float. It is not necessary to know the water, to think about location or where the pike may lie, since the bait is merely going to sit on the bottom, anywhere, until a pike happens upon it. Runs will often be few and far between. Quite honestly, such a style does not deserve success. It's a lazy method, perhaps relying on chance rather than application. Having stated our opinion, we have to admit to having fished in this way many times in the past!

Static deadbaiting does not have to be that simple or boring, and certainly it does not have to be that slow. An intelligent approach can turn 'chuck it and chance it' into a highly efficient and at times extremely fast method of fishing. To fish a water blind is just a waste of time and, we consider, nothing short of stupidity.

In any form of fishing it is important to understand your quarry's habits and know its habitat. This is universally known, or should be – apart from beginners, perhaps – and yet so often this knowledge is disregarded when bottom-fished deadbaits are used. It is essential to ensure that your deadbait is lying in a position where pike will or are likely to pass by or are already present. One can only be sure of this if a thorough working knowledge of the water has been obtained, including the underwater topography. Pike are not intelligent fish

and they are usually easy to catch, but, at the risk of repetition, you can't catch what isn't there. Therefore the first thing to do on any water is to consider the likely places where the pike can be located. On gravel pits, in particular, it is essential to be aware of the location of gravel bars, plateaux, drop-offs, shallows and similar features. Then a static deadbait can be 'left' fishing in a precise spot where there is every possibility that a run may develop.

On a water where there is little scope for changing swims, or where there are very few productive areas, it is essential to find the consistently productive swims and, more particularly, the precise spots within the swims where runs are usually forthcoming, and to concentrate on these. It is surprising how often a particular spot within a swim always seems to produce the runs. This can be critical and on some waters it is essential to have bait precisely placed, perhaps in an area only a foot square. Sometimes the reasons are obvious from observation of the surface features, but more often than not there seems no apparent reason. So it is helpful to remember the areas from which each run materialises and present baits in these in the future in order to discover whether you have found a feeding spot. If you continue to work at your fishing in this way you will without doubt produce dividends on future occasions.

We are lucky in some ways, since we are forced to approach our deadbaiting in a more active style. The Norfolk Broads, by their very nature, are highly inaccessible and the use of a boat is essential. Once afloat on the fishing platform (which is all that a boat really is), even our static deadbaiting becomes more mobile and active. When movement to another swim is not restricted the deadbait method can take on a different perspective. It is not always possible, and sometimes not even desirable, to use a boat. Given the choice, however, we would virtually always opt to go afloat. We will go into this in greater detail later on in the book.

MORE ACTIVE DEADBAITING

Subtle changes in tactics are often necessary on different waters. We have mentioned that there is more to static deadbaiting than 'chuck it out and hope' and that a knowledge of each swim and the location of the pike is essential. Much of this knowledge can be gained only by experience.

Let us assume that we are fishing a large gravel pit or lake for the first time, that we have only deadbaits at our disposal and boats are not allowed. In this situation there is little point in fishing blind: the pike could be anywhere. We can draw on our experience of similar waters, but there is a danger with such a generalisation, because pike certainly vary their habits from water to water. However, there are enough established 'rules' to enable short cuts to be made. A number of these are covered elsewhere, as in Chapter 3. It should be appreciated that the pike will not always be in the same spots and may move because of a number of factors. For example, if the bait fish have moved into deeper water in the depths of winter, the pike may have followed. If you are fishing the water in late February or March the pike may now be in very shallow water as a prelude to spawning.

The first thing to find out about a new water is the topography of the bottom – the deeps, the shallows, and so on. With a very large body of water these essential features have to be discovered the hard way, by means of plumbing. In such circumstances the most sensible approach is to fish as many swims as possible. These first trips should not be concerned with catching the biggest fish in the water, but rather with discovering where some of the pike are. Then static deadbaiting takes on a much more active and mobile approach as swims are changed regularly. No more than an hour is ever spent in an unproductive swim, and the bait is recast to different places in that swim. It is surprising how often a fish will take

immediately, perhaps because the bait has come to rest near by. Fishing deadbaits in this manner will soon make some pieces of the jigsaw puzzle fall in place. A holding area may be found or a pattern begin to evolve. Certain areas will soon become obvious targets for more concentration, others not worth the bother.

Obviously, if other pike anglers are fishing the water further short cuts can be made as you soon discover where they have been successful. A word of caution: don't assume that a hotspot is anything other than a popular swim which everybody fishes, and the only spot on the water where pike can be caught. All too often such areas are created by anglers, not by the pike.

COVERING THE WATER

If you are limited to the bank, there is a dangerous temptation to cast the bait as far as possible in the belief that the pike will be far out in open water. Boat anglers can cover all the water, and they should understand the fallacy of such a concept, having caught many a pike by casting towards the bank. Even boat anglers when confined to the bankside often revert to long-range fishing. Pike are not confined by some invisible barrier fifty or sixty yards out; as often as not they will be found moving close in, perhaps just along the first drop-off or even tight into the bank itself. It is often productive to try these areas first, with one rod, then, after a while, if no results have been forthcoming, put out the bait a little further. Never neglect the stretch of water between the bank and the limit of your casting ability. Pike fishing is not a tournament-casting competition. Indeed, it is possible that the one place the pike will not be is where everybody casts. As so many people appear to cast as far as they can, inevitably there is a band in a well fished water in which most of the deadbaits will lie. Pike do move away from pressure zones, possibly further out, but just as likely closer in.

Obviously, if a boat is permitted on the

water all swims become instantly accessible. There is no need for fishing at extreme range; all that is necessary is to up-anchor and move. Baits can be fished all round the boat so it becomes much easier to establish greater understanding of pike-holding areas, which results in more pike being caught.

This searching technique is not always guaranteed to produce more fish. On a number of occasions we have spent all day boat fishing, moving swims, searching out the pike, convinced that we have fished as effectively as possible – yet we have blanked. Later we have found that a solitary bank angler has had a field day taking numerous fish by sitting in one swim all day, maybe having waited four or five hours before fish came into the swim or came on the feed. Such occurrences make one ponder why the static waiting game is more successful on odd occasions than the more active approach. However, considering the whole affair as something of a lottery, the angler who buys one ticket to fish one zone is less likely to hit a feeding area than the angler who takes several tickets for several swims.

BAIT PRESENTATION

Pike are essentially instinctive creatures and it does not require great sophistication in tackle and techniques to catch them, particularly when the bait is lying on the bottom. But simple changes can improve results on heavily fished waters, and some slight refinements may be necessary. We have discussed deadbaits themselves and coloured baits in earlier chapters. Changes of this kind are obvious refinements which can be made. It is also worth considering the effect of bait density and durability in conjunction with the type of water, the nature of the bottom, and where the particular bait is to be presented. If it is necessary to achieve very long range, most pike anglers will opt for mackerel because of their suitability for long-range casting. However, the pike may not be 'into' mackerel at that particular time;

the going bait may be a soft bait, such as sardine. To achieve the same distance with such baits as can be obtained with mackerel some refinements are necessary. A very well frozen pilchard or sardine will cast like a rocket and if it is fished static it can be fished on a standard deadbait trace. Being extremely soft once thawed, such baits prove very effective.

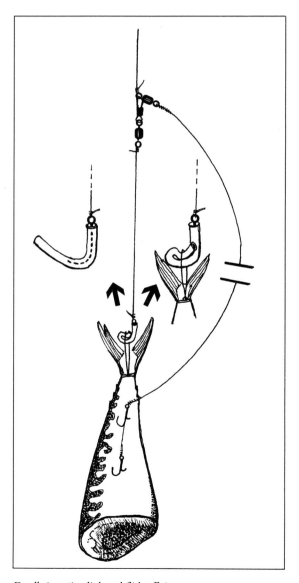

Deadbait casting link and flick-off rig.

However, smaller or less frozen sardines may require the use of a deadbait casting link in order to achieve distance. The bait is tail-looped; the loop, approximately ½ inch long, is made from an 8–10-inch doubled length of line. Dacron will suffice, but Vic prefers Marlow's thin waxed whipping thread, available from boat chandlers. A loop is tied in the thread and the two loose ends are passed through the bait's tail root with a baiting needle, then pulled through to seat the loop. The loose ends are wrapped round the tail root twice and knotted.

The object of the loop is to take the full weight of the bait on a flick-off link during casting, leaving the trace slack so that the hooks can be lightly nicked in a soft bait but will not pull free. The flick-off link consists of an eyed hook, size 4 or 2, with the point and barb cut away and the bend opened. This is tied to a short length of monofilament line about 4 inches long of not less than the breaking strain of the reel line, which terminates in a tiny American snap swivel of safety-pin type. A length of silicone tube is pushed on the hook up to the eye, where it is held in place with Araldite or superglue. This tube should project not less than ¾ inch so that it can be doubled back on itself. The flick-off link is secured to the upper eye of the trace swivel by the small snap swivel. In order to cast a very soft bait such as a sardine the silicone tubing is doubled and held in that position by the tail loop and the weight of the bait. During the cast as the bait is in full flight the pressure on the doubled rubber eases so that it straightens and flicks off the tail loop.

One useful tip: before attaching the hooks to the bait, pass them through the tail loop, then, when reeling the bait back to cast to another part of the swim, even if the hooks pull out they will engage in the loop and the bait will be recovered.

It may be that the bait is masked by bottom debris or weed or sinks in silt. Improvements in presentation can overcome these problems. For example, suspended deads could be used, or the insertion of balsa rods into the mouth of a bait will increase the buoyancy (if enough balsa is inserted the bait will actually float). On silty bottoms the bait can be made buoyant enough to avoid sinking into the silt or the bait could be made to fish clear of the bottom debris. In some circumstances, even on clean bottoms, a bait suspended off the bottom will result in more fish. Our experiences suggest that eel sections and smelt are two of the most effective bottom-suspended deadbaits and that a fresh deadbait suspended on a float paternoster rig can also prove quite killing on certain waters.

A useful tip with balsa rods is not only to sharpen one end, to assist in inserting them, but also to varnish or use a cellulose seal to stop water penetration, otherwise the buoyancy is lost after a time. Middy now market deadbait floater sticks fitted with a small eye. If a loop of line is secured to the eye and the hooks and the

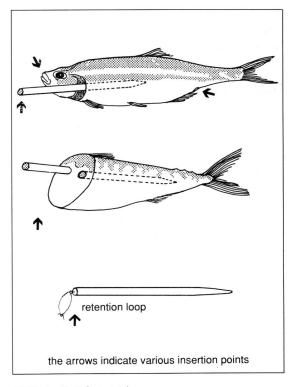

retention loop

the arrows indicate various insertion points

Middy deadbait floater sticks.

trace passed through the loop before the hooks are attached to the bait, the sticks will be recovered even when a hooked fish ejects the bait. Alternatively, Marvic have introduced a deadbait punch which injects a highly buoyant waterproof foam into the bait. The latter method allows a bait to be made so buoyant that it rises from the bottom to the surface with ease. This is particularly useful when baits need to be presented at the midwater level or above.

It should now be apparent that there can be more to a static deadbait than first meets the eye. Suspended deads may be the answer in some circumstances but in others they could work against you. For instance, much of the water on the Thurne system is very shallow and extremely weedy. Logic suggests that it is not necessary to use much weight on the line (there's no real distance to cast) and if a bait were suspended above the weed it could be very efficient. However, the pike on the system do move slowly along tunnels, underneath the weed. When the fish are seen cruising nearer the surface they appear to be interested in active live fish only. It then becomes obvious that the best method of fishing a deadbait

The Marvic deadbait punch.

in the very weedy areas is to use a heavy bait, which will pass quickly through the weed and sink into the tunnels underneath. A reasonable amount of weight is also necessary to keep the bait in place and to avoid any possibility of it being dragged back into the weed by wind action or boat swing. An alternative would be to wobble for the more active pike, above the weed, appealing to their inquisitive nature or tempting those below the weed to strike upwards.

These observations do not apply to the open-water swims, but such places on the Thurne system are few and far between and, not surprisingly in some of the heavily fished areas, the pike rarely venture into the larger open expanses.

This heavy-bait approach has certainly paid off for Martyn in recent years, producing not only his two biggest pike but numerous other large fish at a time when most others have struggled on the same waters.

ADJUSTING TO FASTER FLOWS

We have talked of static deadbaiting, of making it more active and more interesting, and of some of the more versatile methods. In Chapter 11 we devote considerable space to wobbling, an extremely exciting and active form of fishing, nowadays sadly neglected. Indeed, it is possibly the most effective fast-water piking method. But what of rivers generally? Obviously, many of the comments we have made apply just as well to faster waters; they too will almost certainly respond to deadbaits, though sometimes river pike seem to take longer to develop a liking for static baits.

The concept of constantly changing swims can prove more deadly on most rivers. By leap-frogging rods (reeling in the end rod and recasting above or down from the other) every half-hour or so, you can cover an enormous amount of water in a day, until a hotspot is found. The same logic regarding the distance the bait should be positioned from the bank applies as much to running-water styles as to lakes. The pike will often be right under the bank, moving along the first drop-off, or lying aginst the far or near bank. They are not always in the middle. Experimentation is the key. Martyn used to catch a large number of pike from the upper Bure actually under his feet. Those pike preferred to lie in the undercuts under the bank, an ideal ambush lie.

Rivers, fast or slow, will also respond to deadbait techniques. On some it may take time, but eventually the pike will become ac-climatised to deadbaits, or can be weaned on to them. Then their use will produce some start-ling results with big fish.

OF FLOATS AND LEGERS

We have mentioned that the basic tackle for deadbaiting (wobbling and trolling excepted) will involve a leger and/or a float. Obviously, floats impede casting distance so for long-range static deadbaiting they are rarely used. Instead, the simple leger, using as much weight as necessary, tends to be adopted, either with the line passed through the eye of a bomb or buoy-ant leger or by means of a paternoster link (which is more advisable). However, such rigs can lead to problems of bite detection.

This is one instance where the almost uni-versally used Optonic bite alarm is perhaps not

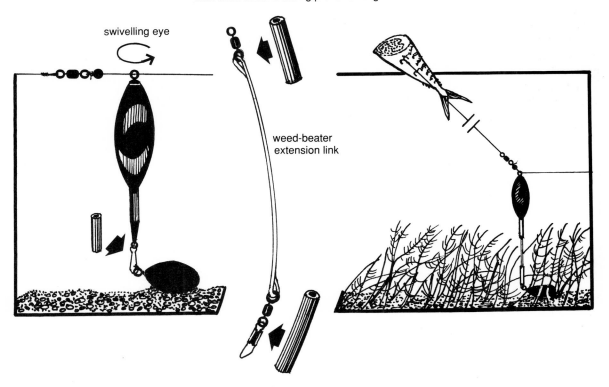

covering swivel and link swivel
with 3mm silicone tubing prevents tangles

swivelling eye

weed-beater
extension link

The buoyant leger.

Drop-off alarms, probably the most efficient indicator with legered deadbaits.

the best indicator. For this style of fishing the drop-off indicator, preferably electronic, is more suitable. The illustrations show how this form of indicator signals the take by dropping back against the back rod rest when the line pulls free on a run. The electronic version gives an audible as well as a visual alarm. This indicator will also signal drop-back bites: the drop-back effect is achieved as the line tension eases. The advantage of using such indicators for long-wait fishing such as this is that one does not have to constantly keep straining to watch near-invisible floats at long range. With drop-offs takes are quickly detected, which certainly helps eliminate the problems associated with deep hooking.

The leger is restrictive. Even though the bait can be varied, suspended, or coloured, it stays in one place until reeled in. Float fishing, on the other hand, offers a number of further attractions, even aesthetically — a float is nice to watch bobbing gently among the waves or lying tranquil on the surface in a still calm. Did it move suddenly? Yes, surely those are ripples coming from the float, and there it goes, away! To us, watching a float glide across the surface as it sinks from sight or realising that it hasn't materialised after the passing of a wave is far more exciting than a leger run. These are the magic moments. The adrenalin starts flowing. They are the times when pike fishing is at its most exhilarating.

In this piking is different from catching other fish. The bite or run of other fish is struck

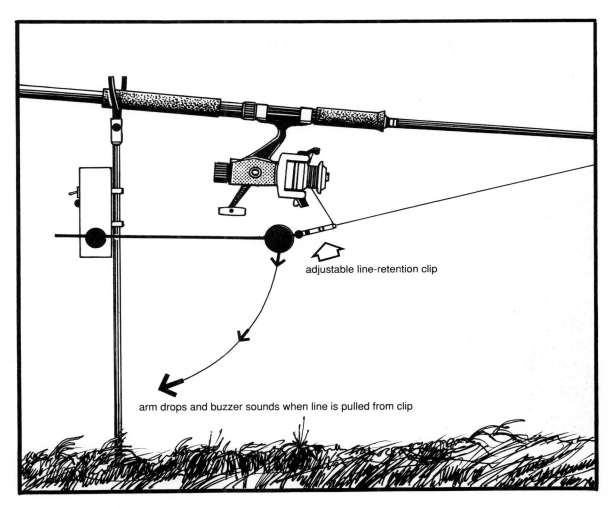

adjustable line-retention clip

arm drops and buzzer sounds when line is pulled from clip

Electronic drop-back indicator.

instantaneously whereas with pike there are a few fleeting seconds to savour the take as one tightens down to strike – a time when imagination can run riot as to the size of the fish on the other end, a period of anticipation and expectation. It's only a few seconds from the time the float sinks to the winding down and making the strike. This is not the past, when, uneducated to the needs of conservation, a complete cigarette may have been smoked and ten minutes elapsed before the strike, allowing the pike to gorge the bait. Nowadays, real pike anglers enjoy these magic moments for only a few

seconds, but they are some of the most golden seconds of pike fishing, before the unknown is revealed.

There is something aesthetic about a float but it has practical purposes also. It is an extremely effective bite indicator: it is nearer to the bait and it gives an immediate and positive indication of a run. A float, even if a pike is only mouthing a bait, will indicate what is occurring, whereas a fish may be deeply hooked before the drop-off sounds.

Floats are essential in boat fishing because the swing of the boat makes other forms of bite

There is something aesthetic about a float . . .

detection virtually impossible. This point is covered in more depth in Chapter 23.

Float design has radically changed in recent years. The Gazette bung is slowly but surely becoming extinct, though a slight revival in the concept of a big round fat-bodied float has re-appeared with the use of polyballs. Neither of these makes an efficient deadbait float, but pike will take baits whatever float you are using. It is too late for a pike to detect an extra-buoyant float if it has taken the bait. No float, however well designed, will affect the number of takes. That is not really the float's purpose for it is merely an indicator. In some circumstances, particularly on heavily fished waters, a large float which creates a great deal of water resist-ance may result in a dropped run.

The rejection by pike anglers of the Gazette bung, particularly during the 1970s, and its re-placement by streamlined cigar-shaped slider floats, was a considerable improvement. Such floats offer less resistance to pike, though in some instances floats are available which are not as visible as they should be. A surface float, unlike the sunken paternoster methods often

used with livebait fishing, needs to be highly visible, with a good proportion brightly coloured. The most visible floats in most light conditions are coloured a very bright flame orange, but on occasions light values, water colour or vegetation reflection will be such that black, yellow or white will show up better. A selection of colours is therefore essential to cope with these varying conditions.

For several years, slider cigar pike floats with the line passed through the centre of the body became fashionable for both live- and deadbait piking. However, they are not the most visible deadbait floats available. Fortunately, manufac-turers such as Middy have listened to advice from ourselves and others and have produced pencil-style deadbait floats. The pencil deadbait float has a long thin body with bottom-end attachment only by means of a swivelling eye. The float is self-cocking to allow approx-imatley half of the float to be exposed above the surface. This portion is painted with a high-visibilty vibrant colour. The float stands out

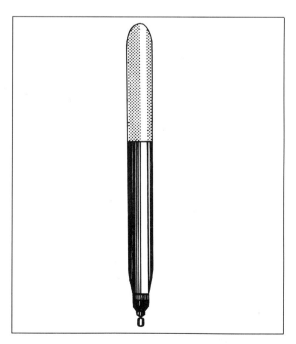

Marvic Middy self-cocking pencil deadbait float.

A standard float-fished deadbait rig, consisting of pencil float, bullet weight, trace and deadbait – in this case a horse mackerel.

like a goal-post on the water and makes an excellent visual indicator. That is the purpose of such floats. These floats do not increase catches but they do indicate takes efficiently and that means fewer deep-hooked pike. In most circumstances we consider that the pencil deadbait float is the best choice available for deadbait float fishing.

Usually a float-fished deadbait is fished with some weight on the line and fished slightly over depth. In bank fishing the line between float and rod tip may be sunk beneath the surface in order to prevent line drag causing the float to drift in. With the bait fished over depth a self-cocking pencil float sits as proudly as a lighthouse. A slider float, on the other hand, would lie flat on the surface, signifying a take

by cocking before submerging or merely sliding across the surface. In boat fishing similar criteria apply, though often much less distance is involved, which may mean that the line need not be sunk below the surface.

At times the wind piles the surface layers of water towards one end of the lake and in these circumstances a counterflow in the form of an undertow moves below the surface layers in the opposite direction to the wind. This causes the floats to drift against the wind, and it can be quite noticeable on some Norfolk broads and big lakes fished from a boat. At such times it is often necessary to increase the amount of weight and the distance between stop knot and lead to counteract the movement. There is no set guide as to how far over depth one should fish, except to say that it should be the minimum necessary to continue fishing effectively. If you want an anchored bait, you may have set the float considerably over depth, and likewise when fishing a river with a strong current.

In either of these circumstances takes will still be indicated promptly because the line will be under tension caused by the bow effect, which in turn ensures positive run indication. Often a run is discernible as the float suddenly drifts a few feet. This is caused by the tension slackening as a pike picks up the bait and moves down current, as opposed to against it. The line goes slack and the float which has been held in

Vic assembling rigs for the next day's fishing.

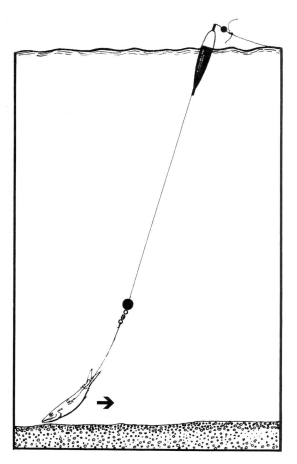

Float adjusted so that the deadbait just trips the bottom.

tension is suddenly free to drift with the surface wind.

We have discussed ways of holding the float in one position so that the bait does not move. This may not always be desirable. An extremely efficient method, particularly in boat fishing, is to allow the bait to drift, and this slow drift can be achieved by utilising surface wind, undertows or current. Keeping the line on the surface or fishing with the stop knot at much the same distance from the bait as the depth of water will result in the bait drifting slowly. A greased line used in conjunction with a cigar slider can prove a very deadly method for covering the water. In these circumstances the slider is more efficient than the pencil because it is bulkier and the bow in the line can give a very slow and attractive drift to the bait. Such styles can occasionally be used from the bank if the wind direction is favourable but they are far more effective from a boat.

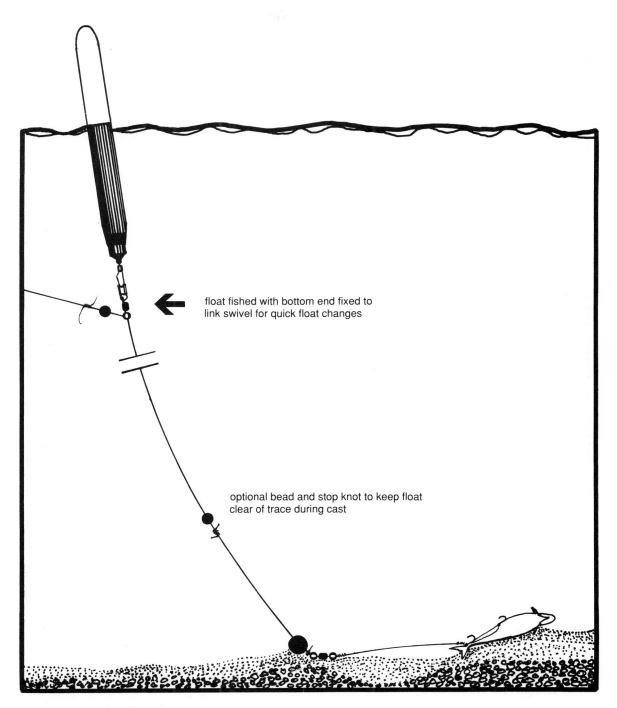

float fished with bottom end fixed to
link swivel for quick float changes

optional bead and stop knot to keep float
clear of trace during cast

Standard static deadbait float rig.

The amount of 'lead' used with the float can prove important. Obviously, over a very silty bottom, such as is found on many of our home waters like the Broads, heavy 'lead' may drag the bait into the silt, which is neither attractive nor desirable. Where there is little or no undertow, wind or current, it is questionable whether any weight is needed at all; the bait can be allowed to sink under its own weight with the float stopped slightly over depth. Again, variation of the stop-knot position will counter a minor wind drift. Most people tend to weight the line with the equivalent of two swanshot, which is really a token gesture. Far more thought should be given to how much weight is desired or whether any weight is necessary at all. It's not that lead will stop a pike taking but the amount used may well result in more takes, as with the heavy weight and heavy bait concept on the Thurne mentioned earlier. Martyn has also experienced a situation on Filby Broad where a large bullet seemed to produce far more results than a couple of swanshot, and yet Filby's bottom is relatively clear of weed. Here there appears to be no obvious need or specific reason to use more lead. It is possible that the pike have a preference for very static baits and any movement caused by undertows – or perhaps even the pike swimming past the bait – arouses suspicion. We have our doubts about this second aspect but have no further explanation for the behaviour of Filby pike. It is always worth bearing in mind that pike preferences change as well, so possibly one day they will prefer the extra movement that can be obtained using rigs without any weight. When one method seems slow we are prepared to ring the changes.

Generally, we fish a float-fished deadbait with a bullet weight equivalent to several swanshot on most firm-bottomed waters, but we would quite happily use weights of more than an ounce in specific circumstances, such as for the firm anchoring of a bait in fast flows. It should not matter even if the water is very shallow, when the weight will create some disturbance – in any event there is quite a commotion as the deadbait hits the water. This may attract pike rather than scare them.

On less firm bottoms we tend to use as little weight as possible and if necessary add buoyancy to prevent the bait sinking in the silk. We consider it most important to experiment with weights and also with the use of slow-drifting deadbaits in addition to pure statics in order to find which style produces the most response on that water at that time.

DRIFTING THE DEAD

Drifting can of course be taken one stage further. The slow drift to which we have already referred is not necessarily meant as a method of catching pike through increased bait activity; the bait is merely rolled slowly along the bottom, much as it probably would be affected by an undertow, and allowed to move in this way so as to present the bait to as many fish as possible.

A more active form of drifting is to follow the present trend of drift float fishing, which is discussed in Part Three but can also be applied to deadbaiting techniques.

Many people believe that drifter floats were designed purely to take a bait to inaccessible areas well beyond casting distance. Certainly this is one function of these floats, but, equally importantly, the float's original designers (several people may lay claim to this, though probably many people were experimenting on the same lines without being aware of each other's experiments) were using drift floats to move baits positively through a swim using a live- or deadbait. The designers appreciated that the float's aim was not only to reach beyond casting distance but to cover a large expanse of water, from the start of the drift through to the end, with the object of covering more pike.

Drifter float design has progressed significantly throughout the 1980s and it is now possible to buy such floats as well as conversion kits which allow any centrally tubed pike float to be made into a drifter. This is a very active and exciting form of fishing, to which Martyn devoted a whole chapter in *Predator*. It provides the bank angler in particular with a means of fishing new water, a means of working for extra fish and ultimately obtaining more satisfaction from his fishing. It should be used, as with every other method, in specific circumstances. It will not always prove the best method of reaching a great distance or even be the most effective, but on its day it can be unbeatable.

If pike are showing a distinct preference for very static baits it may be necessary to drift a bait to the area where they are feeding, if this is out of casting range, and then fish the bait static at that spot. The drifter float might not achieve this but a balloon could be the answer. We include diagrams of both drifter floats and balloon rigs. You will note from the balloon fishing rig illustrated here that there is a simple attachment so that the balloon is not lost. This is a small refinement on early rigs, where the balloon was pulled free from the tackle and ultimately bounced over the surface of the lake

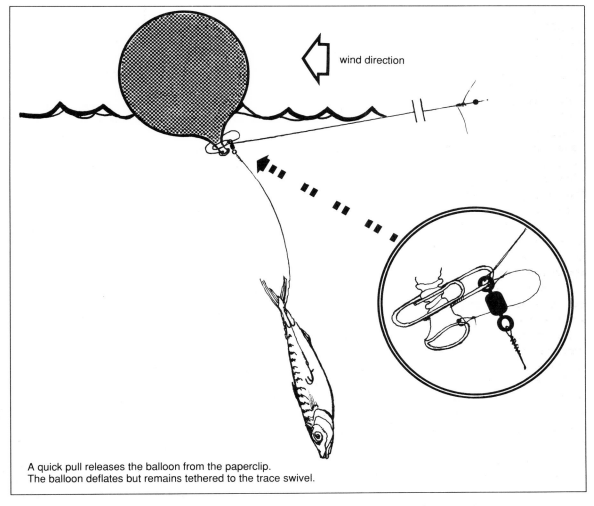

wind direction

A quick pull releases the balloon from the paperclip.
The balloon deflates but remains tethered to the trace swivel.

Balloon rig.

to become part of the usual litter mountain. (Martyn recalls fishing a Norfolk lake several years ago. He drifted a bait out on a balloon, pulled the bait free, and the balloon bounced calmly across the surface of the lake and into the field on the opposite side. Numerous black sheep were grazing peacefully until this great blue object suddenly appeared in their pasture. Being inquisitive of this new arrival, they chased the balloon across the field, up a small hill and over the brow. At this stage the balloon exploded on a barbed-wire strand with an almighty bang. Never have black sheep run so fast or in such terror.)

There are a few points we would stress about

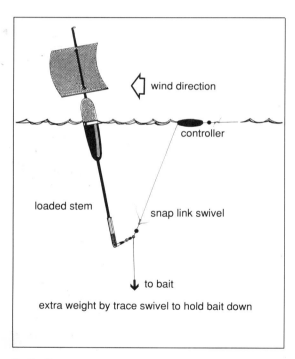

Drifter float rig.

wind direction

controller

loaded stem

snap link swivel

↓ to bait

extra weight by trace swivel to hold bait down

drifter fishing. One is that for long-range fishing the bottom-end-attachment or the pull-away-attachment floats are far superior. The reason for this is that when one eventually strikes, which is perhaps a misnomer at such range, at least one does not have to pull through the float or move it through the water, which creates strike resistance. The effectiveness of the strike is improved, or at least there is less likelihood of the float being damaged on the strike or retrieve. Striking at long range is improved if prestretched line is used; unstretched line stretches and stretches so it is difficult to set the hooks effectively.

A small controller is also an assistance in keeping the line on the surface (see diagram). It is also essential that the line is well greased so that it floats, or the drift will be impeded. Finally, a balloon can sometimes be used in conjunction with a drifter to assist in speeding the progress of the float in the first few yards, in particular if you wish to get the bait out quickly beyond a weedbed or an area of shallow water.

11

Wobbling – The Neglected Art

In this chapter Vic takes a look at the neglected technique of wobbling, highlighting the development of specialised rigs, discussing the application of wobbling and adding a few unique extras for experimentation.

RIGS – THE DEVELOPMENTS AND CHANGES

In the Victorian era, spinning for pike with natural deadbaits was not only popular but an effective angling technique, nowadays all but forgotten. The term 'spinning' when applied to lures (other than plugs) and deadbaits exactly describes the action of the bait, which revolves about its axis when drawn through the water. A number of commercially made spinning flights and mounts were available to our Victorian ancestors, some ingeniously constructed, so as to impart spin to a deadbait to a greater or lesser degree.

Today, with such tackles no longer in our rucksack, those few still in existence have been relegated to a collector's cabinet. The modern angler may be forgiven for not being able to discern the difference between a flight and a mount. Flights were rigs containing an arrangement of hooks whereby a curve could be given to a deadbait, which caused it to revolve slowly. A mount did not impart a curve but caused the bait to spin, usually more rapidly. This was achieved by a pair of angled metal or celluloid vanes positioned by the bait's head. These vanes, each inclined in opposite planes, acted like a propeller, revolving the bait as it was moved through the water.

Mounts were often fitted with spikes, weighted or unweighted, for inserting into the bait's abdomen via the mouth, which not only helped reinforce the body but provided added weight for longer casts and for searching deeper water.

A bait which spins draws attention to itself, and therefore will be attractive to a predatory fish for the following reasons. First, a spun deadbait is drawn through the water fast or slow according to the whim of the angler, and any pike will be acutely aware of movement in its vicinity. As the bait revolves it will produce a strong visual signal, which may aptly be called

Vic wobbling – a deadly technique when practised correctly.

the strobe effect. A revolving deadbait seen from above, below or from the side displays its darker back and silvery underside alternately. The faster the spin, the greater is the strobe effect. It produces what anglers term 'flash', which also emanates from a live fish as it turns quickly.

Finally, a spinning bait agitates the water. The faster the spin, the more disturbance, which takes the form of a helical vortex directly behind and in alignment with the bait's axis at whatever angle in the water the bait may be. This disturbance causes water displacement. Such swirls can be detected by the pike's sensitive receptors.

These three attributes – mobility, visibility and audibility – are exhibited by all fish as they move. Alone or in combination, they are the principal factors by which a pike locates its prey. A spun deadbait exhibits them all in full measure.

One further factor remains to be mentioned – scent. Predatory fish can also scent their prey, as is evidenced by pike finding deadbaits in deep water where little light penetrates, and also in coloured flood waters. With a host of liquid attractors now available, even this fourth factor can be added to a spun or wobbled bait.

There is no doubt that a spun deadbait is very attractive to pike. The Victorians were very well aware of this, but generally the means by which they mounted their deadbaits were sadly lacking in efficiency. In a word, ironmongery! They festooned their baits with a horrendous array of single and treble hooks, often up to six sets of trebles adorning one bait. One would think that any pike grabbing such a mouthful would be held fast. In practice this did not occur as often as might be expected. It takes a great deal of force to drive home such a number of hooks, particularly when so little can actually be transmitted to the hooks themselves for the obvious reason that the bait has to be moved first, and this is impossible when the bait is held hard in a pike's jaws. What little force did get through was further dissipated by being equally distributed to all the hook points.

One complicated mount, the crocodile, whose only virtue was its apt name, was fitted with two flat spiked metal bars. These were clamped on either side of the bait, and like all the old deadbait tackles it was liberally supplied with hooks. Those metal bars could be utilised by a pike as levers, enabling it to unhook itself. Some of the flights, such as the Bromley-Pennell, incorporated three flying trebles, the bait being fixed to the flight by both single and right-angled hooks. This did catch pike, but it would have been more efficient with fewer hooks.

Some of the ancient and not so ancient spinning tackles are illustrated. It is only comparatively recently that the Archer mount, another made by Hardy, and similar contrivances ceased to be manufactured. I used such rigs years ago and found the Archer efficient enough if one of the three trebles was moved. However, there is one serious drawback in using mounts which spin rapidly – their vicious propensity to twist the line. The use of Wye or Hillman spinning weights and celluloid anti-kink vanes certainly helped mitigate this problem, but did not eliminate it. The only answer

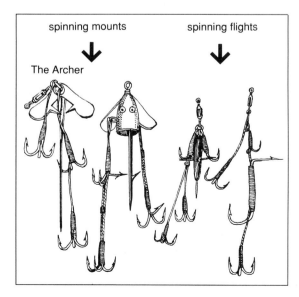

Antique deadbait spinning tackles.

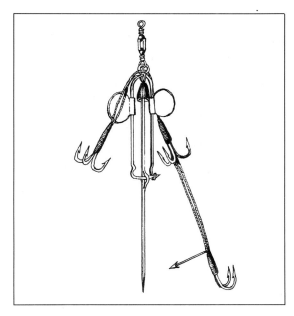

Another Victorian mouthful.

was to purchase spinning mounts in pairs, one with left- and one with right-hand spin. After fishing for ten minutes or so the mount had to be changed for its companion in order to remove the twists the first had caused. I found that much aggravation could be avoided by the use of ball-bearing swivels, which were expensive but worth every penny. Even they did not eliminate line twist completely.

Before describing the most effective flight of all, I will mention the Victorian method of trolling. It was not trolling in the sense that we understand the term today, but the use of a special mount which consisted of a heavily serrated and slighty bulbous metal spike, which could be forced into the deadbait's abdomen via the mouth. As usual, this tackle carried a host of hooks. This monstrosity was fished sink and draw, directly under the tip of a multi-jointed rod at least 16 feet long. The heavily weighted bait plunged down head first when dropped into the water. Just before it reached the bottom the rod was raised and a little line reeled in so that the bait headed back towards the surface. The process was then repeated. As

can be envisaged, this was a pike-fishing method better suited to searching the deep holes and weed-encompassed swims in rivers. When a pike took the bait it was not struck but allowed as much slack line as it needed while it pouched the bait. Richard Walker often mentioned the advice given to him by his grandfather on how long a pike should be allowed to have the bait before striking: 'Let him have it for ten minutes – by your watch.' It was sound enough advice, for unless a pike ejected the bait immediately its hooking was a certainty. We now consider gorge baiting barbaric, and rightly so, but when it was standard practice the main mass of the population was not as affluent as today. Many a needy family would have gone hungry but for a welcome fat jack or two. In that context the method can be more readily condoned.

To return to the best of the Victorian spinning tackles. This was called the Nottingham flight, developed and used by anglers from that region early in the nineteenth century and in advance of many of the more complicated rigs that I have touched on. The Nottingham flight was never modifed until the 1950s, which gives some indication of its merits. At that time, unbeknown to each other, Fred Wagstaff and I modified the flight by the addition of a single hook to lip-hook the bait. In its original design the Nottingham flight consisted of just two treble hooks about 2½ inches apart fixed to a gimp, then later a wire trace terminating in a swivel. It was almost identical to the twin treble rig that the great majority of pike anglers use today, particularly with static or buoyant deadbaits. The main difference was how the bait was mounted on the flight and how it was fished. The old-style anglers inserted one arm of the lower treble into the bait's flank behind the dorsal fin. Then, according to the amount of spin desired, the bait was bent slightly, forming a curve. The more the bend the faster the spinning action, and vice versa. This bend in the bait was held by inserting two arms of the upper treble into the bait behind the gill cleft, keeping tension on the wire between the two

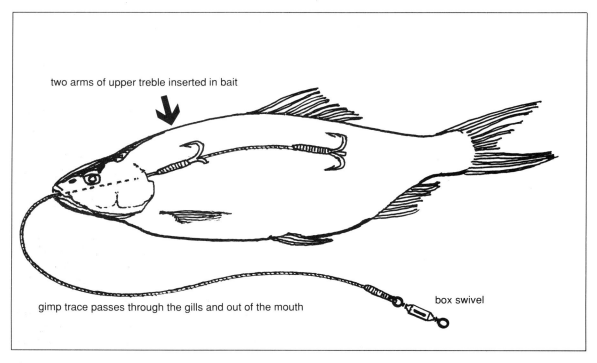

two arms of upper treble inserted in bait

gimp trace passes through the gills and out of the mouth

box swivel

The original Nottingham flight.

sets of hooks. Lastly, the swivel and wire were passed through the gill and out through the mouth.

This was the first true wobbling rig, for it was not necessary to impart a curve in the bait unless it was required to spin. Baits rigged in this fashion could be fished fast or slow and made to rise, sink or flutter, and, by varying the speed of retrieve, they could be fished shallow or deep. It was a successful and versatile rig.

The modification Fred and I arrived at independently was to pass the trace wire through the eye of a single hook before securing the swivel. This hook could be fixed by twisting the wire round the shank for three or four turns or by holding it *in situ* with a rubber sleeve. In the latter case the hook could be moved along the wire in order to accommodate different sizes of bait. The single hook took the full weight of the bait in casting, removing the strain from the hooks fixed to the bait. Also, it was now possible to position one treble further

back, in the vicinity of the anal fin, which considerably improved the rig's efficiency. (It is interesting how Nottingham crops up again and again in angling's history. Apart from the aforementioned flight, there was the Nottingham as opposed to the Sheffield style of fishing, and of course the famous Nottingham centrepin reel.)

My last attempt to improve the Nottingham flight incorporated a bright-red sleeve to hold the lip hook, and the substitution of VB hooks for trebles, which I found equally efficient.

Very little deadbait spinning for pike is practised nowadays. Considering the undoubted attraction a spun bait has for the species it is surprising that the method has lost its popularity. I think that if I live long enough and can find the time I might try to design a modern spinning rig. As I write a couple of ideas have sprung to mind!

Wobbling could be described as spinning in slow motion. All the pike-attracting properties inherent in a rapidly spinning bait are exhibited by one that is wobbled. The strobe effect is slowed to an irregular flash emission, and the water disturbance caused by the bait's movements becomes an intermittent and varied pulse rather than a full vibration. Scent can be improved if an attractor is injected into the bait or if it is anointed with the essence. As wobbled baits can be moved through the water more slowly than ones that spin, the scent is not dissipated so quickly. Wobbling can be all things to all men. The angler who casts out a deadbait and then gives it the occasional twitch, moving it a yard or so, is wobbling his bait for those odd seconds. This is very slow-motion wobbling indeed, but wobbling all the same.

Before I consider the many and varied ways a bait can be wobbled, mention must be made of recent developments in wobbling-rig design. The Wagstaff/Bellars variation on the Nottingham flight was an improvement, but since the two trebles or VBs were on the same length of wire they could be fixed to one side of the bait only. This added weight made it slightly lopsided and tended to throw it off balance, so it limited, even to only a slight degree, the action that could be imparted to the bait. This could be overcome if the hooks were inserted on the underside of the bait, along the keel, or alternatively along the top of the back. The bait could now be moved through the water without a tendency to veer. In the former arrangement, unless the bottom was clear of weeds and debris – which is rare indeed – the hooks collected all manner of rubbish, and a weed-festooned bait is no pike attractor. There was an even worse disadvantage with the latter method. A pike taking a bait below and from the side, which regularly occurs, did not, unless it was small, always take the full cross-section of the bait into its mouth. Thus the hooks situated on the top of the bait could be missed. Tooth marks supplied firm evidence time and time again.

The problem was solved by the design of a rig in which one set of hooks was fixed to either side, which did not throw the bait off balance. This required each treble or VB to be joined to a separate length of wire, both of which were fixed to the eye of the lip hook. It worked well, but unless the lip hook was large, size 2 at least, the eye would not accommodate the two wires and the trace snap swivel as well. Besides, as the full length of the hook shank protruded well in front of the bait's mouth so did the hook wires which led back from the hook eye. It looked untidy, as well as collecting weed far too efficiently. Aesthetically it offended my artisitic sensibilities! In any good design, excellence of form usually implies excellence of function, and this applies as much to fishing tackle as to any artefact.

Since it was proved that covering both flanks of the bait with a set of hooks improved the ratio of hooked pike to takes dramatically, I decided to design a new type of hook which would not only be aesthetically more pleasing but would also do away with the two unsightly wires, leaving the eye clear to take the trace snap swivel.

Designing a new type of hook is one thing; having it produced is quite another. I should know: I have designed a few. A manufacturer will only undertake to make a minimum quantity, usually many thousands. New shapes require new jigs and tooling and even the

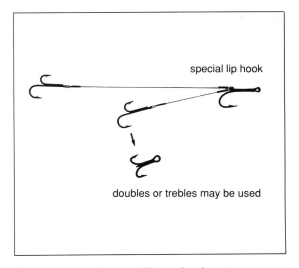

special lip hook

doubles or trebles may be used

The contemporary Marvic wobbling and trailing rig.

development of new manufacturing processes. Prototypes have to be rigorously tested and often slight modifications may be necessary, either to the design itself or in order to ease a problem in production. It can be a very expensive business. In spite of all these difficulties, the Marvic wobbling hook is now being marketed.

The shank of the wobbling hook is doubled back on itself, forming a hook eye in the same plane as the hook bend. A second eye is formed on this doubled shank on top of the bend. To this second eye the two hook lengths are joined. The doubled hook shank is brazed, making for great strength. The hook lengths no longer protrude but fit closely around the bait's head, and the hook eye is free to take the trace snap swivel, or alternatively the trace may be crimped or twisted on if required. Quite fortuitously, and at much the same time, Martyn was involved in the design of his new treble, called the MP. It soon became apparent that this was far more efficient than a conventional treble, not only because of its better hooking properties but because unhooking was simplified as well. The MP makes a perfect marriage with the wobbling hook and the two

combined make by far the most advanced wobbling rig yet devised. The same rig is also better than any dead- or livebait trailing rig I have come across. It may be that the Marvic wobbling rig is at the moment the most efficient rig for its purpose. No doubt our ancestors thought the same about their designs. In one of the chapters I wrote for John Bailey's and Martyn's book *Predator Becomes the Prey* I said that however excellent an item of tackle appeared to be there was always room for improvement. Modern and future technology will ensure this. Perthaps, like the Chapman or the Archer rigs, the Marvic wobbling rig will in the years ahead be a collectable antique.

SOME ENHANCEMENTS

The efficiency of the wobbling technique is due to the fact that a deadbait moving through the water imitates a live fish, the pike's usual prey. I do not usually make dogmatic statements, particularly about any facet of angling, but I am prepared to this once. I am quite sure that a wobbled deadbait is better than any lure

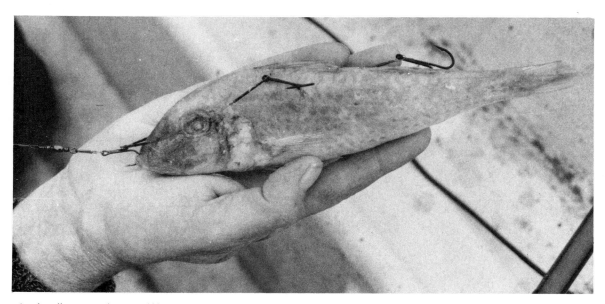

A red mullet mounted on a wobbling rig.

ever devised, excellent as some of them are. Wobbling baits have the edge over lures because when a pike takes a wobbled deadbait it is holding on to soft flesh, not wood or plastic. It is unlikely to reject a deadbait, but unless the hooks on a lure find immediate lodgement the pike will attempt to reject it. Lastly, a wobbled bait can be fished in such a multitude of ways, and so slowly if need be, that wobbling has to be the most versatile of all pike-angling methods.

Good as wobbled deadbaits are, it is possible to make them even more attractive. We have covered coloured baits elsewhere and this addition can be very effective. The problem with bait enhancement is that one never really knows if the enhancement induced a pike to take the bait in preference to a natural one, or if it would have taken an unenhanced bait as readily. However, there is strong evidence that certain colours attract pike and that they prefer one colour one day and a different one on another. I think the preference is strongly linked to the prevailing light values. Thousands of pike have fallen to the tail half of a herring, but I consider that the head half makes a better bait. Both baits smell and taste the same and their different shapes do not appear to effect the issue. It is the colour that matters. A herring's head is coloured with red, particulary round the eye socket, and this makes the difference. There can be no other explanation. If this supposition is correct, and I believe it to be so, wobbled baits can be made all the more attractive if a spot of colour is introduced. (Interestingly, Martyn still considers the tail half of the herring to be better but that, possibly, the head of a mackerel scores over the tail.)

Dying a bait's head or tail, or adding colour to the rig rather than the bait, are worthwhile experiments. I have had a few hooks made in a red-bronze finish, and similar crimps are now marketed. This is not the place to argue the merits of crimps or otherwise; that is a separate debate. However, hook shanks covered with bright-red sleeves are very visible when attached to a bait. So is a little strip of red-,

orange- or yellow-coloured plastic pushed over the hook point so that it remains on the hook bend. The logical development is a streamer deadbait!

Perhaps not so extreme, but a simple way to add a splash of bright colour to a wobbled bait is to make use of the red triangular-shaped tags that are often fitted to spoons. One of these can be slipped on the hook that is pressed into the bait. With the Marvic wobbling rig a tag can be fitted to either side. Because these tags are pierced with a fair-sized hole, to enable them to be fitted to the split ring that attaches the treble hook to the spoon, they can get lost when a fish is being played. They are so cheap that this is of little consequence. Miserly anglers can construct their own tags from sheet plastic, with a hole of smaller diameter, so that they remain on the hook bend and cannot slip over the barb.

Such crazy ideas often led to the development of successful angling techniques. Bait enhancements can be taken to extremes but if such experiments are not conducted it is impossible to tell if a bait can really be made hyperattractive. It may be that it never can — which I suspect — but it is worth a try.

Here is one more idea to set you thinking. Brightly coloured sea-fishing muppets, which look for all the world like miniature multi-tentacled squid, can be threaded on the trace before it is joined to the swivel. The muppet will then rest against a bead — bright-red, of course — by the trace snap swivel. Imagine wobbling a bait with the muppet pulsating just in front of its nose! Now that is real bait enhancement, and it works.

There are a few other anglers prepared to try out such zany ideas. Some years ago I read an article in one of the angling weeklies by Grahame Pullen. He had tried two good-sized discs painted to represent eyes fixed on either side of the deadbait's head. He asserted that when such a bait was wobbled it seemed very attractive. Grahame considered it better than using undoctored baits. I know that not a few pike anglers laughed their heads off. I didn't. I

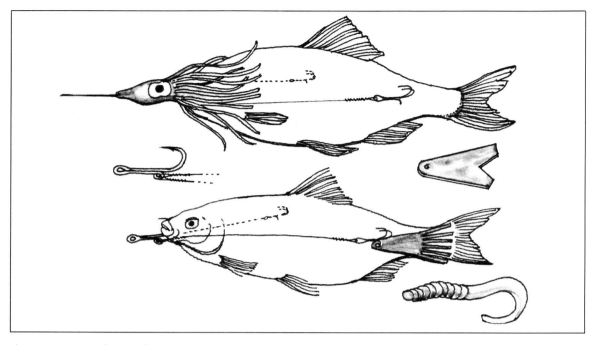

A muppet, vanes, and zany enhancement!

understand that Grahame's writing was misinterpreted by many who added eyes to their baits and left them legered static on the bottom. This was not what was meant.

Naturally, bait enhancement with colour is nothing like as effective in murky water. Then scent and vibration take over as pike attractors. In really dirty water both lures and wobbled baits can be forgotten, and bottom-fished deadbaits are the only hope.

Many years ago I adapted the baited-spoon technique for spinning for perch. It was and still is a deadly method of catching predatory fish, not only perch. I removed the hooks from a 2½-inch copper and silver spoon, passed a short length of stiff wire through the hole at the narrow end of the spoon, introduced some beads on either side and formed an eye at each end of the wire, one for holding the swivel and the other for a snap link swivel. The snap swivel took the lip hook of an early design of wobbling rig and the wire trace could be attached to the other swivelled eye. A small

whole herring was mounted on the rig, so I had a combination set-up consisting of a large lure allied to a large bait. When it was retrieved considerable resistance was inevitable, but the revolving spoon, now acting like a bar spoon, thumped the rod tip with a regular beat, no doubt advertising its whereabouts in no uncertain manner. This combination was launched into the relief channel, not far from Magdalen Bridge. I kept well clear of other anglers, not for secrecy, but so as not to attract undue attention and the inevitable ribald comments. The herring was eventually mangled by what was most likely a small pike. I mounted a new herring and cast across the channel, then alongside the near bank. After another bait was mounted I duly landed a 17lb fish. I did not care who came to watch and comment after that. That was the only pike I caught on that unusual rig. A few days later, on my third cast into a Norfolk lake I lost the spoon after hooking a solid snag. For some reason I have never repeated the experiment. Perhaps the extra strobe effect

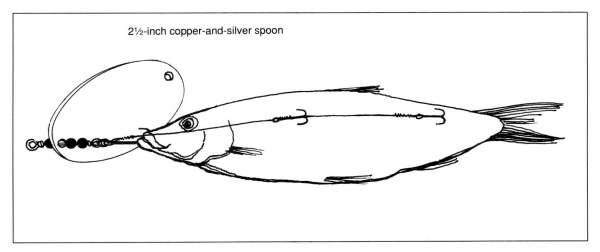

2½-inch copper-and-silver spoon

Vic's experimental combo.

caused by the rapidly revolving large spoon allied with powerful vibrations created enough visual impact and commotion to either scare the wits out of any self-respecting pike or stimulate it to investigate the unusual disturbances. That 17lb fish certainly wasn't frightened when it saw the herring – it nailed it.

Possibly the future may see artificial and natural baits used in combination. What is certain is that a standard method is first modified and, as a new generation of anglers go fishing it is changed, or even allowed to fall into disuse. There is nothing particularly innovative in my baited spoon. Our American friends use jig-livebait or small spinner-livebait combinations with considerable success.

Mark you, innovations in tackle design take time to be accepted by British anglers, unless they are carp fanatics. This is partly due to the natural conservatism inherent in our race. It is also due to the fact that they never hear about them. Ony a small percentage of anglers read the angling press, and even fewer read books. The tackle trade is nearly as bad. A new hook or rig that is manifestly an improvement takes at least three years to be accepted, sometimes longer, before anyone begins to show interest. Europeans and North Americans have a much more enlightened attitude.

WOBBLING METHODS AND TECHNIQUES

Most of the good pike caught in England each year, as opposed to Scotland and Ireland, are taken on static or buoyant deadbaits. This is hardly surprising for that is the method used by the majority of pike anglers. Visit any good pike water and nearly every angler will be sitting behind his rods, electric drop-offs or Optonics set. He fishes for carp and most other specimen fish in the same way; only the bait and terminal tackle differ. It works, but it can be unbelivably boring, as I know to my cost, having spent hundreds of rod hours drowning deadbaits. Sometimes, because the action is so slow an angler will decide to enliven the proceedings by engaging in a spot of wobbling. He reels in one tackle, removes any weight and, without changing or modifying his rig, hooks on a deadbait by inserting one arm of the upper treble through the bait's lips. He then fixes the lower treble where it reaches. Unless the bait is a small one the second treble does not even extend as far back as the dorsal fin. This set-up is cast and retrieved. He may get a fish, but more likely if a pike does grab hold it will not be hooked, for such a rig is very inefficient.

Soon the angler fishes mechanically, perhaps in a desultory fashion, and then convinces himself that this wobbling lark is not all it is cracked up to be.

It is important to understand how ninety times out of every hundred a pike attacks a wobbled bait. Once this is realised it becomes obvious that a normal two-treble rig cannot be anything but near-useless as far as hooking is concerned – except, as I have mentioned, with sprat-sized baits. A pike will chase the bait, overtaking it to one side. It will then turn and take it crossways, aiming for a mid-point on the fish's body. Occasionally it will chase and grab a small bait from behind. A pike's aim is not so perfect that it can make a sure strike every time. Sometimes it misses altogether and sometimes it just manages to grip that section of the bait around the anal fin.

The pike has a problem and I can best describe its complications by reference to my training as an anti-aircraft gunner early in the war. I particularly remember a film that was shown to potential gunners over and over again. It depicted a small boy standing on the pavement with his back to the camera. An old man was passing by, riding a bicycle. The boy aimed a snowball directly at the cyclist's head. It missed behind by a yard or two. Another man on a cycle appeared. This time the boy did not aim directly at his target, but well in front. A slow-motion sequence showed the cyclist moving forward into the line of trajectory. The snowball knocked his hat off.

A target moving across the field of vision can be hit only if the correct amount of lead, or 'aim-off', is estimated. After watching this film many times, even the most simple sailor began to realise that aiming directly at fast-flying aircraft was pretty stupid.

A pike taking a wobbled bait has to solve the same problem, estimating direction and speed correctly. We solve this mentally, the pike instinctively. It has to hit a target moving across at right angles to its own line of advance. By rising or sinking, the target can complicate matters. The pike hits the target often enough

but many times it only manages to connect with the rear end of the bait. A normal deadbait twin-treble rig does not cover that area, and that is why it is such an inefficient wobbling rig. At least one set of hooks must cover this all-important rear section. This is even more essential when using large baits. I always ensure that one set of hooks is never forward of the bait's vent and sometimes, if I think the pike are lethargic, making half-hearted attacks, or coming short, I will place one set of hooks as far back as the wrist of the tail.

BAIT TYPES, ADAPTATIONS AND PRESENTATION

A wobbled bait, whatever the variety, will only stand up to so many casts. Soft baits such as sprats or herrings do not last so well as freshwater species like rudd, roach or skimmer bream, and eel tails make a superb wobbling bait. These, as well as mackerel, trout, whiting and horse mackerel, seem to last longer than others I have tried. Smelt falls somewhere in between.

The short life of wobbled baits is caused by the fact that water is forced into the mouth and eventually fills the stomach cavity. This occurs as the bait is pulled through the water and it increases its weight. When a water-filled bait smacks down on the surface at the end of a cast, the stomach wall will eventually split open. From then on disintegration is rapid. This does not occur with eel tails, which last for cast after cast. A few more casts can be made if, once the stomach wall starts to split, it is fully cut open and the intestines removed. A split bait sinks more slowly and may behave erratically, but pike do not seem to mind. Sometimes such a bait is just as effective as a whole one.

There will be times when pike are lying deep, or it is considered expedient to search deep water. Normal practice is to add weight to the line above the trace and swivel. This is not a very good idea. The bait's action is

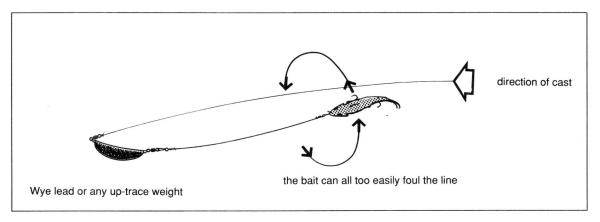

A problem with up-trace weights.

affected, a faster retrieve is required, and casting inaccuracy is impaired. Perhaps worst of all, the bait is held back when cast into a facing wind; the weight, which offers less resistance because of its higher density and far smaller surface area, will fly ahead of the bait, which will swing from side to side. All too often the hooks will foul the line as well. Finally, the up-trace weight is prone to collect weed.

If weight is necessary it can be added to the bait itself. Some anglers put a swanshot or two on a double length of monofilament line, which is pushed down the bait's throat. The small loop formed by the doubling of the line is held on the bend of the lip hook. It works, but it is very fiddly and time-consuming when hands are cold and wet. After suffering this disadvantage I decided to design a better arrangement. The result was the Marvic Deep-water pin. This is a pointed hardened-steel pin

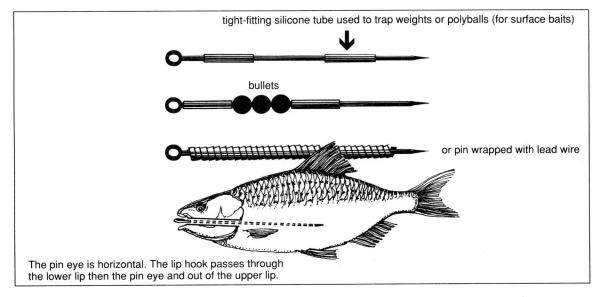

The Marvic Deepwater deadbait pin.

fitted with a good-sized eye. Tight-fitting sili-con rubber sleeves will hold small bullets or barrel weights, if you can get hold of any, firmly on the pin. Wrapping the pin with lead wire is just as effective. The pin is pushed down the bait's throat and into the stomach. The eye is left level with the lips and horizontal so that the lip hook of a wobbling rig can be passed through the bait's bottom lip, through the eye of the pin and out of the upper lip. The pin also works with small polyballs or pierced lengths of balsa rod (I shall be discussing surface-wobbling techniques later in this chapter). A Deepwater pin allows difficult deep-water swims, even those close by snags or overhanging tree branches, to be tackled more easily, for a bait weighted in this manner casts far more accurately.

Normally, when I decide to fish for pike using wobbled baits, I prefer to stick at it for a whole day's fishing. But it is useful to have a spare rod rigged up for wobbling even when fishing bottom deadbaits, or even float fishing from a boat. If a run hasn't developed it some-times pays to wobble a bait around and over the static ones. This can draw a pike into their vicinity and as often as not it will pick up one of these baits. What I think occurs is that a pike lazily follows the wobbled bait and, as it passes close by one lying on or suspended just above the bottom, the pike takes the static bait as the easier option. I can think of no better reason.

As for boat fishing, if a pike swirls at the surface within casting range it can be instantly covered if a rod with an already baited wob-bling rig is to hand.

One very obvious advantage wobbling has over most other forms of pike fishing, other than lure fishing and trolling, is the vast amount of water and the number of potentially feeding pike that can be covered in only an hour or two. If there is a disadvantage – and this can be discounted, as wobbling is as good a method of taking pike as any other – it is that rather more baits are needed, for the reason I have already mentioned. With the recent development of specially designed wobbling rigs now available

to all pike anglers, any pike taking the bait is more likely to be hooked than would have been the case in the past.

Casting and reeling back a bait mechanically will not take pike consistently. It is essential to know how a bait behaves when it is being re-trieved with variations in speed, and what hap-pens when it is activated by short jerks or a longer pull with the rod tip. If you are lucky enough to know an affluent friend who owns a swimming pool, gaining this vital information is easy enough. Most of us will have to resort to experimenting in the clearest river or pit we can find. It is helpful to have a friend who can report on how the bait is behaving.

The actions that can be given to a wobbled bait are so many, so varied, that it is important to know how to use both reel and rod tip to produce a particular type of movement or gyration at will. This skill can only be acquired by watching the bait's performance and how it is affected by variations in speed of retrieve and rod tip manipulation. An angler who knows exactly how his bait is behaving at all times and can make it perform as he wishes will catch far more pike than the chuck-and-retrieve mer-chant.

Angling writers often perpetuate myths they have read in other books. As they are repeated ad infinitum they tend to become accepted fact and angling lore. One of these oft-repeated be-liefs is that the pike thinks a wobbled bait is a sick or injured fish, and therefore represents an easy meal. I do not believe a word of it. That presupposes that a pike has a mental capacity enabling it to reason, which is manifestly ab-surd. A pike cannot think rationally; it only acts instinctively. Admittedly, a pike's instincts, like those of most wild creatures, are rather more developed than our own. Or, perhaps, more correctly, our instincts have deteriorated be-cause our cocooned environment has reduced our need for natural survival behaviour. Pike have to eat fish to survive and, while they are opportunist feeders and the odd watervole or water bird will be taken if offered, fish make up most of their diet. Any fish, healthy or unhealthy, which enters its zone of vision will be chased if the pike is feeding. Sick, injured, dying or dead – it matters not. All are grist to the mill. The fact that a wobbled bait seems to us to give a fair imitation of an injured fish is immaterial; the pike takes it because it is there. Wobbling a bait to represent a wounded or dying fish seems to us to attract pike. The reason that it is successful is that the bait is moving so slowly that it remains in view for longer, and so a pike can take it easily enough if it wants to.

Pike can attack baits not so much because they need food as because their aggressive instincts are triggered. Perhaps because the bait is an intruder, the pike reacts as do many wild animals when their territory is violated. Whatever the reason, when the slower, more enticing method of working a bait has failed, it is worth trying to wobble a bait faster, using vigorous rod tip action, so that it sets up maximum vibration, strobe effect and commotion. It is very possible that this can trigger a lethargic pike into chasing off an intruder acting so aggressively, and in so doing it may grab the bait instinctively.

Enough of hypothetical suppositions. I mentioned earlier that eel tails make long-lasting and excellent wobbling baits. A tail from 6 to 8 inches in length seems suitable. Naturally, it cannot be weighted with a Deepwater pin, nor has it a mouth to take the lip hook. Whilst the pin offers no answer, deeper water *can* be fished if the bait is allowed to sink for longer before the retrieve is begun. A hold for the lip hook can be contrived if you skin some 1½ inches off the thick end of the eel tail. Fold the skin back, then cut away half of the exposed flesh and form the remainder into a wedge shape. Cover the wedge with the skin and use any surplus skin to form a flap which can be laid on the wedge itself. This flap of tough skin gives a firm hook hold, as does the thin end of a wedge. Preparing a bait in such a manner may appear complicated, if not tedious, but it is quite straightforward.

Eels mounted on a wobbling rig should be

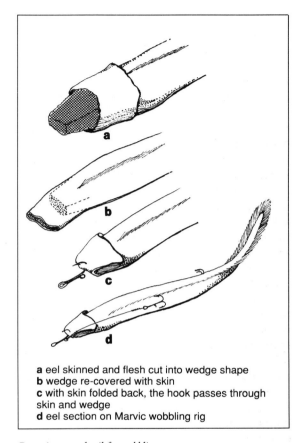

a eel skinned and flesh cut into wedge shape
b wedge re-covered with skin
c with skin folded back, the hook passes through skin and wedge
d eel section on Marvic wobbling rig

Preparing an eel tail for wobbling.

given a slight bend. When the eel is retrieved, this imparts a slow, seductive spin, which pike seem to appreciate. The merits or otherwise of curving any bait, let alone eels, can be debated. Some anglers believe that a bait which revolves gives better results than one which doesn't. This belief may have some validity since a spinning bait emits more flash and vibration. However, any uncurved bait will also revolve more or less, depending on the species of fish used as bait. For instance, a deep-bodied fish such as a small bream has a tendency to gyrate and roll more than a slim dace or smelt. The roll will be irregular and intermittent, just one or two rolls as the bait is retrieved for ten yards or so. It is a wide-looping roll. The bait rises and sinks, describing a helical spiral. It is not the angler who decides if a faster spin is more productive than a slow roll; it is the quarry.

A pike may prefer a certain type of bait presentation one day and one quite different on another, so dogmatic utterances about the best wobbling action are best ignored.

I said earlier that wobbling can be all things to all men, so versatile is the method. The technique can be as leisurely as casting out a bait and letting it sink to the bottom, perhaps to lie there for a spell. The bait is then either reeled in or pulled with the rod tip for 3–4 feet. When twitched the bait will rise, then subside again. This bait activation may be repeated at relatively long intervals or every few seconds until the bait is recovered. At the other extreme, an angler may decide to crank back a rapidly revolving bait as fast as he can. Both methods catch pike. In between are so many permutations that it would take a small book to list all the wobbling techniques that it is possible to employ.

Pike may swim near the surface, hang at any depth, or lie close to the bottom. Their position in the water may alter by the hour, depending on the depth band their prey is situated in, the direction of the wind, the light values, and other factors of which we anglers

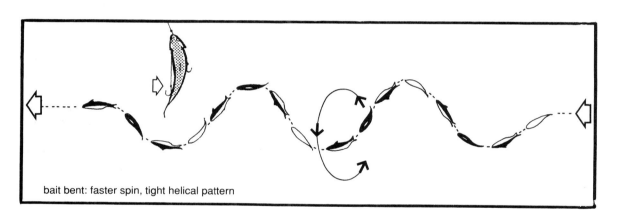

bait bent: faster spin, tight helical pattern

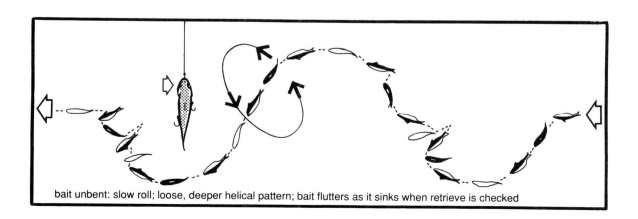

bait unbent: slow roll; loose, deeper helical pattern; bait flutters as it sinks when retrieve is checked

Variations on a wobbled bait's action.

understand little. But at least, when fishing from a boat, we can discover the depth of a pike by the use of a graph recorder, water depth permitting. The bank fisherman can only surmise according to past experience. For such reasons wobbling a deadbait can be more versatile than and just as successful as – and often more so – any other pike-fishing technique, including lure fishing. All depths can be searched, within reason, by varying the action of the bait, the speed of retrieve, even the choice of bait, until one of the permutations proves successful. Then, within an hour, the pike may cease to be interested in the killing method, but at least the changes can be rung again and perhaps a technique found that will succeed once more.

For those who have done little wobbling or none at all, it might be helpful if I describe one cast and retrieve. The bait is cast and at splash-down the seconds are counted until it has sunk to the required depth. This can be ascertained by experimenting with large and small baits, timing the rate of sinking in a swimming pool or a clear-water lake. The bait is then given forward movement by a slow firm pull with the rod tip. This causes the bait to rise and gyrate, even to begin a slow roll. As it sinks, the slack is reeled in until the pull of the bait is felt and the rod tip bends a little. Perhaps after a few more turns of the reel handle a pause may be made for two or three seconds so that the bait starts sinking. This is then arrested by a faster snatch, a short, sharp pull with the rod tip, which causes the bait to rise upwards with a short burst of speed, so emitting a flash. After some more line is recovered a long sweep of the rod will make the bait perform the slow helical spiral already described. Variations on these technqiues can be tried until it is time to recast. Always work the bait right up to the side of the boat or very close to the edge of the water when bank fishing. So often a pike will be following close behind and may grab the bait at the very last moment. If it does, watch out for fireworks. It will hightail it for deep water as fast as it can swim. Usually, however,

it will be scared of the boat or your silhouette. Then you may be startled by a yellow flash or even a boil at the surface as the pike turns away.

It is interesting, in this context, to compare our pike and the North American muskie. Muskies will follow a bait right up to the boat, which enables the angler to carry out the 'figure-of-eight' technique. This consists of moving the bait, usually a lure, in a vigorous figure-of-eight pattern. To achieve this, even the rod tip may be plunged below the surface. In this way a muskie can be stimulated into striking the bait. Our pike, not having quite such an inquisitive nature, never hang around long enough for this unusual technique to be attempted.

When a pike takes a wobbled bait it is manifested in two ways. It may crash at the bait, a powerful thump is felt and the rod tip may slam round. This happens so quickly that any re-action is impossible; the pike either hooks itself or it is lost. Quite often, however, the pike will take the bait gently, with delicacy even, and this occurs quite regularly with a slow-moving bait. The moment a little tug is felt the rod tip is swung backwards towards the bait, so slackening the line, and the reel bail arm is opened. As the pike moves away it will take line as in a typical run to a static deadbait. This run is then struck in the normal manner without delay. With a multiplier the spool must be disengaged or set very free-running so that the pike does not encounter resistance as it swims off.

SURFACE WOBBLING

Certainly one of the most exciting means of catching pike is surface wobbling. It is also highly efficient. This method is most effective in the warmer months and early autumn. The bait is made to float on the surface by the use of a deep-water pin fitted with small polyballs or a short length of balsa rod inserted in the bait via the mouth or vent, or buoyancy can be added by means of a Marvic deadbait punch. Adusting the buoyancy can make the bait sink very slowly indeed, which I consider important. A bait doctored in this fashion can be fished in those intriguing patches of clear water surrounded by weed rising to the surface, and over those excellent pike-holding areas of shallow water where bottom weed is dense and where there are only a few inches of weed-free water near the surface in which to wobble the bait.

Pike love to lie deep in the weed, for with binocular vision and eyes set high in their heads they can scan the water surface. The bait can be retrieved very slowly, even allowed to sink a little at times, and may take many minutes to retrieve. When the surface is well rippled the bait can be made to skip through the waves, twitched in short bursts so that it turns and flashes. Even in a flat calm, these little bursts of speed which radiate vibrations seem to prove irresistible. Pike can take a surface bait savagely, sometimes even leaping clear of the water as they do so. From the moment the bait is cast it can be watched and the sudden appearance of an impressive bow wave moving ever closer to the bait is heart-stopping.

WOBBLING IN RIVERS

If I had to choose just one water where I could only use a wobbled bait it would be a river. In such an environment wobbling is often a better method than most others. For one thing, potential pike-holding swims are easy to detect. There are the obvious ones, mentioned in every book on pike fishing – the deeper holes, the eddies, the slacks, sharp bends with deeper water under one bank, and, of course, weir pools. Perhaps the classic pike swim is where a sidestream enters the main river. The pike will lie off each promontory or even just inside its mouth. The slack downstream of islands and the more subtle swim where the current slackens a little and is hardly discernible may hold a pike or two. All these swims have been written of and the authors are quite correct. Pike are to be found in such places.

What is not usually realised, however, is that pike are not averse to using the current. They will lie in surprisingly fast water, which presses down on their shovel heads and slips past their steamlined bodies, affecting them little. Any glide of moderate depth, even if the current appears powerful, can hold pike. These fish are rarely troubled by anglers.

It is usually better to cast downstream and work a bait up current, for the current itself can be utilised. For example, the bait may be cast downstream and across to the far bank. It is then allowed to swing across the river, held on a tight line, and then worked slowly back close to the bank. The bait can be wobbled just inches from the edge or as far out as the rod can be extended. When the current is running strongly enough a bait can be held and allowed to gyrate by a likely pike lie. Sometimes this will trigger a response even from a lethargic fish as the bait remains in its vicinity for so long.

In fast water, baits can be forced to the surface by the current. In such situations the Deepwater pin is the answer, as weight can be quickly added or subtracted to suit the strength of flow.

When a bait is wobbled up current, and pike lie facing the flow of water, they will not be able to see the bait until it moves ahead of them. If a pike wants the bait it will follow. Moving out to the side, it will turn as described previously and take the bait crossways in its mouth and then, invariably, turn downstream. Wobbling a bait up current creates pressure which can be felt; the rod tip will be bent and the line will be tight to the bait. There will be no doubt whatsoever if the bait is taken. The rod tip should be moved in a downstream direction as quickly as possible in order to let the line slacken and allow the pike to turn downstream without feeling any impediment. Rarely need the bail arm be opened for once the pike has turned it can be struck at once and nearly every time it will be hooked in the angle of the jaw.

There are times when the only way to fish a likely swim is to cast upstream. Inevitably, the

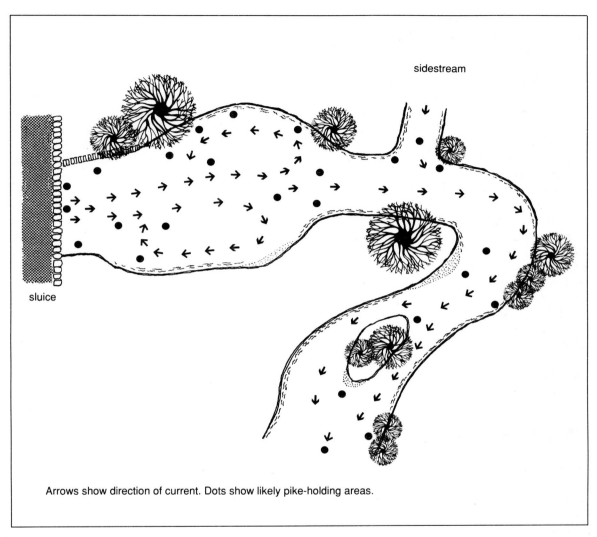

Arrows show direction of current. Dots show likely pike-holding areas.

Pike location in rivers.

bait has to be retrieved faster than normal and the pike has little time to make up its mind if it wants it. If the pike does take, it may hang in the current just holding on to the bait. If this is recognised the fish may be struck and again the hookhold will be in the jaw angle. Usually such pike will also turn downstream. The line slackens and some fast reeling in is necessary to regain contact.

It may happen that a good pike-holding swim is impossible to cast to because of vegeta- tion extending low down over the water. It is possible, by making use of the current, to work a bait into such areas. This little problem can be overcome by the use of a float. A streamlined tubed and camouflaged float is best. The line should pass through the body, for floats fixed bottom end only wobble and skid when brought upstream, and normally coloured pike floats with bright-red or orange tops have been known to be taken by pike in preference to the bait, particularly when reeled in against the current. The smaller the float the better, so use one that will only just support the bait.

The float is allowed to trundle off downstream, taking the bait along beneath it. Once the bait has been carried to where it is required it can be wobbled back normally.

IN CONCLUSION

Perhaps I have convinced some of those pike anglers who sit in bivvies behind a battery of rods and surrounded by enough tackle to fill a van that there are other easier ways of catching pike. I am sure that, like me, they detest humping mountains of gear, often for long distances. Just think, for a whole day's wobbling all that is needed is one rod, a net, and a haversack to accommodate baits, rigs and other odd bits and pieces such as scales and a camera.

Wobbled baits will catch pike but rarely in bitterly cold arctic conditions, then the game is just not worth the candle. I hope that I have shown that there is much more to wobbling than meets the eye. It is a whole fishing system in itself and is immensely versatile. Once an angler has mastered the technique and understood the subtle variations he may be surprised how many large pike will grace his landing net.

PART THREE

LIVEBAITING – THE PIKE ANGLER'S NATURAL CRAFT

12

The Heart-Stopping Second

There is something special about a pike taking a livebait. Possibly it is the knowledge that one is using a completely natural bait to catch the quarry. Perhaps it is the visual stimulation and anticipation.

In livebaiting, there is often some indication of a take before its occurrence. It can be seen in advance, allowing the adrenalin that much more time to flow. There is added excitement when a float which has been bobbing merrily around for the last ten minutes suddenly starts signalling that the bait has sensed danger. Then there is the chase. The bait endeavours to dart away from its predator in an attempt to escape the inevitable. The bait is engulfed in great jaws; there is a cascade of water, followed by a swirling vortex. Those using livebaits will have seen it all happen many times, anticipated the very moment and yet still, for a heart-stopping second, it catches them by surprise. The climax, nature highlighting the roles played by predator and prey, occurs before their very eyes.

After the stimulation of the take, landing the fish, even though enjoyable, can only be something of an anticlimax, regardless of the size of the prize. The extra excitement, the build-up to the take, is usually missing from other pike methods. At times a lure or a wobbled bait may be chased across the surface or followed by a great bow wave, but such pre-take activity is not usual with such methods except in shallow water. Usually the fish is not there one second, then the next instant you find yourself locked in battle, whereas with livebaiting there is so often some form of warning.

There is much more to livebaiting than added excitement. It is unquestionably the most obvious method to use for a predator such

A heart-stopping moment as a fish hits the surface.

as pike since it offers them their natural prey. Nowadays there is much pressure both from outside and within angling itself to control or abolish its use. In Chapter 14 we delve in depth into the pros and cons of the livebait debate. It is sufficient at this stage to mention that the pike angler is unduly restricting himself if he refuses to condone a practice which has been used successfully by generation after generation of pike anglers both here and abroad over many centuries.

Throughout the world livebaiting unquestionably accounts for the vast majority of pike captures, while England is unique in its continued development of deadbaiting techniques. In most countries deadbaits rank behind both livebaits and lures. Admittedly, we have one or two special circumstances, such as limited stocks of prey fish in some waters, which makes livebaits difficult to obtain. Indeed, the pike angler is sometimes blamed for damaging fish stocks, but rarely is this the fault of the pike angler, who is merely being used as a scapegoat. Evidence of the decline in prey fish in England's waters has been linked to agricultural chemical leaching, industrial and sewage pollution, and an apparent lack of effective water quality control over the course of several decades.

If other countries had our problems with fish stocks they would unquestionably solve them in a different way. They would not blame the pike angler but would look for the root cause. Indeed, it is interesting to examine the American philosophy. They actually breed fish for selling as livebait in tackle shops. When we were in the United States we would drive to the local tackle shop each morning at first light to buy bait. All types were available – suckers (a great gudgeon-type fish), minnows (a variety of dace/roach types) and even frogs, water-dogs (salamanders) and leeches, to name but a few. Purchasing bait is very efficiently organised. You can select the size and variety. They are then placed in a reinforced polythene bag which is pressure-injected with compressed oxygen before being sealed. The oxygen

ensures that the fish keep extremely fit and lively, even if the drive to the lake is a hundred miles or more.

The American method would certainly have great possibilities in the United Kingdom. We are, however, bogged down by legislation which restricts tackle dealers or fish farmers setting up such an enterprise. Unfortunately, English by-laws are littered with prohibitions concerning the numbers of fish which may be used as bait or transferred to or from a water. In addition, the by-laws prohibit the commercial sale of livebaits. Many of the rules were introduced in the misguided belief that disease would be transmitted if fish were transported from one water and introduced to another. The reasoning is misguided because most of the likely diseases are already endemic in the majority of our waters. One would need to start again, eliminating fish movement, keep-nets, landing nets and even birds landing, swimming or wading in different waters. There are a whole host of means by which disease is spread which make it extremely difficult to isolate one water from another. In addition, some of the diseases seem to be stress-related and already dormant within the fish. Perch disease may be one such example. If commercially bred disease-free fish were sold as bait, what harm would that do?

As it is we have to live with a number of misguided regulations. Therefore we need to take greater care of our bait to ensure that we use the minimum number to the greatest effect. Once upon a time livebaiting was practised by using a roach for, say, ten minutes, and then taking it off the hooks in favour of a fresh bait. Unquestionably this practice resulted in more pike. Often this is not possible nowadays, through lack of baits. A worn-out bait, in most circumstances, will catch fewer pike since its main attraction qualities – movement and vibration – have ceased. Sometimes such a bait will catch pike, perhaps on the easy-meal concept or possibly because its behaviour is similar to a distressed or dying fish. However, fresh baits mean more takes.

BAIT CARE

Let us now consider in a little more detail how to keep and store baits. We will assume that there are no rules concerning their transport and you may maintain a supply at home in a pond or large tank (practical fish keeping for pike anglers).

We believe that a bait which is well looked after will be more frisky in the water and therefore attract more pike. Bait care begins with its capture. So many anglers take a keepnet on their livebait-catching excursions and catch as many baits as possible, cramming them all into the net before eventually tipping them into a bucket and taking them home. Already damage will have occurred to a number of those fish, which will cause problems if they are to be retained in a fish tank or pond for a number of weeks or even months before being used. If the fish are kept in a keepnet damage occurs when scales and slime are lost, enabling fungus and disease to colonise damaged areas. This is particularly likely to occur if the fish are kept in an overcrowded tank. It is far better to ensure that as the livebaits are caught they are immediately placed in a bucket which, having smooth sides, will ensure that little damage occurs. In addition, you should, if possible, avoid handling the fish with dry hands. It is imperative to retain as much of the protective slime as possible, so handling should be kept to a minimum.

If the baits are to be used on the day it is still advisable to store them in a bucket rather than a keepnet. More fish can be kept in a given volume of water if an effective aerator is used. If you are catching great numbers of baits they should be spread between buckets. It is as well to remember that live fish have already exerted energy during capture even though it may not have seemed so as you reeled them straight in. It is unlikely that they will be as lively then as they will be several days later, provided that you take good care of the baits in the meantime.

Obviously, the baits should be transferred as quickly as possible to your main retention tank. An air pump should be used during transport to keep them in first-class condition.

Anyone who keeps tropical fish or cold-water fish will know that there are numerous problems associated with keeping them in good condition for long periods of time. It would be as well, if you retain large numbers of livebait, to refer to one or two reference works on practical fish keeping. We can only give one or two hints about practices we find effective. For instance, on buying a cold-water fish you will normally be advised to break it in gently to its new environment by allowing the water temperature of the transporting container to slowly equate to that of your pond or tank. We do not usually carry out this practice and have noticed no adverse effects on baits with the system we use, but if you experience problems with fish turning belly up or showing signs of distress on introduction to the tank a sudden temperature change could well be the cause.

Some of the biggest problems arise through overcrowding and you should beware of the temptation to hold too great a stock. It is difficult to give hard and fast rules on this because it depends on the size of the baits and the volume of water in the tank. If you put great numbers of fish into the tank and they begin to show signs of distress, overcrowding may be the cause.

You will be able to retain more fish if there is a moving flow of water. An outdoor tank with a hosepipe from the tap which continually introduces a slow but positive flow, with an overflow pipe taking the excess away to a drain, works perfectly in most circumstances. However, too great a chemical composition in your drinking water supply can give problems and chlorine in particular can cause a total bait wipe-out.

Different fish will react in different ways to being confined in the holding tank. Some will exist in normal drinking water whereas others will suffer. An alternative is to use electric pumps to keep the water moving and the oxygen content at a reasonable level. We have found this less satisfactory than using fresh running water from the tap but if you have problems of fish dying in your tank for no apparent reason (such as fungus or oxygen starvation) it may be as well to eliminate the tap water flow and use an air pump, just in case chemicals are distressing the baits.

Obviously, you can go to elaborate lengths by installing a water filter, but this is not usually necessary. The greatest problem will occur during the warmer months and retaining baits in September will prove far more difficult than during the winter. In early autumn you may need pumps, running water and very few fish in your tank to have any success, whereas during winter the density can be increased and it is not necessary to add so much oxygen to the water since the fish now require less because their metabolism has slowed down. The spread of disease is also less likely.

If you notice any fish in the tank with fungus they should be removed as soon as possible. Similarly, any mortalities should also be taken out.

We know there are differing opinions on the question of feeding livebaits. We do not feed as this causes increased fish activity and waste deposits in the water and ultimately the fish seem to suffer. However, we also do not advocate retaining the same fish in a tank throughout the winter without feeding. We would normally attempt to turn over our bait supply within six or eight weeks or replace the supply with a totally new stock. Otherwise the continued lack of feeding and retention within a confined space naturally affects the fish. Their flesh softens and they become less active and therefore less effective as bait. These fish consume their store of energy over a period of time, and fish should be returned to the water, where they will quickly recover their former strength.

There are one or two extras which can be added to a livebait holding tank. In the United States we were given a number of different chemicals for the purpose of increasing the oxygen content of the water and other chemicals for eliminating diseases. Similar chemicals

An explosive take.

can be acquired from tropical fish shops and they are very effective. Indeed, the oxygen additive really does appear to make the baits extra-lively. We often add a capful of this to a bucket of livebaits on a particular day to vamp them up, so to speak. We also use the chemicals in a livebait tank to minimise the risk of disease and to maintain oxygen levels.

There are countless other things which can be done to ensure that the baits remain in good condition. A used bait should not be reintroduced to the fish tank, for inevitably within a day or two fungus will result and that fish will die. It may even cause an epidemic of fungus which quickly spreads to other healthy fish. Similarly, when it comes to taking a few baits from the tank, for a day's supply, a very soft micromesh net should be used to scoop them out rather than one with a coarse mesh. All these measures are aimed at keeping the baits in as pristine a condition as possible and that really is the secret of ensuring that you always have a high-quality livebait. Once again, as with so much pike angling, just a little more attention to detail may result in one or two more fish on the bank.

13

Dead-or-Alive Theories – II

THE 'ULTIMATE BAIT'

In our introduction to deadbaiting we examined the concept of weaning pike away from their natural diet of live fish to a more energy-conserving food, our deadbait lying on or off the bottom. We are not suggesting that pike will then give up eating live fish but that they begin to feed much more readily on dead fish and come to accept them as part of their 'natural' diet.

Now, we accept that pike do not have our powers of reasoning; they cannot perform mathematical calculations concerning the equation of energy obtained from a dead fish as opposed to a live one. Pike are opportunitists and as such they will take an easy meal when they come across it. If the easy meal becomes much less random within their environment they will begin to spend more and more time in search of such meals and less time searching or hunting for the harder alternative. Hence our reference to a weaning process. The more deadbaits are introduced, the more effective deadbaiting will become.

Unfortunately, it is never quite so simple as it first seems. It may be that some pike actually have a preference for the taste of 'exotic' foods. When they are offered this exotic they quickly show their preference. In some ways this may be likened to some people's preference for a meal from a Chinese takeaway, as a change. Pike might prefer a mackerel to a live roach. Such preferences are unlikely to continue for ever and different pike may have different tastes. This is an idea on which we have not conducted a great deal of research since it has always appeared that when a bait is fishing well

in the water most of the pike are 'on' that bait. Not all people have the same preference for the same foods. Why should pike?

Pike may take a deadbait not so much as a change but as a form of dessert or a sweet, the different taste being quite to their palate but in a totally different way from a live fish. The 'unnatural' dead may at first score over livebaits because it is different. On the other hand, perhaps we are crediting the pike with far too much intelligence – the power to distinguish different tastes. It may be that in the long term deadbaits may score simply because they are readily available.

Ultimately, however, if all deadbaits have been fished out (if this is possible) and have 'blown', the pike will still need to eat to survive. Their natural food is a live fish and we as pike anglers would need to use the supreme natural bait for pike – live fish – if we wish for any degree of success. A comparison of the two major English methods can then be considered. Just as the concept of weaning carp away from natural foods to a 'preferred' diet of unnatural boilies or preoccupation on a particular particle bait can be applied in carp angling, so too may the pike's feeding habits be influenced by pike anglers. A livebait water may be converted into a first-class deadbait fishery, though eventually pressure may tell and all the deadbait fishing methods may decline in effectiveness. They may still provide an easy meal but the pike will have become instinctively aware of the potential danger associated with deadbaits. With livebaits the angler can offer the pike its natural food. A pike must eat to survive, it will always eat live fish, and so we can present that alternative.

Possibly we are carrying a hypothetical

Steve Harper in action with a good fish on livebait.

argument a little too far. It is unlikely that a situation will ever occur where pike in a water *always* refuse to take deadbaits. That would be crediting them with a long memory and a degree of reasoning intelligence. Certainly, pike do become wary of deads after intensive fishing. The next season may see them accepted again, though the 'going' bait may well be different. In the meantime livebaits will catch as well as ever. Deads may catch because they are different; livebaits will catch because they are the norm.

We can of course offer a choice of livebaits, some exotics even, but normally livebaiting is practised in order to present the pike with its normal food. On hard-fished waters problems may arise as a result of the restricting effect of tackle on the way a bait swims. This may deter cautious pike, but generally we must regard ourselves as extremely lucky that we are still able to fish for this species with their natural food as bait. It is certainly much easier than fishing for tench with a natural bait such as daphnia, for example.

14

A Case for Livebaiting

It was the mid-1970s. The dace seemed to be vanishing from the upper reaches of the River Wensum and it came to be believed by many that the problem was caused by the pike anglers taking them for livebait. But, unknown to these critics, a chemical sterilisation of the upper reaches was taking place: as abstraction reduced water levels, phosphates, nitrates and other chemicals leaked into the river.

This insidious and growing pollution was having a far greater effect on the dace population than the relatively few pike anglers catching a few for bait from random swims along the river. The menace of such unseen pollution is recognised now, yet pike anglers are often still blamed for declining sport. There have always been pike anglers taking fish for use as livebaits. Indeed, nowadays, with deadbaiting so popular and anglers by nature relatively lazy, far less livebaiting is practised. If pike anglers were the cause of such a decline sport should now be improving as a result of the popularity of deadbaiting. No. The truth is that pike anglers have been used as scapegoats, and the underlying unseen menace, chemical pollution, has continued its desecration.

It is now time that anglers as a whole united to combat the root cause of reduced fish stocks in our rivers. What price then a few small fish for livebait?

THE CASE EXAMINED

Some years ago Vic decided to give up using live fish as baits for pike. He now realises that it was a decison based on emotion rather than on logic. He even wrote a piece in one of the earliest issues of the Pike Anglers' Club magazine explaining his decision. He did state, however, that he would contine to use small lip-hooked baits. To forgo using these would have been irrational, for whenever he fished, for whatever species, the only way he could succeed was by hooking a fish in the mouth. There was no difference between lip-hooking a bait and catching it on a hook.

We both value our wildlife and the aspect of livebaiting which disturbed Vic was having to stick a hook into living flesh – a sentiment most civilised people would share. So for a few seasons he fished only with deadbaits and noticed that his catch rate dropped – not dramatically, but enough to encourage him to spend not a little time wobbling deadbaits, rather than using them conventionally either lying just on or off the bottom or suspended under a float. What he failed to realise then was that when he was wobbling he was trying to make a deadbait behave as if it were alive. It was some time before the penny dropped – he was livebaiting by proxy.

This further reinforces the belief that livebaiting is one of the best of all pike-fishing methods, even though Vic, at the time, was not prepared to practise it.

Generally tolerant of other people's opinions, Vic was quite happy to fish alongside friends who were using livebaits. Unlike the most vociferous members of the anti-livebait faction, many of whom do not fish for pike, he considered that whether to use livebaits or not was a matter of personal choice and conscience. There is an ever-growing minority of anglers who seem to delight in restricting the freedom of choice of others. Livebaiting, if carried out within the confines of water authority by-laws, is a legal method of fishing, and even when he chose not to do Vic realised that he had no right whatsoever to question the actions of those who did.

He soon came to realise that by not using livebaits he was denying himself the best pike-fishing method of any. This alone was not the reason he decided to reverse his views. In fact it took many months of research, questioning the beliefs and arguments of those, either for or against livebaiting, and seeking the opinion of a most knowledgeable biologist before he came to a decision as to whether he could livebait with a clear conscience.

It was the alleged cruelty aspect that had been of great concern. As an animal lover he had always felt squeamish when inserting hooks into the body of a live fish. To a non-angler, or even an angler who has any feeling for other creatures, sticking metal hooks into a living body looks extremely cruel. That it *seems* cruel it does not necessarily mean that it *is* cruel. To confuse appearance and reality in this matter is to allow emotion to override rationality. Snap decisions based solely on emotion are rarely substantiated for long.

Put simply, this whole matter hinges on the answer to one question: do fish feel pain? Nobody, scientists or laymen, can provide positive proof one way or the other, but what little research has been undertaken, allied to other evidence, seems to indicate that fish do not suffer pain in the same way as warm-blooded mammals. Indeed, it would be surprising if they did, for fish not only live in a different medium from mammals but are cold-blooded creatures. Since mammals and fish are quite different life forms, to believe that they both feel pain in an exactly similar degree is an untenable hypothesis, which would not be entertained by anyone with even a smattering of scientific knowledge.

The RSPCA some years ago instigated an investigation into the cruelty involved in blood sports. Angling was included among the topics under scrutiny. What came to be known as the Medway Inquiry eventually published its conclusions. Perhaps the RSPCA hoped that overwhelming evidence of cruelty in sports, including angling, would eventually lead to their abolition. They were to be disillusioned. This is not the place to list Medway's findings, but they did give fish 'the benefit of the doubt' as regards feeling pain. This phrase does imply that some doubt remains. The National Anglers' Council's own report by scientists, conducted at much the same time, concluded that 'the scientific evidence does not show that fish feel pain as commonly understood by humans'.

The 'benefit of doubt' conclusion of the Medway Report was based mainly on research conducted by Professor J.S. Kelly. Briefly, Kelly discovered nerve endings in fish skin, particularly in the area of the mouth, and these were similar to those which detect tissue damage in man. He also found the presence of two pain-related substances. One is a peptide molecule, called P, which is involved in the transmission of pain. The second substance, enkephalin, is an opiate which blocks the transmission of pain detected by substance P. This would dull or even prevent pain being perceived, provided that the nerve endings are linked to the brain in fish as in humans. Enkephalin appears to function differently in mammals because they do feel pain, yet it is highly possible that fish do not in the same way that we do.

Accepting that the two life forms, fish and mammals, exist in totally different environments and that fish are primitive vertebrates while mammals are more advanced life forms, it is not inconceivable that P and enkephalin function quite differently in each. Such evolutionary changes in the functions of similar substances are well known and have occurred thousands of times.

Without any scientific understanding we can see ample evidence that fish do not suffer pain in the same way as ourselves or other mammals. If I put a handful of pins inside my mouth and chewed them then I would suffer not only laceration and damage but agony. The same would apply if I ate sharp-spined sea urchins and fish, as well as crustacea such as hard-shell crabs and crayfish. Fish can accommodate such items with ease. Cod will happily crunch sea urchins and crabs, while chub – and pike, incidentally – make short work of crayfish. In the nature of things, where fish consume such fare their mouths also become lacerated, but repair is far more rapid than in mammals. If it hurt fish to eat such things they would not attempt to do so. Therefore it must be assumed that it doesn't – which could well indicate that in fish enkephalin blocks the release of *P* effectively.

Bill Giles of Norfolk pike fame once told us that he caught a small perch and the hook point had penetrated an eye. When he removed the hook the eye was pulled accidentally from the socket. That little perch was returned to the water. As an experiment Bill kept the perch eye on his hook and recast. Shortly afterwards he caught the same one-eyed perch. (An almost identical episode was reported in the *Fishing Gazette* early in the 1920s.)

Vic has caught badly injured fish. On one occasion he landed a medium-sized roach so badly wounded that the abdominal wall was ripped open, allowing its viscera to protrude. If he had just had an eye ripped from its socket or his intestines were spilling out he would not fancy a meal, yet both fish did. Martyn once conducted an experiment where, having hooked a chub, he released the reel bail arm so that the chub, with the hook still in it, was able to swim freely. He watched as the chub returned to its shoal and began to feed – again, hardly indicative of a fish in pain. Most anglers seem convinced that when a fish is hooked it doesn't feel pain and it is highly probable that they are correct. Barry Rickards made a telling point when he compared what would happen if someone was hooked in the lip. As pressure was applied the person would follow meekly so as to ease the pressure which was causing great pain. A fish in the same predicament does exactly the opposite, it pulls back, and this, we suggest, clearly indicates that it cannot possibly feel pain as we understand it.

We have listened many times to the arguments of anglers who state that livebaiting is cruel. When it is suggested that sticking a hook in the body of the fish causes no more distress than sticking a hook in the mouth, which all anglers do when catching a fish, they will not accept that supposition. When asked to explain why they think a hook in another part of a fish's body causes pain whereas one in the mouth does not, they are always at a loss to provide a rational answer.

Anti-livebait anglers are fond of pointing out that it is cruel practice to tether a live fish so that it cannot possibly escape the attentions of a predator. This fallacious argument is based on sentiment alone. A fish is a primitive life form: it cannot think and it cannot differentiate between cause and effect. A fish acts by instinct, instinct developed and honed by the evolutionary process over millions of years. A fish's instinctive behaviour is concerned with survival, food and reproduction. It instinctively reacts to danger, usually collectively as a shoal member. If alone, it can only protect itself by flight. If it is tethered on a livebait tackle it will react by trying to swim away from that which is restricting its movement. A livebait doesn't say to itself: 'If I have to stay here a pike will come and eat me.' It is not a cerebrating life form: it is totally unaware of its predicament. Mental cruelty cannot be involved. Those who take the view that it is cruel to use live fish for catching pike are crediting the bait with mental faculties akin to our own, which is manifestly absurd.

Another argument why livebaiting is unnecessary to catch pike is that they can be caught on other baits – lures and deadbaits, for example. This is correct, but we should hate to restrict ourselves to lures, for not only do pike become wary of them eventually but there are times, particularly in bitter winter conditions, when lure fishing is a waste of time. It can also be near-useless if the water is cloudy. Deadbaits are effective but, as every experienced pike angler knows, there are times when deadbaits are ignored by pike in favour of livebaits. We repeat, a livebait is the very best pike bait of all and it is important to fight restrictions on the freedom of the use of any bait, provided it is legal.

One would expect the anti-angling lobby to single out livebaiting for attack because it looks cruel and can so easily be presented in that context to the public via the media. Anglers should know better and should realise that when they attack an angling technique used by their fellow anglers they are helping to weaken the case for angling as a whole. Internal bickering encourages our enemies and diminishes our united strength.

To ban livebaiting could so easily become the thin end of the wedge. Most anglers would not hesitate to impale a worm on a hook, yet it too is a livebait, and so is a maggot. There is not a great deal of difference between a worm, which is an invertebrate, and a cold-blooded primitive creature such as a fish. The dividing line is narrow and to allow one to be used as bait and not the other, without sound scientific evidence, not emotional sentiment, is foolish in the extreme. What seems equally ludicrous is that some angling clubs have banned livebaiting on their waters. Not one official will have carried out any research into the matter, few will be pike anglers, and not one scientist or fishery biologist or even an experienced pike angler will have been consulted at all. On what they base their decision, which profoundly affects other anglers, is never divulged.

We can only conclude that such decisions are based on well-meaning sentiment, with the perpetrators remaining in complete ignorance of any relevant evidence one way or the other since they have not researched the matter. A strange way to take decisions! Club officials may ban livebaits because their waters do not appear to be fishing well and they consider that the taking of livebaits will only compound the problem. We find it hard to believe that taking a few roach of 4–6oz affects the biomass of cyprinids in any water to the slightest degree.

Quite recently, in one of the monthly magazines, an angler debating the livebait issue from an ethical viewpoint offered the opinion that you can do anything with a deadbait that you

A pike spins in the water in an attempt to throw the hooks.

can with a live. Certainly, you can give an appearance of life by wobbling deadbaits. One thing that is impossible to achieve is to make a deadbait alive. We defy anyone to make a deadbait behave like a paternostered livebait, which not only signals a particular pattern of vibrations but remains tethered in one small area. If anyone has solved this problem we would gladly attend a demonstration.

Those anglers who do not use livebaits, for whatever reason, should have their opinions respected. Equally, those who do use livebaits when they consider that it is necessary to do so should also be allowed their freedom of choice.

The freedom of choice and the freedom to act as we think fit within the law is a precious commodity, sadly eroded in many parts of the world. This should not be ignored by those who endeavour to curtail our freedoms. There can be no justification in banning the use of livebaits for catching predatory fish until there is irrefutable evidence that pain and suffering is being inflicted on another creature. At present the evidence points to the contrary.

15

A Livebait is a Livebait?

A livebait is a livebait; if it wriggles use it is the generally accepted criterion for livebaiting. Little thought seems to be given to whether there is any merit in adopting a more selective attitude for particular circumstances. Certainly it is true that a hungry pike will take a live fish wriggling frantically, whether it is a humble roach or an exotic goldfish. But is it possible to increase returns with a little more thought about which bait is used?

Quite often there is no choice. Quite simply, you fish with whatever livebait you can obtain. This will usually be roach, since they are the most common fish in many waters, and that is

where it will end. If, however, you are able to arrange for a supply of other species, some baits have particular characteristics which can be used to your advantage. Let us examine some of the likely livebaits and highlight some of their good and bad points.

ROACH

This bait must account for the majority of pike caught on livebait, simply because it is the bait most commonly used. It is an easy bait to use. It may not be as hardy as some of the others,

The battered results of a pike take.

but it is nicely shaped, not so deep in the body as to present a difficult mouthful. Another advantage is that roach often average the 'right' size to be easy to control, weighing 2 or 3oz.

The roach is a relatively attractive fish with its bright silver sides and reddish fins, and it is relatively visible to the pike unless it is lying dormant on the bottom. Generally one cannot go far wrong when using roach. In the majority of our waters roach form the staple diet of pike throughout most of their growing years. But, and this is a big but, in the average size range roach may not prove particularly attractive to some of the bigger pike. They may prefer something a little more substantial.

RUDD

How often we have heard anglers cursing about the tangles resulting from using rudd as bait! Being partly surface feeders, rudd have a propensity to swim upwards, knitting paternoster rigs into veritable cobwebs. In spite of this drawback they are not a bait to avoid. On some waters, they are vastly superior to roach.

On the Thurne system, for example, a system noted for its big rudd in the past, these fish are at one with the shallow-water environment and they can be made to roam most effectively, covering large areas of water. Indeed, they have proved to be a deadly attractor for the system's big pike.

Perhaps the rudd's brighter brassy colour and its deep-red fins add to the appeal, or perhaps it is the way it tends to swim in the upper layer of water, above the dense weed, that makes this bait more visible and so effective. We have noticed the same effect on other shallow waters and have even paternostered rudd effectively by means of a buoyant leger rig with the main line sunk along the bottom, out of the tangling reach of the rudd swimming above and towards the surface.

The rudd is not a bait to be ignored just because of its tackle-tangling reputation but one to be used, particularly in shallower water

on a rig that helps to avoid such tangles. It is perhaps best used as a roving bait.

BREAM

A small skimmer bream is obviously a highly desirable target for a pike. Its silver sides are extremely visible, while its flat-sided deep shape may give it the appearance of a larger meal than it actually represents.

Small bream can cause one or two problems, however. Their very shape may prove difficult for the pike, forcing it to follow tradition by taking hold of the bream across its flanks and then turning it before swallowing. Sometimes a pike may find that it has taken on more than it can chew. As a result, more fish tend to be lost on bream baits, with hookholds often poor, or, more correctly, the hooks never getting into the mouth of the pike in the first place. These are usually smaller-sized pike and one should not delay striking unduly just because a bream bait is being used.

Another problem with bream is that the shape is not really suited for paternostering, and they do tend to 'give up' quickly when used on such rigs. They make another excellent rover, however, and it often proves possible to encourage them to work large areas and, one hopes, to cover more pike on their travels.

We have found that roach × bream hybrids perform that much better and, being a little more slender across the body, they make quite an excellent bait without presenting the hooking problems encountered with true bream. The roach × bream hybrid is also usually hardier, livelier and longer-lasting.

Bream have an added attraction. On those waters containing large bream shoals it is often found that the big pike follow the shoals and feed on them in preference to smaller prey. If you use a bream of ½–1lb (which is still controllable) it is far more likely that you are presenting to the pike a bait which they are accustomed to taking. In other words, your bream will be taken in preference to a 2oz roach. It is certainly possible that on some waters big pike feed on little other than bream.

Big Baits

Perhaps this is the appropriate place to discuss the 'big bait equals big pike' theory. It does not always hold true. Indeed, if you use only small baits you will catch big pike sometimes, but you may well be lengthening the odds.

We are currently experiencing difficult times with regard to fish shortages. This means that one must exercise some discretion as to what baits are used. Nevertheless, we would be remiss if we did not emphasise that a big pike needs to expend considerable energy in obtaining numbers of small prey fish whereas it can often achieve the same return for less expenditure of energy by taking a 2lb bream.

We all like sweets now and then, but these are titbits taken in addition to a full meal. So it is with the pike. Big pike will prefer to hang around the *best* available food source in a particular water. If that source if big roach, bream or carp then that food will form the basis of their main diet and hence the most likely livebait to catch them.

Big baits are therefore more likely to select bigger pike in a particular water. They do, however, present problems with presentation. Naturally, there will also be occasions when such a philosophy does not hold good. Fry-feeding pike are a case in point, when the pike are herding up and feeding on an abundant supply of tightly packed tiny fish. They merely have to charge through the trapped shoal with mouth agape, taking in great numbers of fry at a time. This usually occurs in the early autumn months and then the pike may become totally preoccupied on such extremely small fry.

Bream as bait fit well into the big-bait equation and certainly results can be quite dramatic with a bream livebait between ½ and 1lb, particularly on some big Dutch waters.

DACE AND CHUB

Dace and small chub make quite remarkable livebaits. They are more difficult to retain in tanks and buckets since their oxygen requirements are high, but as a livebait they are hyperactive compared with baits caught from still waters. What is more, they are the perfect shape, and their thin body is easy for a pike to grip, so hook setting is more positive than with bream. They are often readily available at 4oz or so, at which size they make a bait which is very versatile and easy to control. If the bigger-bait philosophy is applied, obviously chub are easier to obtain in the larger sizes than dace, though a 12oz-plus chub livebait is quite a handful.

In the smaller sizes these baits are among the most effective for use on paternoster rigs and of course their bright silver or bronze sides make them extremely visible.

CRUCIAN AND OTHER CARP

Some pike anglers place crucian carp on a pedestal high above other livebaits, considering even that other types of carp are not as effective. The crucian does indeed have many attributes. It is a virtually indestructible livebait, it can be used for hour upon hour, and seemingly it appears to suffer few after-effects – until a pike takes it. Crucians are incredibly hardy. Not only that, when used at the right time of year they will work constantly. Other livebaits usually display periods of activity then lie dormant for a while. As the time passes the periods of activity lessen in favour of greater periods of rest. The crucian just works on and on. The bait is therefore quite special, but only during the warmer months. Until the water temperatures fall considerably the crucian will display all these characteristics throughout the early autumn and perhaps into late November.

Crucians become active again towards the end of the season as water temperatures begin to rise. In the depths of winter, however, crucians become lethargic and virtually dormant and at times prove to be quite useless as livebait. There are ways round this. Retaining them in warmer water, for instance, may help; but, inevitably, when they are being used the cold quickly reduces their metabolism and they become less active than more conventional livebaits.

Other carp, such as small mirrors and commons, display similar characteristics to the crucians. Although they are probably not quite so hardy they tend to be a better winter bait with less tendency towards the lethargy displayed by crucians. There is an important difference, however – the crucian tends to swim in a different way. Its actions whilst working, particularly on a paternoster rig, tend to be more frantic, with lots of short sharp bursts and fluttering dashes. We are sure that this unusual characteristic accounts for much of their success. They are different, and their frenzied activity appears to prove irresistible to pike.

Quite a different bait is a goldfish. Some farm ponds contain great goldfish and large numbers of fish from 4 to 8oz can be caught easily. Obviously this is a unique bait. How can a pike resist a bright-orange or yellow fish swimming past it? It will stand out like a sore thumb in all but very coloured waters. Goldfish tend to very hardy and where pike have seen everything else a goldfish livebait can prove a refreshing last ace to play. Eventually, however, that very attribute – its 'unnatural' visibility – may deter a cautious predator.

TROUT

In the chapters on deadbaiting we mention that we have not found trout to be a particularly effective deadbait. As a livebait, however, trout can at times be very special.

The action of trout as a bait is totally unlike any other livebait. They swim powerfully, towing tackle all over the place. As a roving bait they will cover much ground in a short space of time. Indeed, they can be something of a headache in weedy water, because they are so powerful that they can easily bury themselves into any weed. Fortunately, only a slight pull will normally get them going again and they will break themselves clear and go dashing off – in search of pike! The effect of all the frantic movement emitting vibratory signals throughout the swim will arouse even dormant pike, winding them up until eventually they strike, perhaps out of anger or as an instinctive reflex.

Sometimes you can have a problem as a pike will chase the trout across the surface but fail to catch up with such a super-powered bait. Martyn can remember Eddy Turner, one of the great exponents of using trout livebaits, telling of an occasion when a pike chased his trout across the surface of the River Thurne. When it failed to catch the bait it settled for the nearby live roach fished by Bill Hancock. Bill was quite satisfied with his twenty. On that occasion using trout worked against Eddy. Normally trout livebaits can result in fish, and big fish, when others baits have failed, merely because their hyperactivity seems to wind up large pike.

The only time Vic fished Broadlands lake in Hampshire he used a fair-sized trout livebait which was so lively that a heavy bomb had to be used on the paternoster link to hold the bait in position. Nearby he cast out a small legered smelt. Whether the trout wound up the pike or not, it ignored it in favour of the little smelt. At 22lb 6oz that pike could have made short work of the tethered trout. Perhaps its powerful vibrations attracted the pike, which found the smelt en route to a more substantial meal.

Unfortunately, even though trout are first-class baits they can create problems. We have mentioned their propensity to outrun pike and the sheer difficulty of controlling a 4oz-plus trout livebait on pike rigs. There can be

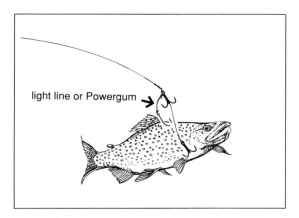

light line or Powergum

The ET breakaway rig.

other disadvantages – striking, for one. Trout have very tough skins and if the hooks are deeply embedded in the bait they do not easily pull free on the strike. Also, the weight of the trout can often help loosen the hookhold as the pike thrashes or shakes its head. There are ways to circumvent this. You can use a rig in which the hooking hooks are not embedded in the trout, which is held on 'breakaway' hooks attached by light line to the main trace (see diagram). Alternatively, ensure that the hooks are only very lightly nicked under the skin of the trout so that they will come clear on the strike.

Most trout livebaits are obtained from fish farms. It is rare for them to be less than 4oz and often the bait will weight as much as 8oz. Tackle for these baits should therefore never be light. We strongly disagree with the use of light lines for pike fishing, but with a bait such as trout strong tackle is even more important. Eleven-pound line is an absolute minimum for trout livebaits, and indeed for any form of pike angling.

Another difficulty with trout is keeping them alive and in good condition. Many anglers acquire a supply from a fish farm and by the next morning find that every single one has perished. The trout is a hyperactive fish, requiring high oxygen levels, and there is absolutely no way that it will survive unassisted overnight in a bait bucket. Even a well oxygenated fish tank is unlikely to keep trout alive for long. The answer is to use a bait cage and to keep the trout in a river which has a good flow of water and oxygen. In this way they can be kept fresh and lively for long periods. When the baits are moved for the day's fishing it is essential to keep them well oxygenated. Obviously, air pumps will have to be used during transportation and during the course of the day the baits should be kept in a small bucket-sized bait cage in the water, where the oxygen content will be higher and the water will flow more freely.

You can buy a bait cage from a tackle shop or you can make one by drilling holes in an ordinary bucket. The lid is firmly secured and an opening flap is cut into it for removing fish. A string of wire passed through holes in the flap and the lid will keep the flap closed. A cage bucket which fits inside a standard bucket offers a convenient means of carrying bait from one swim to another. It also means that you can keep your hands dry and warm. Lift the cage clear so that its contents drain, select your bait, and reimmerse the cage in the larger bucket.

Bait cages can also be used to keep baits other than trout in better condition, particularly in the warmer autumn months when baits can suffer through oxygen starvation if kept in a bucket alone.

Trout livebaits are rather special in their effect on pike, particularly on dormant non-feeding fish. They are not a cheap bait to use, unless you can catch your own supply, and they do present a whole host of problems. Unfortunately, dead trout are not particularly effective except for wobbling. For some reason a live trout will work incredibly well for a period but then it will suddenly keel over and die. This means that you can use quite a number of trout on a particular day and end up with a number of dead fish, which adds to the cost. Even if trout do not make particularly good deadbaits, the loss can be recouped – they may taste good on a plate! This is certainly not a bait to be neglected.

PIKE

The use of small pike as a livebait is an emotive subject. Many pike anglers would condemn such use on the grounds that it was against the interests of pike conservation. We cannot see that one can condemn this in one instant yet condone the use of other live fish in the same breath. It is all a question of degree and for those who wish to use small pike as baits we have no objections.

A small pike bait is used in order to appeal to the cannibalistic nature of the pike. Some anglers have achieved considerable success with their use (see Paul Snepp's chapter in *Predator Becomes the Prey*). However, the use of such a bait can present problems. Martyn can recall one instance from the few times he has used small pike as bait. It was many years ago on the River Bure. He had caught a jack of about 2lb

and thought that this might single out one of the very large Bure fish. He set about mounting the bait on a double set of snap tackles. The bait was then slowly trailed behind the boat. This was quite some task, with the lively pike kiting all over the river. It was necessary to keep the check on the reel and at times to hold the rod to stop it being pulled out of the boat. He was just on the point of giving the whole thing up as an impossible task when the pike's movements became even more frantic. Sensing something was afoot, he quickly disengaged the check and opened the bail arm. Now untethered, the pike bait shot to the surface, crossed the river and disappeared into a side dyke, followed by a great bow wave and a crocodile-like back breaking the water as the bait was taken in one almighty explosion. Unfortunately, the bait ultimately proved too much for its attacker. After slowly easing back into the main river with its quarry, the pike

The jack livebait was taken in one almighty explosion.

ejected the bait and Martyn disconsolately reeled in an extremely lacerated jack.

The practicalities of fishing a pike livebait require very careful thought about rigs, tackle and presentation. Tackle must be stepped up if one is to present a 2–3lb pike as bait. On the other hand, if a ready supply of baby pike can be obtained there is very little difference in using them compared with other livebaits.

Perhaps some big pike are purely cannibalistic and feed only on other pike. If this is the case, though it would be difficult to establish, the use of a small jack pike as bait could result in one or two eye-opening surprises. Our thoughts are that the pike baits will prove better around spawning time, but this is purely supposition. It is not a bait we have used with any frequency, though we would not be adverse to doing so when the opportunity is offered.

OTHER BAITS

Tench

A number of other species can be used as livebaits. Tench, for instance, have been used with success by some anglers. This is contrary to the old Victorian idea that the tench was a doctor fish and that because of this the pike would not eat it. Although, when discussing jack pike, we said it was somewhat hypocritical to condemn the use of one livebait type, we personally find it very difficult to contemplate the use of a tench as a bait. This is just natural reluctance, and unquestionably tench will catch pike. Incidentally, tench have a well proven reputation as a supreme livebait for catfish. They are of course not generally available in the right sizes for pike livebaits, small tench being notoriously difficult to catch except in little ponds as abound in Kent, where Vic in his youth used to catch little 4-inch tench one after the other.

Gudgeon

Gudgeon are of course a very good pike livebait, though in most circumstances, because of their smaller size, their use brings the attentions of numerous jack pike. In addition, because of their camouflaged colours it is essential to keep them off the bottom so that they are more visible. They are a very hardy bait and where extreme distance casting is necessary (which can be achieved with smaller baits) they can often prove far more effective than small roach and the like, which do not survive such treatment.

Perch

Perch are an interesting pike bait. The old fallacy about the spines discouraging pike should not be believed. In recent years perch have not been readily available as a result of the ravages of perch disease. Perch do, however, make an excellent pike bait. Indeed, in Holland a perch in the ½–1lb range appears to bring far more takes than most other baits on the large waters. Possibly perch form the staple diet of those pike, though this is extremely unlikely when one considers the vast amounts of prey fish in these waters. Ruffe fall in the same category, though, like gudgeon, they should be fished well off the bottom as they would be virtually invisible lying doggo.

There are of course several other livebaits which can be used for pike. We are sure that eels would make a remarkable pike bait if anyone could find a way of mounting them. We have concentrated on those baits which are more generally used and available and hope we have provided pointers to why a particular bait may have the edge over another in certain circumstances.

16

Techniques

It is probably true to say that there has been little change in livebaiting practices over the last century. There have, of course, been advances in tackle, with modern technology providing new improved materials. But, this aside, developments tend to a large extent to go round and round in circles, as new generations rediscover forgotten rigs of the past, merely substituting the new materials in their construction. This is particularly the case with paternostering and the current experimentation aimed at avoiding bite-offs.

It is of course not surprising that there have been few changes. Man has been livebaiting for centuries and is an inventive creature, so it is to be expected that most modes of presentation will have been considered at some time in the past. In this chapter we follow tradition and distinguish between roving, legered and paternostered baits, adding our own thoughts to the vast literature already available on the subject of livebaiting techniques.

ROVING METHODS

The Standard Approach

Whereas deadbaiting is traditionally known as the slow method, livebaiting has built up a reputation for producing smaller pike. We hope that we can dispel both myths. Nevertheless, it is probably true to say that most anglers who practise roving livebait techniques will at first conclude that roving is a recipe for taking small pike. There is logic in this, too. Smaller pike are more energetic and perhaps, like many of nature's inexperienced young animals, will chase anything that resembles food, not always

with success. Larger, more experienced pike can afford to be more selective. When they do strike, success is more probable than failure. The larger pike may lie dormant for longer periods of time and not follow the almost incessant feeding behaviour sometimes apparent in their smaller brethren. When a larger pike does feed it wants value for effort, and a small roving livebait may not prove tempting enough unless it virtually dances on the predator's nose. If this factor is appreciated then it immediately becomes apparent that a roving bait must generally be of a larger size in order to attract the bigger pike. Compare this with paternostered livebaits, where larger baits can be a problem to restrain whilst smaller baits can be tethered in likely holding spots.

Not only are bigger baits more tempting to the larger pike, they can also be made to rove more effectively than a small bait, which will quickly become worn out. The roving bait technique aims at presenting a live fish swimming as naturally as possible in the vicinity of a pike. A larger bait is better able to 'drag' the tackle along.

It is well known that Dennis Pye was one of the leading exponents of the true art of the roving technique and – while some doubt has been cast on his claims – it is unquestionable that he caught an enormous number of large pike with his refined method of using roving baits on the Thurne system. Indeed, that system provides an environment perfect for the technique – extremely clear water (although unfortunately the prymnesium blooms now often effect this) which is shallow and weedy.

With the line greased heavily so that it floats and the float set to keep the bait off the bottom or above the weed, large livebaits can be made to work all over a particular area. It is not even necessary to cast. Merely drop the bait into the water and the bait can be encouraged to swim against line pressure. The greased line will bow in the wind and the bow will cause pressure against which the fish will swim. A good-sized roach or, even better, a bream or rudd can be made to rove long distances above weedbeds and tempt any pike it encounters to strike. A dormant or semidormant pike may not strike instantly, and if a small bait is used it may not strike at all, when a paternostered bait placed in front of its nose may be more successful. However, if it is a case of discovering the whereabouts of one or two large pike in a large and barren area of water, a big roving bait is far more likely to succeed because of the extra water it will cover. If it is suspected that there is a fairly dormant pike in a particular spot, then either a paternostered or an active 'wind-up' livebait, such as trout, is more likely to invoke a response than a standard roving bait.

In the development of his techniques Dennis Pye designed a particular 'dumb-bell' float. At first observations it would appear that a standard streamlined slider would achieve the same results as the dumb-bell. However, experimentation has shown that for working livebaits on shallow waters the dumb-bell is more efficient. It provides greater control of the bait, actually assists in enabling the angler to make the bait rove away from the boat and does not seem to wear the bait out as much as more standard floats. Some anglers use polyballs with a tube

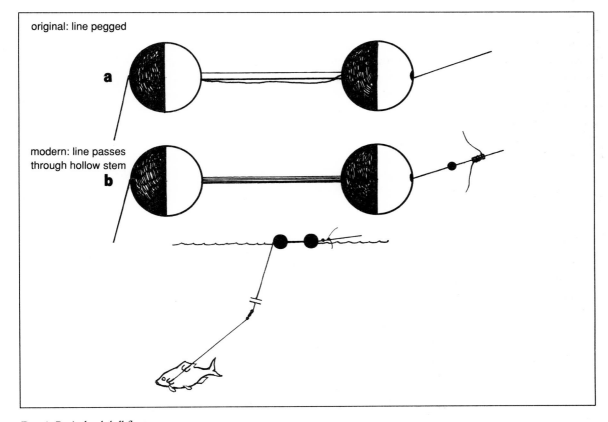

Dennis Pye's dumb-bell float.

through the centre. These are effectively a half dumb-bell and again seem to work better than more standard streamlined floats. This is one instance where an improvement in float design aimed at eliminating resistance to a taking fish, perhaps in the form of a cigar-shaped float, has not succeeded.

It must be remembered that Dennis, like most Broadland anglers, was always afloat. This form of roving is usually less successful from the bank, where there may be less wind to assist bait movement and all too often it becomes difficult to encourage the bait to swim away to open water.

With roving baits there are fewer problems with bite-offs, though occasionally a pike will hit a bait on the surface and continue moving forwards with mouth agape, which risks severance of the reel line. This is more likely to happen if your line is not adequately greased and no longer on the surface. We cannot stress too strongly the importance of greasing the line for this technique, not only to reduce such occurrences but also to assist bait action by reducing tackle drag. Similarly, it is essential to use fresh baits. A worn-out bait will just remain in one place or go round and round in small circles. Occasionally, however, this rule, like many a rule in pike angling, does not apply. Sometimes a worn-out bait will present the pike with a very good image of a stressed fish, which may be more to its liking than a livelier bait. Possibly the easy-meal concept applies. This is more likely to happen when you have found a number of pike and the bait is presented among them, rather than when you are using the roving bait as a means of locating pike. The roving bait is really a search-and-locate technique. Once a number of pike are found in a particular area it sometimes pays to change method in order to maximise success.

We have been discussing roving in shallow waters. Obviously, the method need not be confined to such water or to the use of specialised dumb-bell floats. The method works at all depths, though, obviously, the deeper the water the more line is underwater to create line

drag on the bait. This leads to some difficulty in encouraging the bait to rove extreme distances, as it will tire that much sooner. A standard method used nowadays is to fish a streamlined cigar-shaped slider float with the stop knot set so that the bait roves at a suitable depth, either just off the bottom or above the weed. The method anticipates that the pike will strike up towards the bait; the bait is not intended to reach the bottom, where it would lie in relative sanctuary. The rig is very simple. In addition to the slider float, as little weight as possible is required, for the greater the weight the greater the energy drain on the bait. On shallow waters weight could be eliminated entirely, but in deeper water it is desirable to keep the bait down to some degree, and this becomes more important when the water is coloured. In extremely muddy waters roving techniques are unlikley to prove particularly successful.

The best method of hooking a bait for roving in still and slow-flowing waters is for the top hook of a tandem trace to be inserted just under and towards the back of the dorsal fin and the bottom hook to be nicked into the flesh around the pectoral fin. In this way a correctly mounted bait will hang slightly nose down, not horizontal, before casting. It will tend to enter the water nose first as opposed to a belly flop, so there will be less damage to the bait at splashdown. It may be necessary to cast the bait rather than merely dropping it over the side of a boat, perhaps in order to clear an intervening dense weedbed or to get it moving when bank fishing. Baits can be mounted in a similar fashion when using a paternostered rig. However, if you are trotting fairly fast waters it may prove better to hook the bait with the upper hook through the top lip and the bottom hook nicked into the back of the dorsal. This prevents the bait being caught across current and dragged downstream with a flank opposed to the flow. Hooked in this way the bait will find it far easier to work against the current, and will fish more effectively. Obviously, this all depends on the speed of current.

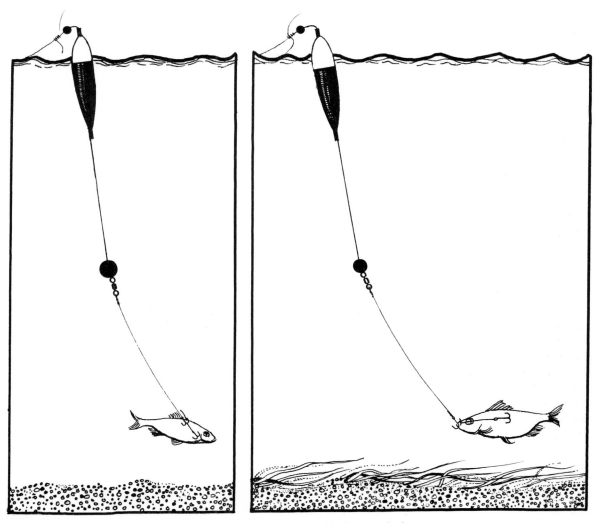

Roving livebait rigs: left, for still or slow-moving waters; right, method of hooking bait for flowing water.

Trotted Baits

Now is perhaps the time to mention trotting. Roving, as with wobbling techniques, really comes into its own on clear faster-flowing rivers, where pike generally tend to be very active feeders. They expend more energy than stillwater fish as they have to contend with currents, and because they require more food to replace the energy loss they tend to be more active and aggressive. It is far less likely that many dead fish will be available to them because any fish that die are quickly carried downstream. The pike are unlikely to be active feeders on static deadbaits. That is not their way; they have to be true working predators throughout their lives. A trotted livebait can be made to work through all likely swims – into eddies, down steadier-flowing straights, round bends – searching out all likely holding areas. Even the shallow faster water is not to be neglected. The pike will often be found on these gravel runs, perhaps feeding on the dace or just passing to another resting spot. Whatever the reason, it is likely to take the opportunity to strike at your passing offering.

When trotting a river it is necessary to have some understanding of the depth variations and to take account of them. At one instant the river may be only 2 feet deep and then suddenly it may drop off to 8 or 10 feet or even more. If the bait is fished only 2 feet deep some pike might be caught from the deeper water but others would not be tempted to strike a bait passing so high over their heads. Usually fishing from mid-water to three-quarter depth will produce most fish in these situations. Assuming you are using a sliding float, it will be necessary to alter the position of the stop knot constantly. The ultimate material for stop knots is power gum. The nylon line will eventually cut through it and you'll have to tie another stop knot, but constantly sliding a power-gum knot up and down does not damage the main line whereas sliding a nylon stop knot generates heat, which can weaken the line, leading to a breakage and a lost fish.

Another trick which can be used in rivers is to trot a bait down to a likely swim and then hold the bait back so that it works in the current, or you can allow it to trot through the swim and then ease it slowly back against the current. Such river piking is an active form of fishing; both bait and angler can cover long distances in a day. Tackle should be kept to a minimum as this is truly mobile fishing.

Drifting

An adaptation of the roving technique which has received considerable publicity and promotion in the last few years is drifting. Its history dates back many years and it is difficult to attribute its origins to any particular angler or group of anglers. Certainly in the 1970s pike men such as Colin Dyson, Archie Braddock, Andy Barker and, of course Vic, all produced vaned drifting floats. There were no doubt many others. The upsurge in popularity, however, must be attributed to Eddy Turner and colleagues, and to the introduction of their large-vaned drifting float. Now numbers of efficient drifting and other vaned floats are

available and it is no longer necessary to take to the workshop to create one's own. The basic essentials for drifting are a greased prestretched line, an efficient drifting float and an understanding that the drifter is being used to cover water, not just to get from A to B as fast as possible. The purpose is to fish the whole length of the drift from start to finish in order to show the bait to any pike along that line of drift. If a specific swim out of casting reach is the target, it is often better to use an alternative method, such as a clipped-up balloon or even a powerboat. Some carp anglers use a remote-control powerboat to deposit baits which could not be introduced by other means. A pike angler's bait can be carried out in a similar way and then pulled free of a clip fixed on the boat. More sophisticated models incorporate an electronic drop-release system. Perhaps, this is carrying things to extremes, but some anglers are using these boats and they do succeed in getting baits to new areas on lakes were rowing boats are prohibited. Perhaps one day an enterprising pike might put paid to the idea by taking the boat, under the impression that it is some vast lure. It would certainly make quite a sight – a miniature Jaws in real life!

Drifting may be fashionable but it is not a magical method. It is no more than fishing a roving bait but it has one advantage – far more water can be covered. Drifting has its problems. Setting the hooks at long range, for example, can be an almost impossible task. It is essential to start reeling in and keep reeling until enough pressure builds up to set the hooks. There can be problems, too, with deep hooking, so it is essential that the strike is made as soon as the float goes under. Fast-retrieve reels and long, relatively powerful rods assist in picking up line from the water and setting hooks, and pre-stretched line also helps. The use of a controller (illustrated at the bottom of page 82), along with heavy greasing – which helps to keep the line afloat – is essential not only during the drift but also on the strike. Perhaps drifting's greatest potential, apart from reaching fish beyond casting range, is that it encourages active angling. It is not a lazy man's sport, but then neither is normal roving. The whole technique involves effort in order to ensure that the bait fishes effectively and covers the maximum amount of water. Only in this way can the full fun and success with drifting baits be achieved.

Other Variations

A few other roving techniques must be mentioned. One is trolling or trailing. This is such an important technique that we devote separate chapters to it, one following this chapter and another in Part Six.

Trolling can be described as a form of controlled and 'tethered' roving, as the bait is towed behind a boat with the objective of covering water and locating pike. Another much-neglected method akin to true trolling we call drift trolling. Instead of being towed over specific areas the baits are left to rove by themselves while the boat is allowed to drift along propelled by wind or current. However, some degree of boat control is called for and nothing could be so efficient in controlling drift as an electric outboard. The boat can be manoeuvred with great accuracy and the motor is quiet when running. Altogether it offers a more efficient means of boat control than oars, which rattle in the rowlocks. The Shakespeare model has a considerable range of forward and reverse speed settings and is perfect for this technique. The addition of a foot-pedal adaptor improves control still further. On shallow waters where active trolling might spook fish the electric outboard can prove deadly.

We often allow a boat to drift downwind as a means to pike location and also to present a bait to as many fish as possible. It is a searching technique similar to trailing without the fatigue of rowing. Such drifting is feasible only in a light breeze and even with an electric outboard it becomes impossible in strong winds. With a drogue, however, drifts can be made when the wind blows more strongly.

When a drogue is needed to restrict the speed of drift it should be streamed from the stern so that it holds into the eye of the wind and the boat drifts bow first. This helps in two ways: minimal hull area is presented to the wind, which is better than allowing the boat to drift beam on; and drifting bow first scares fewer fish and the baits will cover undisturbed water if the rods are positioned in the boat rests so that they project at right angles to the fore and aft line of the boat.

Most open water is snag-free but if any snags are present drifting will find them. The information can be put to good use when the area is fished by other methods.

Soft bottom weed can be a nuisance and weed-festooned baits do not catch pike effectively. Various rigs will eliminate the problems entirely but by far the simplest is merely to suspend a live- or deadbait on a standard float rig about 2 or 3 feet above the bottom weed. It pays to experiment, however, and the depth of the second rod should be varied constantly, for pike do not always feed on or near the bottom.

It is important to hook the bait so that it follows the drift as if swimming naturally. Deadbaits can be made to float horizontally if the section behind the dorsal fin is made buoyant. We use Middy deadbait floater sticks inserted via the vent. The Marvic wobbling rig, described elsewhere, can prove very effective for trailing and drifting.

Bottom dragging, with whole or cut baits, has proved effective but because of the very real possibility that the baits will collect weed and debris they should be made buoyant. Once again the floater sticks or foam injected by a Marvic deadbait punch will give all the buoyancy needed. A bomb is then stopped on the line above the trace swivel, heavy enough to hold the bait down and, equally important, to stir up silt. For some reason the disturbance appears to attract the attentions of pike and possibly advertises the bait. Livebaits on simple paternoster rigs, the less complicated the better, and provided the hook length is longer than normal so that the bait remains well away from the bomb link, also displace silt and are well worth trying.

Drift fishing is best employed in medium to shallow water with a comparatively even bottom. It is difficult to control a drifting boat so that it follows the contour of a drop-off. For that purpose trailing under oars or with an electric outboard just ticking over is preferable, as the boat is not at the mercy of the wind. We often practise such methods when we are alone in the boat and it is therefore important to stop the boat's drift by anchoring when a fish is hooked. Vic devised a simple system to achieve this. A full-sized loop is tied in the mooring rope a couple of feet above the anchor. Another loop is fashioned at the end of a separate short length of mooring rope and the free end secured to the thwart where Vic sits. The anchor hangs over the boat's side, close to the water. The two loops are laid side by side and a piece of tapered broom handle is passed through them. The weight of the anchor causes the loops to remain taut so that the broom handle is held in place. A quick pull on the handle releases the loops and the anchor falls away. One last point: the anchor line must be stowed neatly along the floorboards so that it can run out freely.

We use the drifting technique when conditions are favourable and fish have not been forthcoming from promising swims. Obviously, the larger the water the better. The floats are adjusted so that trailing techniques can be employed while rowing or motoring upwind to commence further drifts. This ensures that the baits are in the water at all times.

As far as we know few anglers seem to try fishing on the drift. When the wind is fair and not blowing half a gale, drifting is more than worth a try. Apart from techniques we have mentioned, drogue-controlled drifts enable a vast amount of water to be covered with lures or wobbled baits – yet another option for the more enterprising angler.

Freelining

Freelining, in which the terminal tackle consists of only a trace, must be mentioned. It is not a technique we would normally recommend. Its biggest problem is that with no form of visible bite detection, such as a float, and because no weight is used, perhaps as many as 75 per cent of takes could occur undetected,

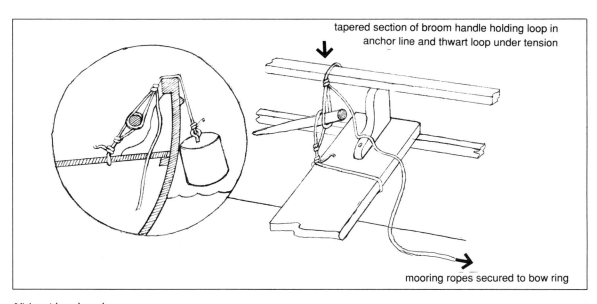

tapered section of broom handle holding loop in anchor line and thwart loop under tension

mooring ropes secured to bow ring

Vic's quick anchor release.

with the obvious result, a deep-hooked pike. Only if the pike takes the bait and swims away from the rod will an indicator such as a drop-off signal a take. In addition, freelined baits tend to lie dormant on the bottom or bury themselves in weed, making their discovery by a pike less likely. A float showing on the surface alerts the angler when the bait is taken, and in whatever direction the pike moves off. Free-lining has some relevance where in very hard-fished water the pike have become suspicious of tackle drag.

Suspenders

Finally, there is currently some experimentation by pike anglers with a variation of the standard float rig when a slightly different action is required from the bait. The technique – which, for want of a better description, has been described as a suspender rig – has been developed with legered livebaits, though it also has some application in roving techniques. A tandem trace is secured to the line and neither float nor weight is used. A polyball is tied to one end of a length of fine nylon and the other end is tied to an arm of the treble placed in the bait's dorsal fin. The rig is improved if the bait is hooked with the upper treble in its tail and the lower in the back of the dorsal, so that the bait hangs head down (see diagram). This encourages the bait to swim away from pressure while the polyball prevents it from reaching the bottom or submerged weed. It also provides

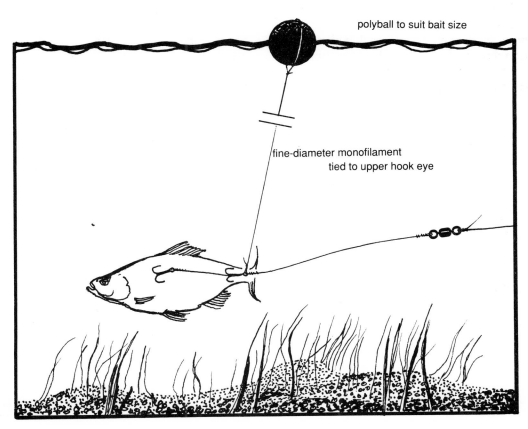

Roving suspender rig.

bite indication. This suspended freelined rig overcomes the disadvantages of the standard method of fishing a freelined bait. Obviously, there is nothing to stop the bait swimming constantly near the surface and therefore this method tends to be limited to shallow waters or presenting a bait to surface- or near-surface-feeding pike. The rig is most likely to be particularly useful where pike have become wary of standard presentations.

LEGERED LIVEBAITS

We have mentioned the use of freelined and suspender-style baits. Legering is an obvious alternative. On first examination the effectiveness of legered livebaits must be questioned. For instance, what sensible livebait would do anything other than lie on the bottom trying to avoid drawing attention to itself? The dark backs of most fish camouflage them so they blend with the bottom and a bait fish will certainly try to bury itself in weed and debris. In addition, pike have a habit of striking at their prey from below, and the position of their eyes is not conducive to bottom predation on live fish. Of course, smell is an important factor in seeking out food lying on the bottom, and bottom-fished livebaits do catch pike. If the required distance cannot be achieved by roving techniques, ballooning, or the like, legering must be resorted to. In such circumstances we would still prefer to use more standard paternoster rigs.

Adaptations to standard legering can improve results, including a number of sunken-float paternoster/leger rigs discussed below under 'Paternostered Livebaits'. One rig which we feel can be classified as a leger rig improves on the basic legering technique considerably. This is the use of the suspender method already described. A standard legering set-up is used incorporating a buoyant leger so as to make the rig more sensitive. The bait can be mounted tail first, which we prefer, or, if the bait is required to work with a different action, either

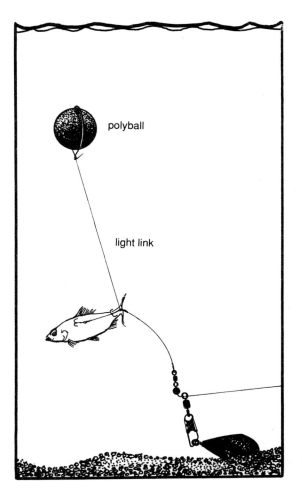

Legered livebait with suspender to keep bait clear of bottom.

the standard roving or river roving method of hooking the bait can be used. Each type of mount will cause the bait to behave differently, which can lead to success on hard-fished waters. It pays to experiment. For long-range fishing we prefer to use a small streamlined and hardy bait such as gudgeon, a small dace or a baby chub. The suspender is incorporated into the rig as before and ensures that the bait is kept up off the bottom so that it remains visible.

Obviously, you must be prepared to lose polyballs since the pike's teeth inevitably cut the fine nylon now and again as it takes the bait or during the playing. It is not necessary for the

1 *An ambition and dream fulfilled; Martyn with his 30lb 2oz fish.*

2 *Bright sunny conditions, dead bait and a large fish – so typical of the Thurne system.*

3 Horse mackerel mounted on a standard pencil float deadbait rig.

4 The best of a catch of three 20-pounders at 29lb 1oz.

5 *Roger Miller armed with a graph recorder goes in search of fish.*

6 A well nourished 20-pounder caught by drifting.

*7 Steve Harper's personal best to date – a huge
Thurne fish of 32lb 9oz.*

8 In-Fisherman's *editor Doug Stange keeps his lures*
  neatly stacked – in a bucket!

9 *Vic with an American pike caught on a lure.*

10 *Martham Broad, scene of several big pike and angling notoriety.*

11 *In search of pike on the Dutch peat bogs.*

12 *A Dutch pike caught with a spoon.*

13 *A Dutch angler displays a good fish to the camera.*

14 Deep, clear water means long and hard fights from
   these Dutch pike.

15 A long, lean specimen is well protected by the carpet
   on the floor boards.

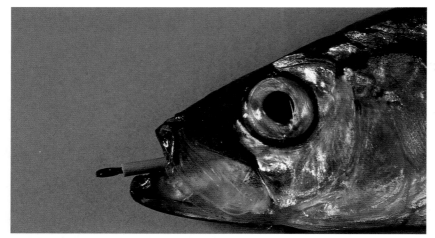

16 *A Marvic deepwater pin inserted in a herring head.*

17 *The Marvic wobbling rig with deepwater pin.*

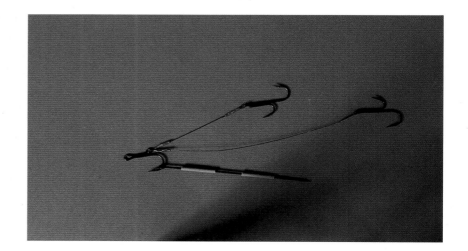

18 *Bait mounted on a wobbling rig with bend.*

19 *A herring mounted Vic-style with a plastic worm attachment for wobbling.*

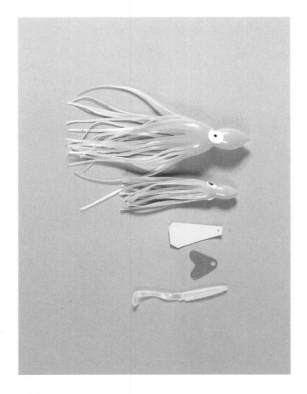

20 *Wobbling enhancements, muppets, colour tags and plastic worms.*

21 Nearly beaten, this Dutch pike grudgingly comes to the boat.

22 In the mouth of the Endrick, Loch Lomond.

23 *The mystique of pike angling is captured in this shot of a frosty morning.*

24 *Carl Garratt with his enormous 44lb 8oz pike from Llandegfedd.*

25 *John Watson and Martyn well wrapped up against the coming storm at Ardlui, Loch Lomond.*

26 *Martyn cradles a magnificent end-of-season fish.*

27 The lure angler silhouetted against a peat bog sunset.

28 Martyn with a 20-pounder taken on slow sink-and-draw techniques using the wobbling rig.

polyball to be fished on the surface; its sole purpose is to support the bait and to prevent it hiding on the bottom. It is sometimes necessary to secure the polyball up the trace with a small piece of soluble PVA string, otherwise the polyball link will gyrate and can tangle with the reel line during casting. Perhaps suspender-link bite-offs can be eliminated to some extent if it is tied to the trace swivel. Curing one problem can lead to another, however, as this can also lead to tangles, because a section of reel line will also be supported, making it more prone to being snagged by the bait.

With this technique the depth at which a bait can be fished is infinitely variable – one of the rig's great advantages. Simply releasing or tightening line will make the suspender raise or lower the bait. One can effectively fish a legered bait a foot from the surface in 20 feet of water and the bait will still be tethered. The size of the polyball is obviously determined by the size of bait. A 1-inch or 1½-inch polyball will be more than adequate for most small baits, and a small bait does help long-distance casting. If a large bait is used it will be necessary to change to a heavier lead, together with perhaps two or three larger polyballs substituted for the more normal size.

Unquestionably this variation on a standard legered rig adds considerable scope to a method which we rarely use in its simplest form.

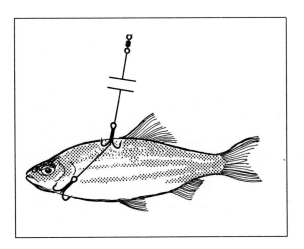

PATERNOSTERED LIVEBAITS

Throughout most of the 1970s and 1980s various types of paternoster rigs have been devised as more and more pike anglers have come to realise that paternostering is the most efficient means of consistently catching big pike on livebaits. The logic is obvious. Roving livebaits can readily move away from a particular area as well as being difficult to control, whereas a paternostered livebait is tethered in one place, its movement is restricted and the bait cannot escape or hide. A paternostered bait can be presented off the bottom and its constant struggles disseminate vibrations which attract pike. Even if they are not in a particularly hungry mood, the tethered hyperactive bait seems to trigger an aggressive or feeding response.

Just as it is necessary to consider bait size to get the most out of roving techniques, so there are certain fundamental points to appreciate in order to get the most from paternostering. First, deadly as it is, the paternostered livebait will not produce if you are fishing your bait in barren water. A paternostered bait, like any other, must be presented in an area which holds pike or where they pass. You can fish it hunter or trapper style, searching for the pike by constantly moving the paternostered baits, perhaps every three-quarters of an hour; or, alternatively, you may know of a specific passing area where the bait can be held until a pike passes and the trap springs.

It is also necessary to appreciate which baits and which bait sizes fish best on paternoster rigs. We have already mentioned the problems that can result from the use of rudd and bream. Bait sizes are important for there is little point in fishing a paternoster rig if the bait is so large that it tows the whole rig all over the place. Ideally a bait of 2–3oz anchored by a bomb of 1½–2oz will prove most effective. Very small baits tend not to perform well for long periods; they tire easily and are liable to attract a very high proportion of jacks, though some of our biggest pike have fallen to quite small baits on a paternoster rig.

There are tricks of the trade which can significantly improve success. The most important is to appreciate that even a bait suspended off the bottom will not keep working all the time. Eventually it will tire, move intermittently, and even lie quiet, which reduces its effectiveness. Baits can actually 'freeze' when pike are near. They have no escape route and perhaps an instinctive reaction to danger causes them to play possum. This is one reason why a paternostered bait should never be left to work by itself hour in, hour out. Every now and again the bait should be 'woken up'; tweaking or tugging the line which will get the bait working once more and often enough the bait will be taken within seconds of being activated.

In addition to activing a bait it also pays to move its position by easing the bait back a few yards now and again. Leave the bait for perhaps thirty minutes in one position and then move it three or four yards. Sometimes a take will occur as the bait is being moved, in much the same way as waking up a bait seems to agitate pike into taking. Perhaps the pike thinks it is about to lose a meal, or perhaps the increased activity causes a pike to home in on the disturbance.

Throughout this book we stress active fishing whatever the technique. In normal circumstances we can see little point in leaving a bait for several hours in one spot. Even when you are fishing a known passing zone, the pike must be coming from somewhere – perhaps from a holding and/or a feeding area. Paternostered livebaiting covers water much more slowly than roving baits but there is still no reason why reasonable areas of water cannot be explored by this method. Generally, it proves to be a very efficient and thorough method and in the course of a few sessions careful grid-searching of a water with paternostered livebaits should provide a detailed knowledge of the water and its bottom structure.

Livebaiting tends to be more effective in clear rather than coloured water. Poor visibility

is obviously one reason why a pike may hunt by means of its other senses, such as smell and detection of vibration. We can discount smell to some extent when using a livebait. However, the vibrations picked up by the very sensitive lateral line are certainly almost as important as sight to a pike for locating live fish. Even so, the success rate of roving baits climbs rapidly as water clarity improves. In comparison, the paternostered bait can often prove effective in quite coloured water, no doubt because of the vibrations emitted by its struggles. By using its senses to detect vibration a hunting pike has longer to home in on a tethered target. In very coloured water even a paternostered bait may not prove effective, but if there is at least a foot of visibility we will fish a paternostered bait with confidence.

In clear water the pike can obviously home in on its prey quite easily. It must be remembered that a paternostered bait does not behave naturally. It is restricted in its movements, tethered to a particular area. It will tend to 'flutter' as it swims first in one direction, then in another, until it reaches the end of its lead, where it will often cease swimming and 'flutter' as it sinks slowly back. This action can prove extremely tempting to pike which have never been caught. After a while, however, the very action will be associated with danger. The pike will become suspicious of paternoster rigs and at that stage variations will be necessary, either

Steve Harper with a magnificently marked 26lb fish.

another method or a change in the rig or the way the bait is attached to the hooks.

A paternostered bait is very effective but it does have some limitations. Generally it will account for far more double-figure pike than standard roving techniques, provided it is fished intelligently. It satisfies the well quoted concept of conservation of energy in that the bait cannot escape, so the pike does not need to expend a great deal of effort in capturing its prey. However, we doubt whether the pike has such capabilities of reasoning. It doesn't know whether the prey will suddenly dart away in an attempt to escape; it doesn't (or shouldn't) realise that the bait is tethered. This is not the reason why the method is so effective; it is more simple than that. It is more likely that because the bait is anchored firmly in front of the pike, constantly catching its attention until, if it was not feeding before, it is stimulated into doing so.

Whilst the paternostered livebait has been very popular in the last two decades it isn't an innovation devised by the modern pike angler. The effectiveness of paternostered livebaits has been appreciated for centuries. As with all things in life, trends tend to come into and go out of fashion. The late 1980s saw an upsurge in lure fishing and, possibly, a realisation that paternostering is not the supreme method, just another very effective means of fishing.

Paternoster Rigs

A number of different paternoster rigs can be used. Indeed, in the last few years numerous variations have been suggested in angling journals. Many of the variations are unnecessarily complex and in our view impractical. The standard paternoster illustrated is still the most widely used of all these rigs. One or two points must be stressed. First, far too many anglers fish with too short a bomb link. The pike is used to striking upwards towards a bait, so the bomb link should be long enough to keep the bait well off the bottom and working above the pike's head. If the link and trace are much the

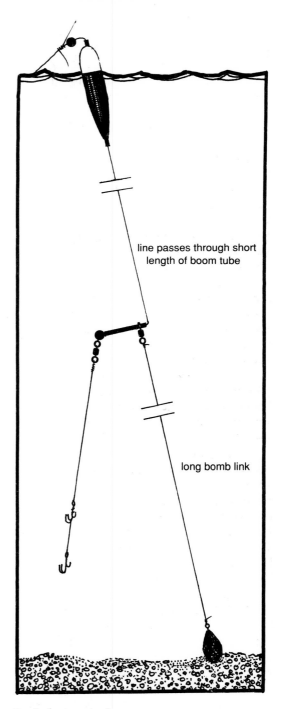

line passes through short length of boom tube

long bomb link

Standard paternoster rig.

same length the bait is able to reach the bottom and the rig is nothing like as effective. Second, it is essential that if the float is required to show on the surface it must be set at the correct depth so that all the underwater paternoster line is under tension in order to keep the bait off the bottom. If the float is fished substantially over depth the paternoster will hang slack and the bait can bury itself in bottom weed or lie motionless on the bottom.

Bite-offs

As with roving baits, in shallow-water situations the standard paternoster can cause problems with surface-striking pike. As the pike takes the bait it may continue with mouth open and trap the main line with its teeth, which will result in a bite-off, probably above the float. This can largely be overcome by greasing the line heavily to make sure that it remains on the surface, away from the striking area. Unfortunately, in very shallow water even this may not prove effective. There is a limit to the extent of up-trace wire which can be incorporated into a rig and therefore this type of bite-off cannot be totally eliminated. Fortunately, it is a rare occurrence with well greased lines.

The standard paternoster rig has recently received considerable criticism because of the possibility of up-trace bite-offs. This is similar to the shallower-water situations where a pike striking upwards traps both bait and the up-trace line in its mouth, leading to a bite-off or a cut-off when the strike is made. This is more likely to happen when a rig is tangled. It certainly pays to examine the rig every so often rather than leave it fishing for several hours. Tangles are more likely as the bait tires and begins to work more slowly and closer to the main line. Some of the more complex forms of sunken paternoster rigs can also be prone to bite-offs but there are ways of virtually eliminating them. For instance, with the standard rig the bomb link can be tied halfway down the trace. This restricts the movement of the bait and reduces tangles. We have had no problems with bite-offs on this rig. For suspicious pike on hard-fished waters such restricted action may signal danger. On the other hand, as the bait action is unlike that associated with the standard paternoster rig, it may be regarded as different, and therefore could even promote more takes.

An alternative is to use a rig incorporating an up trace or simply to tie the bomb link to one hook prong on the trace. This second alternative eliminates any problems of kinking but

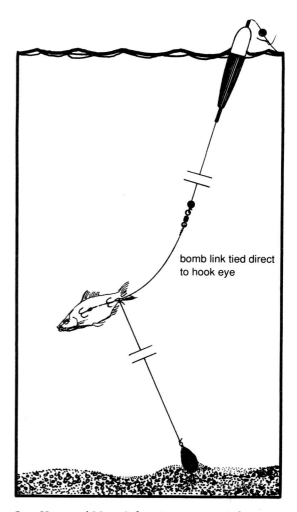

bomb link tied direct to hook eye

Steve Harper and Martyn's favourite paternoster rig for avoiding bite-offs.

does restrict the movement of the bait severely. When using this method we usually tie the paternoster link to the treble which is inserted behind the dorsal fin. Interestingly, we have found that the action caused by this method does not seem to put pike off; indeed, at times the catch rates increase. It avoids the kinking problems associated with tying the bomb link halfway down a trace, where it can twist round the paternoster knot. If, however, the pike are proving cagey with this method, a full up trace can be incorporated into the rig.

Numerous suggestions for up-trace rigs have been illustrated in angling journals in recent years. Many of these incorporate superfluous accessories and are, as already mentioned, unnecessarily complex. Possibly the simplest up-trace rig can be made with a three-way swivel, with standard trace, paternoster link and up trace tied to the three eyes. Obviously, the hook trace must be much shorter than the up trace. Unfortunately this rig suffers from two deficiencies: it is prone to tangles and a taking pike has to tow all the tackle behind it. The

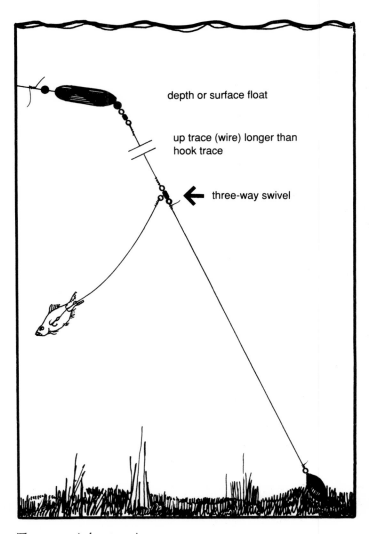

depth or surface float

up trace (wire) longer than hook trace

← three-way swivel

Three-way-swivel up-trace rig.

second problem does not usually result in dropped runs, except with suspicious pike on hard-fished waters.

Bite-offs are nothing new. In the past paternoster rigs incorporated various metal booms in an attempt to eliminate tangles and bite-off problems. Nowadays we can make use of modern materials, such as longer plastic booms, or insert a small plastic boom (such as the Robert's boom) between hook trace and up trace. This helps reduce the possibility of tangling but does nothing to reduce resistance. We include a diagram of one of the most satisfactory up-trace rigs we have used.

Whatever rig is tried it is not possible to guarantee that it will be tangle-free or that it will totally eliminate bite-offs. It is inevitable that if a bait can gain access to the up trace or any of the nylon line it will tangle. Long plastic booms can be incorporated into the rig but a live fish can perform amazing tangling feats and we re-emphasise that the paternoster should be checked every now and again to ensure that the bait hasn't knotted the terminal tackle.

Finally, it is important to keep bite-offs in perspective. We fish shallow waters most of the time and yet Martyn can recall only three bite-offs in the last ten years. Vic's experiences are similar and when we recently discussed this topic with John Watson he also had not found them a problem. It seems that fashionable trends tend to exaggerate what is a relatively rare occurrence.

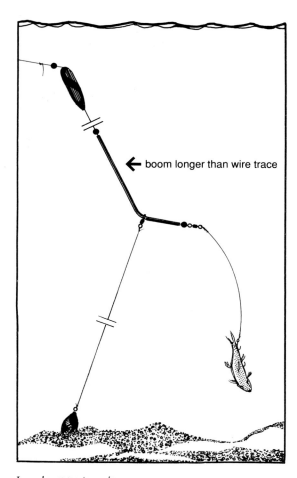

Long-boom up-trace rig.

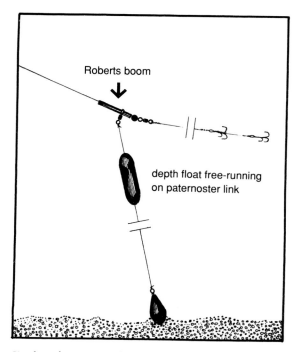

Simple sunk paternoster rig.

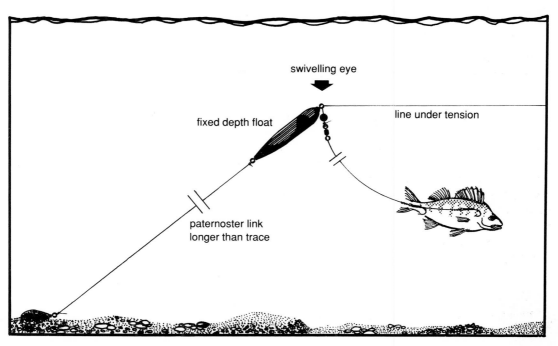

The VB paternoster.

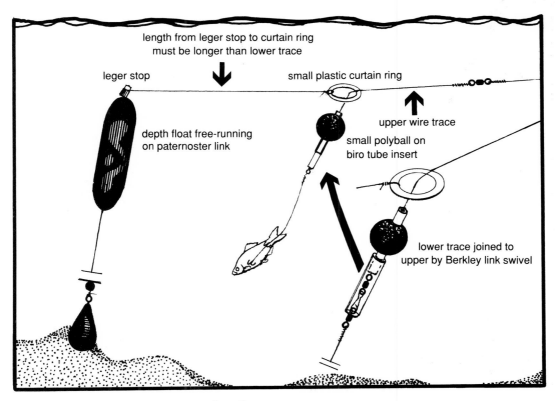

Colin Dyson sunk float paternoster rig — anti-bite-off version.

Sunk Paternosters

We have mentioned that the standard paternoster float can be fished so that it shows on the surface or fished as a sunk paternoster rig. The sunk option is particularly appropriate in water of varying depths or from a boat. We have also mentioned the standard leger rig and the suspended variation. There are a number of other leger-style paternosters which can prove very effective. We include diagrams of three of these. One is a very simple extension of a buoyant leger system. It incorporates a paternoster link on which a camouflaged cigar-shaped pike float or polyball can slide. The line is attached to a swivel joined to a standard Robert's-type boom free to run on the main line down to the trace. With this method the bait is usually tail-hooked, in order to encourage it to swim away from the point of tension and away from the float. This is a particularly sensitive method in that none of the terminal tackle will move at any time during the take

(provided the bomb is of sufficient weight) and is very useful when fishing for suspicious predators. Variations of this rig include the VB paternoster and the CD paternoster, which were developed by Vic and Colin Dyson respectively. Colin's rig incorporates a degree of bite-off protection which is absent in the other two, though we have experienced few problems with any of these rigs in this respect.

All three rigs have advantages over the standard paternoster for bank fishing. Casting distance, particularly with the first rig, is slightly improved. There is no need to worry about varying depths, and tangles are virtually eliminated (a very important point). In addition, the bait has considerable freedom of movement and, as already mentioned, these rigs are extremely sensitive – an advantage on hard-fished waters. *None* of these rigs, however, is suitable for boat fishing, except perhaps Colin's, when the standard sunk paternoster is more appropriate.

17

To Troll and to Trail

We conclude our deliberations on livebaiting with yet another variation, river trailing. (Trolling on lakes and reservoirs is discussed elsewhere.) Although trolled deadbaits can prove extremely successful, both trolling and trailing techniques are more often associated with livebaiting. In the past there has been much debate as to whether 'trolling' or 'trailing' is the correct term. We have no prefer-ence, and will certainly not split hairs. We consider that both terms adequately explain the basic concept.

Like most pike angling methods, trailing has been with us for many years. Trailing livebaits was certainly practised on the River Bure, at Wroxham, in the 1920s – exactly where Martyn and some friends were to 'rediscover' the style some fifty years later.

Trailing in the backwaters.

EARLY DAYS

Martyn discovered trailing as a lad of fifteen whilst fishing the slow meandering bends of the Broadland rivers, in particular the River Bure at Wroxham. Even now that stretch of the River Bure is still famous for its superb pike fishing and numerous large fish are caught every season by the very method that Martyn and his friends 'pioneered' some two decades past.

It all started by accident, really. We were young inexperienced schoolboys. We knew how to catch chub after a fashion from the River Wensum, and we could catch little perch by the hundred. My limited experience with pike was mainly confined to an occasional capture whilst perch fishing. Pike, however, had a certain magic, the 'menace' of the rivers. Those small pike we had caught were by designed accident – gudgeon fished for perch, eels and anything, including pike that would take the bait. But we dreamed of great crocodile-sized fish. Steve held pride of place at the time with an 11lb fish, an absolute monster, and my claim to fame was the proud distinction of having two ten-pounders to my credit. One of these was caught during a night of full moon. I will never forget the image of this leaping giant silhouetted against the moon as I played it from the mill pool bridge, with Simon shouting 'It's a salmon, it's a salmon' – in Norfolk! Inevitably, the fish was gaffed, very badly, and as it lay bleeding in the torchlight we all vowed there and then never to use a gaff again. It seemed to us in spite of our elation a crime to mutilate such a beautiful fish.

Fotunately that fish survived and was to be caught several more times from the mill pool, but the hole in its belly was a reminder of the error of our ways – or, more correctly, of the ways of so many at that time. But then large nets were only just beginning to feature in tackle shops. Once upon a time there was little alternative but to use a gaff. Today I can find no justification in, and accept no argument for, the use of a gaff for pike fishing. And yet grown men, not fourteen-year-old lads, still use them.

I digress, however. Every Saturday we would cycle to our destination. Wroxham was close by and so, inevitably, it was not long before we discovered the boat dykes, full of prime roach sheltering for the winter, an absolute haven for young lads. We would risk the wrath of boatyard owners in our quest for the best dyke and caught hundreds of roach, bream and hydrids. Soon our perch-fishing experience in the Wensum led us to consider using small livebaits fished round the stagings. As a result, many perch found their way into our nets. Occasionally, though, a strike would see our roach rods taking on an alarming bend and a powerful fish would swim out into the main river before biting through the line. Our thoughts turned increasingly to pike. What monsters lurked in this great river, we wondered? How were we going to catch them? In 1970 I wrote in my diary a summary of our thoughts of Wroxham and my only comments concerning pike were: 'Pike, although hard to find, grow big!' Just under that there is a small rider written in September 1974. It reads: 'Not that hard once you use the right method!'

Weekdays at school were spent planning ways to land one of the monsters. It was even rumoured that fish as large as 20lb were present, and once, many many years ago, a 40lb fish had been caught from the great Wroxham Broad, somewhere downstream. Naturally, our imaginations ran wild. We would be the heroes of the school if we could land such fish and, with that new enthusiasm to conquer the unknown, we became pike anglers.

From then on the quest became serious. We saved all our pocket money to replace our inadequate tackle and eventually, with every penny we could find, we visited the tackle shop at Wroxham, the centre of our quest.

I will never forget my visit to that first shop. On the wall was a monster of a pike. At last we could comprehend the full size of a twenty-pound pike. The 22lb glass-case specimen proudly yet sadly held us hypnotised while we were told the story of its capture many years ago. Once over the initial awe we set about the serious business of buying expert tackle. Unfortunately, our limited funds could only stretch to 6-foot solid-glass boat rods, some tough line, a gag, one or two Gazette bungs and a couple of traces. However, we pooled the remainder of our resources to purchase a large landing net, remembering the lesson we had learnt. No one could deny that we were now pike anglers. All we needed were the pike.

As we left the Wroxam Angling Centre on that first visit, with our new grown-up tackle and heads swimming with advice on how to capture our quarry, a further schoolboy dream began to grow in my mind – to own a tackle shop. Or, indeed, that tackle shop with the great pike on the wall. With each weekend visit that dream was reinforced. If only I had known then that many years later it would become a reality.

The rest of that season was something of an anticlimax as far as pike were concerned. I did manage one eight-pound fish, to christen our new net, but that was it.

Things began to take a turn for the better early the next autumn. We were bream fishing from the banks at Wroxham and beside us were two expert matchmen whose catch rate suggested that they would empty the Bure of bream within two or three hours. Fish after fish filled their nets and then, when both played bream, one of them suddenly found he could reel no further. His bream had turned into an unseen force swimming slowly upstream. In those days most matchmen cursed pike. This is an attitude which has been changing as a result of PAC education over the years. Thus what first made us aware that something was amiss was foul language, with the word 'pike' thrown in at intervals. Quickly we gathered round and for what seemed an eternity (at least 10 minutes) the unseen monster swam up and down the river. There was little the matchman could do. He was clever, however, and with gentle coaxing the pike came slowly to the surface. A large audience of anglers had gathered and we all had one fleeting glimpse before fish and angler parted company. That fish was huge. Everyone gasped at the sight. Without a doubt it was much bigger than the one on the tackle shop wall. As the water calmed, everyone stood silently, lost for words. Minutes later my 6-foot rod was assembled and out went a ¾lb bream livebait, the smallest in my net. Nothing happened, or at least that is the way it seemed, until I reeled in the legered bream an hour later. The bream was gone, as was the trace. Something had apparently taken my bait, caught the line in its mouth and bitten it through without any sign of a run. We realised from this that the only traces available from shops, at that time, were not long enough and decided it would be necessary to make our own. We also vowed that that season we would catch a big pike from Wroxham.

SUCCESS AT LAST

At about that time Kevin joined our circle of friends. We were city lads; he was from the country. What is more, his grandfather lived in a great house at Wroxham which led down to one of the dykes downstream from the town reach we were used to fishing. Kevin told us of incidents with pike in that dyke and of the great perch that inhabited his grandad's boatshed. We were intrigued and had soon arranged to fish with him in his dyke. Needless to say, the following weeks saw us concentrating intently on this new-found virgin water.

We then found a new freedom. Kevin's grandfather had two rowing boats and we were taught to row. As a result we soon adventured along the dyke towards the river mouth. We caught a few pike in the dyke – not large, but at last success was coming. One day we ventured into the river and on that very first occasion we caught three nine-pounders and I lost a *big* (to us) fish. At last Wroxham was beginning to reveal one or two of its secrets.

One of them suddenly found he could reel no further.

A week later, quite by accident, we turned the key and walked through the door into what at the time was a piking paradise. We had caught our livebaits in the morning and by ten o'clock we were in the river swim where we had caught the fish the previous week. Nothing happened, so we moved. As the anchors were taken up and I started rowing, Steve had not reeled in one of his baits. Quite by accident we had discovered trailing. Within

seconds Steve's float shot under; the result was our first Wroxham double. Fortunately, we did not pass that success off as an isolated incident but tried towing our baits behind the boat again. Minutes later I caught my own first Wroxham double. That day ended with an enormous fish for Steve, weighing in at a magnificent 19lb.

Over the next few seasons we were to meet with incredible success, each of us catching between twenty and thirty doubles every season by our trailing method. Yet, on reflection, we never put in that much effort. We would usually start about ten or eleven in the morning, having caught our livebaits, and finish at two or three in the afternoon in order to go back to fish for roach in the dykes for the last couple of hours, when the roach always fed best. We had the rivers to ourselves in those early years. The great prymnesium kills on the Thurne system seemed to have left the majority of Norfolk pike anglers at a loss as to where to go. Very few seemed to fish Wroxham. Possibly some were still shell-shocked, while most of the others took to the Ormesby system. But things always change. As young lads we could not resist talking about our exploits. Some of our reports were not believed. Who had ever heard of two schoolboys catching nine doubles in a day to 19lb, and the following day one of them having a brace of 19lb fish while his friend took three others over seventeen? But these were the sort of results trailing was producing for us – doubles every session and many fish over 15lb.

Inevitably, people began to come and see if our reports were correct. Initially they would sit moored in the middle of the river but soon, seeing us catch pike after pike as we trailed past, they too began to tow livebaits behind their boats and also started to catch numbers of pike. By 1974 the method had become widely known as the 'in' style for Wroxham. More and more people flocked to the Bure, with the result that it became nationally famous. Incredibly, however, it made its reputation in the mid-1970s for the vast number of twenty-pound pike reported. And yet of all the fish we caught there were only a handful of twenties, even though we had numerous 19lb fish. I can only conclude that some very suspect weighing and reporting was taking place, and the large head of nineteens were being elevated to that grand twenty status.

With the increased popularity, one or two professional pike killers arrived. I hope they are a thing of the past. On one day we witnessed the massacre of twelve good pike. They would not listen to the ravings of 'immature' kids and week in and week out these murderers set about their task. Presumably they were selling their victims to hotels. We never did find out. Their selfish behaviour led to the decline of pike fishing at Wroxham. I believe that the river has never fully recovered from the massacres which took place during the mid-1970s. Certainly in the later years of that decade the vast numbers of mid- and upper doubles disappeared and we experienced a jack explosion. Since then things have settled down. Nowadays there is a head of pike of all sizes, including fish in the 25–30lb class, but the average size of the pike is still lower. But I will never forget the schoolboy days when fish of fifteen to nineteen pounds really were two a penny.

TRAILING EXPLAINED

Let us now look at what we mean by trailing. Perhaps this description is a misnomer. We are of course talking about a form of trolling but we have decided to use the name trailing in order to distinguish between a form of river trolling which Martyn practised for many years on the Bure compared with large-water trolling, such as that described later in the book by Vic and Bert Rozemeijer. Trailing is perhaps best described as small-water trolling.

The Method

Obviously trailing almost inevitably requires the use of a boat and Chapter 23, on boats and handling, applies equally to trailing and trolling. Trailing, however, requires rather more boat-handling expertise. It is the handling of the boat which assists in control of the bait and has much impact too on the bait's action, which helps make the method so deadly. Assuming that you are fishing two in the boat, one person is effectively responsible for working both rods, the bait's action depending entirely on how the boat is handled. The other is largely redundant until a take materialises or a bait snags.

The method consists of towing livebaits fished on float rigs behind a boat. It is usual to use two rods, one fished further behind the boat than the other. This helps avoid tangles, though there is another important reason which will be mentioned shortly.

The basic rig for trailing is a standard roving livebait rig incorporating a streamlined sliding float. We would usually recommend a reasonable amount of weight on the line to keep the bait down, though in a water which has not been bombarded with trailed baits this is less important.

In recent years there has been some experimentation with floats designed to trail and plane out to the side as the boat moves. A number of prototypes are being tested with a view to making a trolling/trailing float generally available. I hope the results will soon materialise in tackle shops.

How the bait is attached to the hooks is important. A towed bait should swim head first in order that it is presented naturally and also so that the bait does not drown. The up-trace hook of a two-treble rig should be inserted in the lip of the fish and the bottom hook nicked into the flank. This method of hooking does concern some pike anglers, who consider that the hook-set on the strike is not over-efficient. Logically, if the pike grabs the bait and then turns to swallow it head first the hooks are pointing in the wrong direction. We think that they are worrying needlessly. Pike striking at a trailed bait often take it tail first. But this aside, we have not noticed any significant difference in numbers of pike hooked and lost compared with a more conventional hooking arrangement.

There are some specialist tackle items which can assist in trailing, notably outriggers, which aid in keeping the baits apart from one another. Martyn, being a firm advocate, recommends the use of multipliers or, alternatively, the new generation of fixed-spool reels which allow controlled tension to be applied to a spool and

released by pressing down a bar as soon as the pike strikes.

In the early days at Wroxham fixed floats were not only the fashion but the only floats available. Indeed, pilot floats were even used in those days. Streamlined slider floats are obviously vastly superior. However, if a strong current is flowing a slider will tend to slide down the line, causing the bait to be drawn back up towards the surface. In Chapter 29 we mention an ingenious device to defeat float slip when trolling on large waters. The same lock can also be used to overcome this problem where there are strong river currents. Alternatively, the float should be fixed and/or even greater weight used to keep the bait down.

Boat control is obviously very important. At first we used to catch pike at whatever speed we rowed. If a wind caught us and we were out of control, drifting at an alarming pace across the river, pike would still come snapping at the baits. The more the Bure at Wroxham was fished the less this occurred. Our method became more and more refined and we found that we had to trail much more slowly. We were nearly caught out, however, for suddenly our catches tailed right off and we were catching fewer pike in a day than we would have if we moored up and just fished statically. Obviously, the pike were wising up. About that time deadbaits came into their own for the first time at Wroxham. However, there was another reason for reduced results, and a very significant one, as you will see.

Although most trailing will be done by means of control exercised through oars, by far the best method is to use an electric outboard. It may seem an expensive luxury item but in fact it gives infinitely superior boat control in so many circumstances, whether for trailing, for controlled drifting and roving over an area or down a river, or for a silent approach to swims. We currently use the Shakespeare 38, which is available from any Shakespeare tackle stockist, retailing at £250 (1990). It is well worth every penny.

Trailing has a number of advantages over the

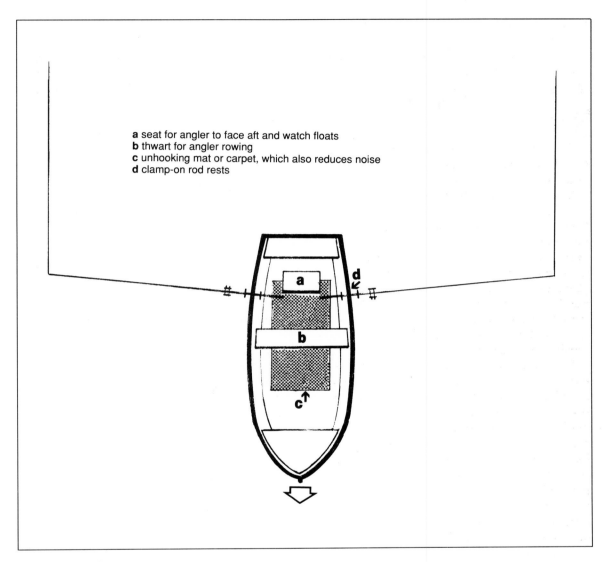

a seat for angler to face aft and watch floats
b thwart for angler rowing
c unhooking mat or carpet, which also reduces noise
d clamp-on rod rests

Boat rigged for trailing.

more static approach. It will locate pike. By rowing or motoring up and down over a stretch of river of lake you can cover more water than by the static approach and eventually the method should locate the pike, and in particular any hotspot where several pike are lying. Sometimes trailing can be used to locate an area and then a static approach applied once a hotspot is established.

This form of location may or may not be achieved by trailing in its strictest sense. For example, you may allow roving baits to drift slowly downstream, or with the wind, controlling the boat so that it follows quietly behind. This is a deadly method at times, but is really only a more active roving livebait style. It does not make use of the positive bait action which can be obtained through trailing.

In covering a vast area it is inevitable that one will pass over more pike. Not all these fish

An electric outboard, where permitted, assists in trolling – but beware of moving too fast.

will be feeding but the law of averages will result in a greater number of feeding pike having a bait pass over their noses. Theoretically, this should mean a greater number of pike on the bank, or, more correctly, in the boat.

Another important point is often missed. We discovered it when we eventually realised that our speed of rowing had slowed to a snail's pace. A trailed bait is something different, it is something which flutters past a pike. It does not give the pike the opportunity to think, consider and decide to take. It invokes an impulsive reaction – more than a spinner or lure, we think, because it is the pike's natural food. If the pike does not take the bait quickly it will have passed and the opportunity will have been lost to that particular fish. Applying this logic, it becomes obvious that the bait must pass positively over the nose of the pike. If you are

trailing very slowly this will not happen. Instead the bait will be swimming around freely and only gently ease through the area. The pike will have the same length of time to inspect the bait as it would an ordinary moving livebait, and if that fish isn't particularly hungry it will have the time to make the decision – not to take. In contrast, a bait moving faster through the swim may cause the pike to strike on impulse. We are convinced of the wisdom of this and that you can row too slowly. The only caveat we would add is that on very heavily fished waters, for a while at least, the pike may become wary of active trailing and only take baits which are fished by dead-slow trailing (the form of free roaming mentioned) or by other methods.

We believe it was Barry Rickards who once wrote that you should see some form of gentle ripple coming from your float while trailing. Obviously Barry also appreciated the point about active trolling. Martyn's records show that he caught far more pike trailing against the current than with it. It is a question of the different action of a bait being pulled compared with a bait which merely flows down river with the current behind the boat. When trailing downstream with the current it is necessary to row considerably faster in order to achieve any form of fluttering action to induce quick impulse strikes. On the other hand, trailing against the current means that one does have to row in order not to drift downstream. There is far more tension on the line and bait so a much more attractive action can be achieved at a relatively slow pace. We are therefore suggesting that a fine balance is necessary, rowing at such a pace as will not drag the bait too fast over a pike's head but will tow the bait at a positive rate. The speed should be regulated so that the bait can swim on its own accord but it will still be slightly restricted swimming. Obviously, this requires considerable practice and experience in boat handling.

With practice, it is possible to use the bow in the line between bait and rod tip to make a bait move to a particular place. This is very useful, not only in keeping baits apart from one another but also in trailing a bait past a particular feature. If you have a river to yourself it is possible to make one bait swing right across a bend while the other follows a straight course. This is achieved by rowing at an angle across the bend and mending the line on one rod only. The method really becomes quite fascinating and certainly cannot be accused of being boring in the way of some forms of static deadbaiting, where the angler may have to wait for hours with little else to do. Trailing is an active method and a full day's rowing can be totally exhausting. It can be so very rewarding at times.

Much has been written of the distance between boat and bait. We would be reluctant to be drawn on any specific distance. Martyn once caught a pike on a bait which had been reeled in and left bouncing on the surface while he quickly rowed across the river to cover a pike strike. Another pike launched itself into orbit to grab the bait, which was dangling two feet from the stern of the boat. Obviously, we would not recommend that as standard practice, but it does illustate that there is much latitude when deciding how far a bait should be trailed behind the boat. Sensibly, one bait should be closer than the other to avoid tangles when turning. This can also be put to further advantage. Let us say that the near bait is fished close to the edge and the more distant one allowed to fish more in mid-stream. Because the near bait is closer to the boat it will react more significantly and quicker to any changes in the pace or direction of the boat. This is very useful where you want to avoid snagging on a known underwater obstruction or shallower area. Very often these areas are close to the bankside whilst mid-river tends to be clear of such obstructions. If you keep the bankside bait nearer to the boat you can avoid many such hazards with a quick pull on the oars to lift the bait higher in the water.

With two anglers in the boat we usually make it a policy to swap sides after each fish. Very often the bankside rod will produce the greater number of fish, though not necessarily the biggest. It seems fairer for each angler to alternate in this way.

A few words about bait size and type, perhaps to re-emphasise some of the points made in Chapter 15. The thinner fish such as roach and dace make the best trailing baits. In most waters these do not need to be large, in contrast to the large-water trolling methods described elsewhere. Many people also find that dead natural fish or even small herrings and the like mounted to give a wobbling action can be very effective used in the same manner as livebaits. Ideally, we would usually opt for a 2–3oz bait. This size provides a reasonable meal while being easy to keep under control.

Finally, let us consider ideal trailing water. Again there is no golden rule, as most waters respond to the method. Martyn has caught fish trailing fast-flowing rivers such as the Waveney and the lower Bure; he has caught twenty-pound fish trailing in shallow dykes less than 3 feet deep, and fish on the Thurne in gin-clear water. Another notable twenty was caught with the Bure at Wroxham 3 feet higher than normal, carrying snow floodwater with a visibility of only inches. On that occasion a 21lb pike was tempted from a known underwater depression by means of a trailed bait. The outrigger was swung round at the crucial moment to allow the tension to ease and the bait sink into the depression for a second, before being eased away once more by the momentum of the boat. At that instant the pike struck. However, we would not generally recommend trailing in very coloured water. Best results are usually obtained when there is good visibility (though not necessarily gin-clear water). If underwater visibility is only a foot or so other methods will prove more productive. The size of the water is rarely a deciding factor and the method is worth trying on most venues and in most conditions. It is not always necessary to use a boat. Some of the smaller rivers and fenland dykes can be trailed effectively if you walk slowly along the bank towing the bait behind. This is where a kiting float can be so useful. Similarly, although we have mainly talked of rivers, the method can prove equally effective on lakes, pits and broads, be they shallow or deep.

In conclusion, trailing – or, if you like, trolling – is generally neglected by pike anglers. It is highly effective, it is active and it can produce some dramatic takes. We would possibly be so bold as to say that trailing and trolling, whether on rivers or large open waters, is one of the most effective methods known today to locate and catch large pike consistently. This applies not only in Britain but throughout the world.

PART FOUR

ARTIFICIAL DECEPTION AND SUSPENDED ANIMATION

by Chris Liebbrandt

We invited Chris to write this part of the book because he is one of the handful of British pike anglers who use lures for much of their piking. Over the last few years Chris has practised the method exclusively and has acquired an in-depth knowledge not only of the multitude of lures now available to the pike angler but also of how they should be fished. After reading Chris's contribution just once we both felt we were far better lure anglers than we had been a few minutes earlier.

While we have caught pike on lures, and perhaps Vic can claim to have some idea how to catch perch on artificials, we both felt that we were not sufficiently experienced to tackle what is, and what will certainly become, an increasingly popular method of pike fishing.

We have both spent three weeks in America, and were privileged to fish with such fine anglers as Al Lindner and Doug Stange, two of the In-Fisherman team. Their enthusiasm and experience made us realise what fun we had been missing, and how much we needed to learn. Perhaps with the natural reserve peculiar to the British, we said little, but thought much!

Until then, between us we possessed a few ancient and nondescript plugs, fitted with well rusted hooks, and rather more spoons and spinners, equally rusty. Now we own what may still be regarded as a relatively small but rather better selection.

We would lay odds of ten Kwikfish to a Crazy Crawler that when you have finished reading what Chris has to say, your whole attitude towards lure fishing for pike will be rather different from what it was before you started.

18

Resurgent Interest

Lure fishing in this country has had a rather chequered career, never really achieving a serious status amongst the majority of pike anglers. This has always seemed strange, for in our Celtic regions (Scotland, Ireland and Wales) lure fishing has always been popular, including trolling spoons, wagtails and Devon minnows, besides trolled and spun deadbaits, both of which are still popular methods. So why have these techniques not been used in English quarters? One suspects that the lack of large waters

– except in the Lake District, and a few large reservoirs which are not in the same league as the magnificent Scottish lochs and Irish loughs – has led to this phenomenon.

There are, however, signs of a revival in lure-angling techniques, and with ever-growing poularity one would hope that this present peak will overshadow some of the more recent troughs.

During my lifetime there have been two peaks in lure-fishing interest. The first in the

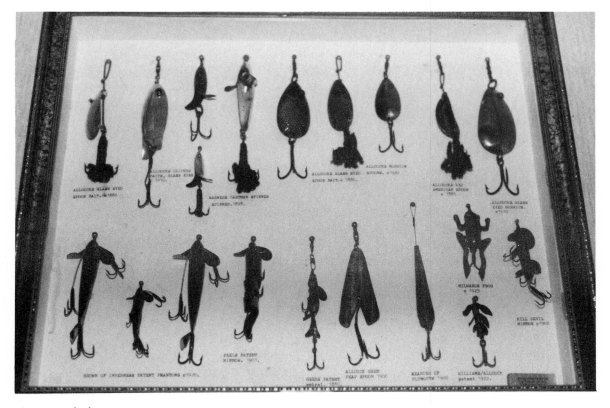

A Victorian display.

1960s coincided with the Norfolk Broadland pike boom of that decade, before prymnesium, increased boat traffic and other factors led to a rapid decline in the 1970s. It is well documented that most of us who own large collections of lures owe a great deal to Ken Latham of Potter Heigham and his foresight in importing American products.

Now lure angling has ended a period of suspended animation. (Perhaps lure angling is suspended animation!) The revival occurred in the early 1980s. Lure imports virtually ceased, and apart from the Shakespeare Paw-paw range of plugs the choice of available lures became very limited indeed. Most of us who were keen enough sent to America for our lures, but this can be difficult, expensive and discouraging to all but incurable angling freaks.

During the early 1980s trout-fishery owners and water authorities began to realise that money could be made from pike angling on their waters. Unfortunately for the pike, the pike anglers and in the end trout anglers, those who allowed pike anglers on their water did so in order to achieve a pike cull. I have seen the decline of what could have been some of the best mixed fisheries in the south of the country due to this misguided policy. (Trout fishery administration is considered in Chapter 26.)

You may wonder why I mentioned this, but it is my belief that these culls were the catalyst necessary to rekindle an interest in lure fishing. How can I make this connection? You need look no further than the restrictions imposed on anglers wishing to take part in these culls. The rules appear to be designed to minimise the amount of fish caught, and usually state that only deadbaits and lures are permitted. Even the lures had to be a minimum of 5 inches in length. This was apparently designed to prevent trout being caught, but, as anybody who has fished these waters know, the spotty terrors still make a nuisance of themselves.

The lures 5 inches in length or longer available in this country in the early 1980s could be counted on the fingers on one hand. Home-

An unusual Heddon Dowagiac minnow, c. 1917, in its original box.

A pair of 1920s Creek Chub Wigglefish lures from the United States.

made spoons and plugs had to be constructed in order to fish those early culls and they worked well. As the culls progressed, so the interest in lure fishing also increased, to a point where the TG lure company was formed specifically to import the best of the American and European lures then available. We now have a varied choice of lures, thanks to those enterprising individuals.

I suppose we should also thank the misguided pike culling activities of the fishery owners and water authorities for helping in this resurgence of lure fishing, but on the other hand we must condemn them for a great disservice to anglers in general in destroying what could have been great mixed fisheries.

We are all indebted to the Pike Angers' Club which has changed, and is still changing, these attitudes, enlightening fishery owners and water authorities as to the folly of culling pike from their waters. One can only hope that in another ten years time the sheer weight of scientific evidence that can be levelled against this practice may finally win the day. We live in hope!

19

Tackle

RODS

One of the more pleasant things about lure fishing is that there needn't be a specialist element. If you want to confine yourself to just half a dozen lures, then you can make use of one of your lighter rods for lure fishing. It is indeed a shame that the modern trend for pike rods is so oriented to 'weapons' of 2½ and 2¾lb-plus test curves. If you don't own a light rod, perhaps a tench, chub or carp rod of about 1½–1¾lb test would suffice. The casual approach to lure angling, half an hour here and there, to wile away the time, is all well and good, but one mustn't expect too much in the way of results.

On the other hand, if you want to be consistently successful you need to be prepared to indulge yourself a little. For the self-indulgent amongst you I will list some of the items of tackle that I use when lure fishing.

The choice of rods always seems to become a debating point whenever two anglers get together. This is particularly so when lure and spinning rods are under discussion. I am not a great lover of heavy rods, as perhaps you will have gathered, and I don't enjoy playing fish on them, ideal though they may be for casting large or heavy baits. With the increased use of longer specimen rods (up to 13 feet) it rather goes against the grain to be seen using the more unconventional short crank-handled American rods. They are, of course, designed for use with multiplier reels, more of which later. These rods have for me become a case of 'once bitten, forever smitten'. I suddenly became aware of what I had been missing all those years. I am a great believer in getting rods built for a specific purpose because then there is no need to compromise. If you are going to use these rods consistently you must be happy with their balance, their test curve, their length and weight and their action.

Unlike other pike rods, your lure rods will not spend most of their time in their rests. You will handle these rods all the time you are fishing, hence the importance of their inherent 'rightness'. My more traditional lure rod is one that I had made specially. It consists of an 11-foot carbon-fibre blank of between 1½ and 1¾lb test curve, and has a progressive action mainly confined to the top two-thirds of the rod, the butt section being very stiff. The action is ideal for casting lures up to 2oz, but it comes into its own when playing fish. The forgiving tip section is an essential for all lure rods since a high percentage of takes occur very close to the bank. When a big fish takes off at such short distances you need that sort of give. Pike are quite capable of accelerating from 0 to 30 knots in a distance of 3 feet, which can generate a force of some 8g, enough to take any of us by surprise. Being relatively long, this rod also gives plenty of control for retrieving alongside reedbeds, sunken trees and similar obstacles, and in playing fish.

I have had this rod fitted with silicon carbide rings which, although expensive, are an investment when one considers the amount of casting and retrieving that they have to put up with. After such a glowing report I now have to admit that this rod has fallen into disuse and I didn't handle it at all last season. The reason is that I have discovered the delights of using crank-handled rods.

Using these rods has the same sort of effect as using centrepin reels for livebaiting – not that they are more effective but because they bring me more enjoyment. This last point is one of the essentials of lure fishing, as it has to be an enthusiast's method. Anyone who has spent five or six hours lure fishing without success (it can happen) needs to enjoy it enough to come back for more. This is my general philosophy when angling. It tends to keep one away from the 'big fish and results' syndrome which leaves many anglers worrying about how they are 'performing' rather than enjoying themselves.

For the most part, crank-handled rods tend to be much shorter, and this is primarily because of the predominance of boat fishing in North America. Casting and retrieving all day whilst afloat can become tiresome with a longer rod so the shorter rods have become the standard tool for lure fishing in the United States, Scandinavia and, increasingly, in this country.

I now own three of these rods. The first is an ABU rod 6½ feet long. This started life as a single-handed rod with a typical pistol grip. I have since had the handle extended to lie along my forearm, which is a decided advantage when playing a fish. Although these rods look weak and fragile they are surprisingly powerful. This, coupled with a slightly different technique in their use, can put quite a strain on your wrist. I found this very uncomfortable, but the modification cured the problem.

I mentioned a slightly different technique when playing fish on this type of rod. The higher, more vertically, the rod is held the less of the stronger butt section can be used to exert pressure on a hooked fish. In effect, you are exerting pressure with the tip only, and, this being the weaker section of the rod, it doesn't really make a great deal of sense. When using the shorter rods and multiplier reels you need to hold the rods at a lower, more horizontal, angle. This means that you can play a fish 'off the reel', using the more powerful butt section of the rod. This all sounds very fine in theory, but does it work? Next time you are fishing try for yourself. It is quite surprising how much more powerful such a rod will feel.

Playing the fish off the reel means exactly

that. Multipliers in the main do not have a back-wind facility, which means that you are totally reliant on the drag and clutch system when a fish is taking line.

The second crank-handled rod I possess is a custom-built rod from Peet Bros. It is just 9 feet in length, a nice compromise for bank fishing. It is long enough to exert pressure on hooked fish but also short enough to make mobility round the waterside simple. It has a soft action and is ideally suited for its purpose. Once again I have had it fitted with an extended handle. The pleasure of playing fish with such a rod has to be experienced and I must admit that it would take quite an inducement to part me from it.

Another type of rod I use is a 9-foot ABU, which is quite powerful. It is really a little too strong for my type of lure fishing as it is quite capable of casting out a half-mackerel or a 4oz livebait. Because of this I prefer to confine this rod to boat fishing with fish baits, wobbling, and the like.

None of these three rods will catch you any more fish than the 11-footer but they do enhance the enjoyment of fishing.

REELS

You can't really go wrong with the modern fixed-spool spinning reel. Everything you could ask for is there, and more besides on some of the contemporary models.

There are a number of features which I find essential. Perhaps the most important is that the spool should have a generous line capacity. This is particularly useful in trolling or boat fishing. Another attribute which is of the utmost importance is that the reel should be fitted with a very good clutch system – again essential when you consider the speed and viciousness of some of the takes you may encounter in the summer. If you are likely to be engaged in more boat fishing or fishing in the winter, there are two other points to consider. The first is a reel incorporating a stern drag, which is so much easier to adjust than those with a clutch tension facility at the spool face. A stern-mounted drag is useful when you are trolling with the drag slackened off so that the line can be taken by a striking fish. The last thing you want to have to do is fiddle about in front of the reel in an attempt to alter the spool tension when a pike is running off with the bait.

A large reel-handle knob is useful when you are cold, your concentration is waning and you get a take. It is the easiest thing in the world to let go. At least with the larger sizes you have got something for cold hands to grip.

Having promoted the delights of the modern fixed-spool reel, I must admit that my eighteen-year-old Mitchell 440 has yet to fail me.

Increasingly pike anglers are beginning to use multipliers for lure fishing. They have been used for years by salmon anglers and our Continental and American counterparts. I often question why it has taken so long for them to become popular in this country. Perhaps expense has been a limiting factor, though for this sort of engineering you are looking at an investment. Personally, I have always believed that another factor which has tended to inhibit the use of multipliers is the totally illogical habit of manufacturers who insist on putting the handles on the wrong side of the reel. When one has been brought up with left-handed fixed-spool reels it just doesn't seem to make sense at all. There is a parallel with fly-fishing reels: it is necessary to change hands all the time. Why on earth do they do it? Until about

Two Kwikfish lures lie proudly beside a first-class baitcasting reel.

five years ago only one left-handed multiplier on the market was ideally suited to lure fishing and that was the ABU Ambassadeur 5001C. However, there must be a revolution going on in the States because now ABU have introduced the left-handed Ambassadeur 521LH, which is a superb little reel. The Shimano Company also produce several left-handed multipliers, the most readily available being the Bantam Quickfire LH. One of the very latest designs of multiplier available, and these are making quite an impact, are the Ryobi T1 and T2. These are an improvement, possessing not only an ambidextrous capability but an innovative clutch design which does away with the traditional star drag system. Multipliers, once mastered, are as efficient as a fixed-spool reel, the only slight disadvantage being that small light lures are more difficult to cast. Even this has been alleviated to a degree with the advent of the magnetic or mechanical breaking systems that are now fitted to almost every reel on the market. One other decided advantage when using these type of reels is that heavier lines can be used than with a fixed-spool type.

There is an aesthetic pleasure in using multipliers. They just feel right, and they instil a great deal of confidence. Lure fishing is a confident man's game. I was talking to a friend, John Milford, recently and he reckons that a blind man could select a lure from his box, and you couldn't help but catch fish on it. (It appeared to me that the blind man had selected John's socks that day, but that is a different matter.) Can such confidence be unfounded? It is no surprise to find that some of the country's leading lure anglers are an egocentric and extrovert bunch – none more so than myself.

LINES

As I have mentioned, multiplying reels allow one the freedom to use higher line strengths than would normally be used for lure fishing. I have never been an advocate of light lines for any form of pike fishing but especially not for lure fishing. You are that much more likely to get snagged up on the bottom or, one of my failings, to cast into trees. This can become quite a problem in the summer when there is so much more bankside vegetation. You must also take into consideration the behaviour of the pike during the summer months. During this time they are at their peak and, as I have mentioned already, they have an amazing power of acceleration from a standing start. Hence the need for soft-tipped rods, good clutches and sensible line strengths. Finally, you have to consider the price of the lures themselves. They are expensive and it makes sense to protect your investment.

As I have never had occasion to use any type of line another than nylon monofilament, I have no practical experience of other lines available, such as braided Dacron. During the last five years considerable and ongoing research has been applied to the manufacture of monofilament lines. Complicated processes have changed and improved the molecular structures. This has led to reduced diameters for given breaking strains. As a consequence the angler has a greater choice than ever before. He can either fish finer with the same breaking strain of line or fish with the same diameter line as before with a higher breaking strain.

It is unwise to fish with lighter breaking strains and finer diameters. This would only lead to problems. Because these lines are thinner, their resistance to abrasion is reduced, and abrasion has a far greater effect on the finer diameter than was previously experienced.

The lines I have been using recently are a monofilament sold under the name of Brent. It is very similar to the old Sylcast. This is an ideal line for the bigger multipliers such as the ABU 5001C and also my Mitchell 440. I use 12lb test. The smaller of my multipliers, the ABU 521LH, is ideally suited to one of the new-generation lines, and the one I am currently using is Bayer Ultima. This line is expensive but 'behaves' itself superbly on the smaller reel. I have been using the 15.5lb BS without any problems.

So I use two entirely different lines, one a traditional thick monofilament that you could tow a boat with, the other a product of advanced technology. It seems strange that they both have a place in my tackle.

TRACES

I have spent some time experimenting with traces for lure angling and to be honest I really don't know what is best. I am currently using traces 10 inches long. I have read in the past that 6 inches is recommended but feel that this is a little too short, whilst I would say that a maximum length for a trace would be 12 inches. Any longer than this and the weight of the ironmongery involved may adversely effect the action of the lure.

The standard trace I use is fitted with a diamond-eyed barrel swivel for line attachment and a snap link to take the lure. The snap links that I prefer are the big Creek Chub safety-pin type, the Berkley Cross-lok or the Cotton Cordell lock. All of these are ideal and allow the lure to move freely on the trace.

ENHANCEMENTS

Another experiment I have been engaged in is adding material to the trace 2 inches up from the snap link. This produces what is known as 'intra-specific feeding response' in predatory fish. Like so many things in angling, you think you have a good idea only to discover that you are years behind. I don't pretend to have discovered something with such a technical name, just that parallel thinking is quite prevalent. This response was originally discovered by an American angling scientist, Dr Loren Hill. He has also been responsible for the Colour-C-Lector concept which will be discussed later.

This feeding response is based on the idea that fish are at their most vulnerable to predation when they are feeding. The addition of fly spoons, spinners, coloured beads and feathers up the trace is supposed to represent food items which the lure is chasing. The pike, seeing that the lure/bait is preoccupied, attacks it with greater confidence. Whether fish have enough grey matter to reason in this way I seriously doubt. However, if this response is an involuntary one I have every confidence in it. That is the theory. Proving it is rather more difficult. It would be nearly impossible to produce any accurate form of scientific control. However, I am confident that such additions do not adversely affect one's results. Indeed, any of these innovations tends to increase confidence. No doubt Vic's muppets work on the same principle!

One lure on the market, the Angler's Pride Chowhound, has been produced to take advantage of this particular feeding response. It is fitted with a small boom to which is attached a little spoon which revolves half an inch in front of the lure.

20

Lures, Spinners and Spoons

THE AMERICAN CONNECTION

It is quite important to consider the origins of most of the lures available in this country. Let me first of all apologise to any American readers for any generalisation I have had to make to simplify this background information.

A limited amount of Scandinavian lures are produced for pike anglers, and those by ABU, Rapala, Nils Master, and, of course, the superb Kuusamo lures, are well known. Generally, the lures we tend to use for our pike fishing are American. In America pike are only one of the many predatory fish, and are by no means considered the most important game fish. This is reflected in the type of lures that are manufactured there. It is interesting to note that lures and artificials form the basis of many of their fishing techniques, bait fishing as we know it coming a poor second. This predilection for lure fishing has given them an understanding of

A largemouth bass..

lure fishing techniques which, at present, leaves British anglers far behind. Allied to this skill, Americans also pay due attention to water temperature and clarity, not to mention pH value. Such factors determine not only the type of lure to suit the conditions but also how it should be fished. Those of us who read that excellent magazine *In-Fisherman* have had our eyes opened, and we are learning fast.

Arguably the premier sporting fish in the United States are the three types of black bass – the largemouth, the smallmouth and the spotted bass. The latter behaves similarly to the smallmouth and I have for the purpose of simplicity included it with them. There are marked differences in these fish apart from the size of their maxillaries.

Although these three bass can quite happily live alongside each other in the same waters, they tend to inhabit differing environments. This is understandable since it reduces competition for food. It also illustrates the differing conditions that the bass enjoy. It is interesting to note that the largemouth, if it is to grow to its largest size (15lb plus), needs to have access to water more than 5 feet deep. The largemouth can even reach weights of more than 20lb. These fish are widespread across the southern states, inhabitating more fertile water than the smallmouth. The higher temperatures induce increased activity and this is an important determining factor in the type of lure designed to catch them. A big bass is very catholic in its tastes and any suitably-sized prey that moves can fall victim to its appetite. Bait fish, such as shiners (like a cross between a roach and a bream), frogs, worms, water dogs (lizard-type creatures which look rather like our newts but are actually the aquatic state of the salamander), as well as mice and voles – all are grist to the mill. Generally speaking, the lures which have been developed for these fish are designed for surface use, shallow- or medium-depth-running. Such are the majority of lures available in this country at the time of writing. You will find a sample list at the end of Chapter 22.

Smallmouth bass are indigenous to the more northerly states, including such massive waters as the Great Lakes. These deeper and huge expanses of water are consequently cooler and not so fertile. As has already been mentioned, smallmouths can quite happily coexist with their big-mouthed cousins, but they feed more actively at lower water temperatures and in deeper water. The record smallmouth weighed just over 11lb.

The deeper-diving and sinking lures as well as spoons, jigs, rigged soft plastic worms, spinner baits and deep-diving plugs have been found to be effective lures for smallmouth bass. Some of the more commonly available lures which fall into this category are also listed.

I mention these two American species since many of the lures which originate in the United States are designed primarily to catch these most popular sport fish. It is fortunate that such lures are equally attractive to our native pike. There are many predatory fish in the States, certainly more species than we have in this country. Perhaps most interesting from the pike angler's point of view is the muskellunge – surely a magnum pike! Many large lures have been produced for muskies and they are of

In calm conditions the Crazy Crawler can prove irresistible.

great interest to the British pike angler. See the chart of lure types at the end of Chapter 22.

Apart from the ever-popular spoon, for years the floating/diving plug has been the most widely available lure in this country. All this has changed in the last two or three years with the advent of the TG Lure Company, and others importing many up-to-date American patterns.

It is very difficult to explain the success of lures like the Shakespeare Big S. The popularity of this lure has possibly been helped by the lack of competition. Fine lure though the Big S is, I still wonder whether its results would have been quite so staggering if some of the other patterns now available could have been fished alongside it. As I mentioned earlier, the introduction of more accurate scientific controls in fishing is virtually impossible. Do we catch more on a favourite lure because it is a better and more effective lure, or because more time is spent fishing because of confidence in its fish-catching potential? This is a problem I have often pondered and I have still not reached a conclusion either way. Perhaps it is best not to search for conclusions at all, but to allow ourselves the privilege of playing hunches whenever we can. I think that we have all at some time changed lures, moved swim or changed baits for no obvious reason other than that we felt it right to do so. The results have often proved this to be entirely justified.

When considering the waters where you intend to lure fish I think that it is a useful exercise to think of the water divided into a series of layers. For example:

Surface to 2 feet
2 feet to 8 feet
8 feet to 15 feet
15 feet to 20 feet
20 feet plus

It seems logical to start either at the deep or the shallow end of the lure-fishing spectrum, so I will start with perhaps the most misunderstood of all, the surface.

SURFACE LURES

It has taken me many years to understand how to get the best from the surface lures I have owned. Indeed, for years they lay dormant in my tackle box.

In my collection there was a Heddon torpedo and a Chugger Spook, both of which were acquired by a friend of mine who visited the United States. He remembered my interest in lure fishing but didn't indulge in any angling activities himself. Yet he brought me back these two little beauties. At that time my knowledge of the art of surface-lure fishing was lamentable (there has been a slight improvement) and I spent a long time casting out these lures, which steadfastly refused to disappear below the surface. God knows what a fool I must have looked trying to get these things to behave 'properly'. It was a good two or three years before I discovered that these lures were supposed to be worked on the surface. This may sound like the sort of mistake only an idiot would make, but I can assure you that it happens more often than many people would be prepared to admit.

Most surface lures are designed to represent frogs, mice, voles, lizards, young waterbirds, dying fish, and similar life forms. Some of these lures defy description. Spoons do not normally come into the surface lure category but a few do. One such is the thick plastic Heddon Moss Boss.

Some of the baits that have gained a good deal of popularity recently are the offset-spinner baits and buzz baits. These are two entirely different types of bait. The buzz baits are the ones which fit into the surface-lure category. They have been designed so that they rise in the water as they are retrieved. When worked properly, a large propeller breaks the surface, creating a wave of bubbles behind the lure. I will be dealing with the intricacies of these lures when looking at the spinner baits.

Other surface and subsurface lures are designed to be retrieved so that just the tail of the bait remains on the surface. Three Heddon lures, the Lucky Thirteen, the Wood Vamp and the Meadow Mouse, are very good examples of lures that work best in this way. These lures should be worked over shallow bays and sand and gravel bars, which may include a drop-off into deeper water close by, which so often harbours fish. It is quite amazing how an apparently fishless-looking bay or shallow, gin-clear water can produce pike as if from nowhere. There is nothing in pike angling to compare to a surface lure being smashed into by a summer feeding pike – a heart-stopping experience!

Working these lures alongside reedbeds and lily pads can also produce some spectacular action. The Meadow Mouse fished *very* slowly is perhaps my most successful surface lure, but this was not always the case. It took me ages to discover how to use this lure to its greatest effect. For many years I had worked this lure like any other floating/diving plug, retrieving the bait some 6–12 inches below the surface, with little sucess. One day I watched a water vole swim through my pitch *on the surface*. A flash of inspiration struck me – why not use the lure in this way? I had been taught a crucial lesson. Mice and voles rarely swim underwater! So what on earth had I been doing with my mouse bait? A very important point, this – the obvious may take a little time to click.

One last thing to remember about these surface lures is that they have been designed to be tied directly to the line. Wire traces can affect their action adversely. This is well illustrated by perhaps one of the best-known of surface lures, the Heddon Crazy Crawler. It is so important when using this lure to hold the rod top as high as possible in order to nullify the weight of the trace. Try this next time you use this lure and see how much the action can be improved by this very small change in fishing technique. Because the retrieve speed is so critical, surface lures are probably the most difficult but also the most rewarding to master.

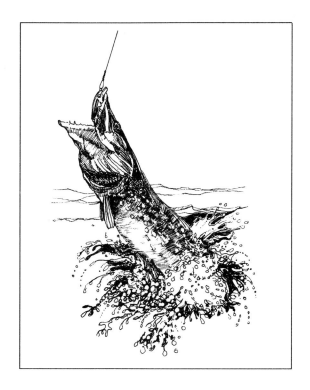

FROM 2 TO 8 FEET

The next fishing layer has probably accounted for more pike than any other in the list – more, I suspect, because of the greater availability of the range of lures, apart from spoons, which are suitable than for any other reason. Most of the lures I own fit into this category. Nearly all the baits discussed in this section are of the floating/diving type typified by the ubiquitous Shakespeare Big S. Many of us must have one of these and similar baits are made by other companies, such as the Bill Norman Big N and Big O. This type of lure is usually described as a crank bait in the United States.

Perhaps the most efficient of all floater/divers are the Heddon River Runt and the 4-inch Creek Chub Pikie. These are indispensable. They fish with a lovely rolling action and dive to a depth of 3–4 feet. I often start my day with one of these in order to search out the swims. The reason I use such baits is that they are not too large to scare fish which are having difficulty in making their minds up, those not actively on the feed. After a few casts I may change to another bait, but it is interesting how many times you move a fish on the lure's first run through. I have no fixed ideas on why this should happen but suspect that it has much to do with the type of response the lure can induce. There are two distinct types of response, which I term the 'interested' and the 'killer'.

The 'interested' type of response usually leads to the fish following the lure, often right up to the bank. The 'killer' can slam the rod top down into the water as the pike hammers the lure and takes off at speed. The art of lure fishing is to change the former response into the latter and many times this is brought about more by luck than judgement. A change of lure and a change in retrieve speed and direction as the lure is worked can lead to success, provided the fish is not spooked in the meantime.

A good analogy is our own response to food. Sometimes we are not really hungry and do not fancy a three-course meal. If somebody offered us a Mars Bar, however, we might be tempted. The opposite of this behaviour is equally common. Such responses may be very similar to a pike's feeding behaviour when confronted with various lures and baits.

The baits which fall into this category are almost endless, but one other collection of baits is worth mentioning. We have already looked at the crank baits (Big S and Big N) and the 'straight' baits (River Runt, Creek Chub Pikie). The last group is the 'banana' baits, so called because of their shape rather than their colour. There are several classic types. Perhaps the best known are the Helin Flatfish, Lazy Ikes and the more recently introduced Kwikfish. These lures do not rely on a diving vane; the shape of the lure itself imparts their action. Banana baits work with a violent wobbling action. Retrieving these baits in the larger sizes – and jointed versions of such lures can be obtained over 8 inches long – can be a strenuous exercise. It is interesting to note that these baits

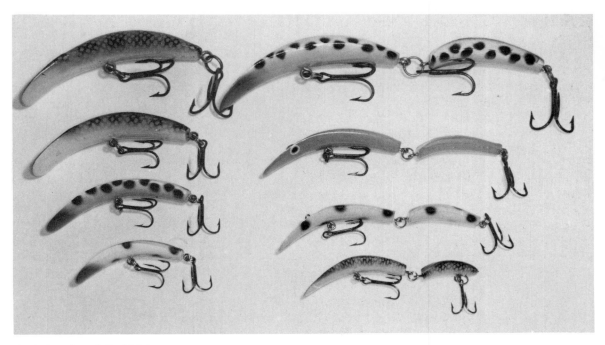

A selection of superb Kwikfish lures.

have been designed to be used with up-trace weights, which certainly helps the bait to sink even deeper. I had overlooked this for many years and I have found that it can considerably enhance the action. It rather tends to slow down the wobble but the magic part comes when you stop the retrieve. The up-trace weight naturally sinks and this makes the bait gyrate from side to side in a very seductive manner. Try it in clear water and see for yourself. I have to confess a prejudice towards these lures. I still have a Woolworth's copy of a Helin Flatfish with which I hooked what would have been a personal best pike – by any method – had the hooks not pulled free. This point is perhaps their only disadvantage. Because of their shape the belly hook can be shielded by the body of the lure. On some models, lure companies have solved the problem by including two treble hooks on a boom which holds the hooks clear.

These baits are excellent for trolling and have also proved devastating for perch, particularly the 5-inch chrome pattern. Trolling with these baits has to be done at a moderate speed. Indeed, it is essential because of their extremely aggressive action. On occasions, I have had these lures flip over on to their backs as a result of excessive speed and increased water pressure. It is also interesting to note that these lures account for some truly enormous pike when they are trolled on some of the big Dutch waters.

FROM 8 TO 15 FEET

The next depth layer to consider is water from 8 to 15 feet deep. Here the selection of suitable plugs begins to thin out. There are, of course, spoons, spinners and sinking lures, but as these can be fished at depths greater than 20 feet they will all be covered later.

This particular layer has until recently been the most difficult to deal with, mainly because of the lack of available lures. Also included in this group is a type of bait which has gained a fair amount of popularity in the United States but is still something of a mystery to us in the undertails of lure fishing in this country. The baits I refer to are a range of lures known as the 'suspenders', or neutral-density baits.

Acquiring a collection of deep-diving baits which do not require the addition of extra weight is quite a simple proposition. In general they are very easy to identify visually. They all have horizontal diving vanes on the longitudinal axis of the bait. The diving vane is larger than normal and in some cases a small weight is included in the lip. The lures which have these weighted inserts are very deep divers, and claims that they can dive to depths of more than 20 feet are not uncommon. A high percentage of these lures are designed to imitate crayfish, as these crustaceans are a staple food item of the deeper-swimming smallmouth bass. Nearly all of these deep divers have the trace connector built into the lip of the lure rather than attached to the body.

What I have written and described in connection with diving plugs has been in relation to a static fishing position. When trolling a bait, you are in reality dragging a bait along behind a boat, which produces a much deeper retrieve pattern. This is because the movement of water over the diving lip or body of the lure is constant, pushing the lure further and further down in the water. Medium divers can easily be fished at depths of 12 feet and more. Once again a word of warning is necessary as many baits, when trolled, can become unstable if the trolling speed is too fast. The correct speed can be critical, but I think that it is fair to say that we all troll our baits too quickly to begin with.

I have given trolling only the scantiest of space. This fine art is described in greater detail elsewhere in the book. In addition, a great deal of literature is available on the subject, such as the chapter in *Predator Becomes the Prey* by George Higgins, who fishes the loughs of Northern Ireland, and of course Gord Burton, who has practised a great deal of trolling on Loch Lomond and other Scottish Lochs.

For us in the British Isles, the advent of the

neutral-density lure is a fairly recent phenomenon. I know of only one which has been specifically marketed and that is the Arbogast Arby Hanger. A few dedicated lure men have discovered that the Heddon Magnum Clatter Tadpolly used in conjunction with a wire trace of the right length has the same characteristics. Generally speaking, the weight of the trace is critical as a few milligrams can affect the balance. It does, however, reaffirm that the majority of American lures are designed for bass, where wire traces are unnecessary.

Whilst on the subject of the weight of the trace affecting a lure's action it is as well to consider the size of the hooks that are usually fitted to most lures. On many occasions I have read that changing the size of the hooks would adversely effect the action. On several occasions I have changed the hooks over to a smaller size but made sure that I have wrapped lead wire around the shank of the smaller hooks so as not to unbalance the lure. One day I ran out of lead wire and this made me think again about the whole issue.

There is no doubt whatsoever that hook sizes change the action of most lures. The bigger the hooks, the slower the wobble. Changing to smaller hooks makes the lure wobble more violently. This is generally considered an improvement but such modifications can be open to question. Take for example the Creek Chub Pikies. The whole reason for their success is their slow and laconic action. To increase or speed up this action *may* lead to fewer takes – the subtle changes which occur can be as critical as that. Pike, like other fish, are endowed with special sensory organs called neuromasts, which consist of nerve cells open to the water. These organs are extremely sensitive to vibration and water displacement. Neuromasts are the fish equivalent of ears and there are many of them. Pike have a slightly different arrangement which has been adapted to its predatory role.

Reducing the size of the hook increases the vibration frequency of the lure and at these finer frequencies the water displacement is not transmitted very great distances through the water. The slower lower frequencies travel far greater distances (because of the greater water displacement) and are therefore detected at a longer range. This is a complete contradiction of what we tend to believe – that the more violent the action of a lure the more effective it will be. There is nothing that inspires confidence like the vibrating rod tip when retrieving a lure. The only problem is that it may not inspire the pike, and that is the most important consideration.

Just one last point concerning the hooks used with lures, and that is the use of barbless hooks. This question seems to produce violent reactions in anglers but I have never seen the issue as that contentious. Either you like them or you don't. Personally I have been using them for the past twelve years for bait fishing and have no complaints. But I cannot accept the practice of using barbless hooks on lures. I did try them on lures while I was still worried about such things but had a disastrous time with fish becoming unhooked. This problem happens more often in lure fishing than in any other form of pike fishing, so it seems silly to assist in the process. In summer, tail-walking and head-shaking pike are commonplace, so hook holds tend to be that much more tenuous. However, whilst discussing barbed hooks, if you are leaving the original hooks on the lures do file the more prominent barbs down to a more acceptable size.

FROM 15 TO 20 FEET

Sinking lures tend to cause not a little confusion when first encountered. It is all too easy to fish them inefficiently. The nearly universal practice of fishing them too quickly is perhaps the most common failing. This is perfectly understandable. We try to protect our expensive lures by keeping them from hooking the bottom. Such a natural tendency leads to fishing them too high in the water – nowhere near where they were designed to be fished. It is therefore very sensible to adopt the widely recommended 'countdown' technique of fishing these baits. This technique involves counting the number of seconds it takes the lure to sink from hitting the surface of the water to the moment the bait reaches the bottom. Once you have worked out the time involved it is that much easier to fish the bait deep down with increased confidence.

There are almost as many sinking plugs as surface and deep divers, and they are listed at the back of Chapter 22. Most sinking plugs tend to be on the small side and this is understandable when one considers the density of the material from which they are constructed. Some are made of metal, which can create problems in identifying whether they are plugs or even spinners or spoons. Spoon plugs and spinner spoons are interesting hybrids. More traditional metal lures are the Heddon Solar and the Cotton Cordell Gay Blades. This type of lure has a very fast vibratory action which can be quite difficult to produce, the speed of retrieve again being quite critical. So it is worth experimenting with these lures until you become familiar with each one. Baits with fast

vibratory actions normally have high trace attachment points just forward of the middle of the plug. Some have several of these attachment points quite close together. The different attachment points affect the retrieve pattern and the depth at which the lure can be fished effectively.

Other more classic types of sinking lures, which are normally slower-sinking than the vibratory types, can be very useful. Examples are the sinking versions of Creek Chub Pikies, Heddon River Runts and ABU High-Los.

Spoons

Perhaps the most universal of all sinking lures are spoons. They have been used for centuries in one form or another. The earliest of these baits were fashioned from wood or pieces of shell. Probably the best-known spoon bait is the Jim Vincent, which originated from a copy of a carved wooden lure by North American Indians. It is said that the spoon bait as we know it has its roots in the middle of the nineteenth century. The idea of using spoons was seized on when a servant dropped a tablespoon into a lake, whereupon a pike was observed to swallow it. Spoon baits derive their action not only from their shape and the bend of the metal but also from the weight and the gauge of metal used. The more pronounced the bend or dish in the spoon, the more pronounced the action. The physical size of the spoon makes a considerable difference to the action. The bigger the spoon, the more it oscillates rather than rotates. This may sound relatively unimportant but it can be quite crucial. It is interesting to note the large spoons which are available tend to be very shallow-dished and long and narrow in shape.

The gauge of metal can also make a difference to the way the spoon behaves. Very light-edged spoons can spin, no matter what their size. These are particularly useful for fishing weedy, shallow waters, but they can be difficult to cast. There are other spoons which can almost be classified as perks and these sink

A selection of pike spinners.

like a stone, but they have their uses in fishing fast rivers or very deep waters.

Spoon baits would almost always be my first choice of lure for fishing running water of any kind. They can be real killers on rivers, where the weight of the lure is counteracted by the flow of the water. Because of this extra water resistance it is quite possible to fish a spoon very slowly and accurately in mid-water or at whatever depth is desired.

I have to admit that it has taken me some time to come to terms with using spoons. A spoon disappears from view as it sinks and I find I often lose track of the position of the bait in the volume of water. This may sound strange, but when you use a floating/diving plug you have a very accurate idea of where the lure is working.

I had no confidence in spoons fished with weedless attachments until recently. My limited experience has been restricted to the ABU Flamingo Giller. This spoon has a strange device which enables the treble to be clipped to the weed guard and swing free when a strike occurs. I found this desperately annoying and soon I gave up using this arrangement. However, I have become converted to the weedless spoons since I discovered the merits of the method which the Kuusamo Bait Company employ. As usual, the simplest ideas are the best. Kuusamo cleverly fix their hooks directly to the spoon's body, with the weedless brush attachment fixed at the same point. This seems foolproof. The hooks do not swing clear of the weedless brushes. I have now used these weedless spoons to good effect on many waters and have never had any undue problems. In fact, at Ardingly I was able to fish through the marginal reedbeds, which are about 7 or 8 feet thick, with no fear of hang-ups or a weed-smothered lure.

Spinner and Buzzer Baits

American hybrid bar spoons, which have become known as 'spinner' or 'buzzer' baits, have recently gained a great deal of popularity. Buzzer baits are intended to be fished as surface lures. This may be difficult to envisage when you examine one and find that the hook arrangement includes a weighted head, but it is the case. The large propeller is the key. This has been designed so that when the lure is retrieved it rises in the water. The correct way of fishing these baits is to whiz them across the surface of the water, which creates a bubbling wake. And they work! After all, the Americans wouldn't continue to produce them if they didn't. Once you have tried using Meadow Mice, Dying Flutters and the like there is no problem in gaining confidence in such interesting lures. The unusual shape of the lures is designed to balance the lead head, which acts as a keel and counteracts the natural tendency of the lure to spin round. This acts on the same principle as the rear rotor of a helicopter, which prevents the aircraft spinning on its axis.

Spinner baits, on the other hand, are designed to be fished at all depths. These lures have a blade where the buzzers have a propeller. Indeed, it is possible to get these lures with more than one blade, or combinations of blade and blade colour. Spinner baits can be fitted with different types of blade. The two most common are the oval-shaped, or Colorado, and the Willow Leaf. Another, a cross between the two, is called the Indiana. These different shapes obviously produce different actions. The Colorado has a very pronounced low spin, which you can feel thumping when you are retrieving. The Willow Leaf has a faster rotation with the blade staying much closer to the axis of the line, producing a less violent action. The Indiana is less common than the other types and I am not quite sure what are the advantages of this blade. No doubt one in the lure box would at some time or another become invaluable. These subtleties are part of the charm of lure fishing – you will never know it all! These lures are fished with a large single hook rather than the standard treble and this certainly enhances their weedless, snag-free properties. There is no problem with their ability to hook fish, however. If you are

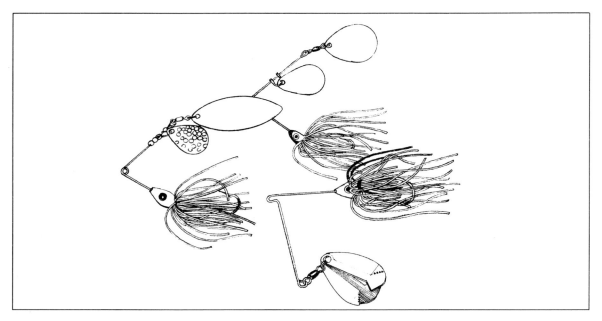

Spinner baits.

unconvinced then the addition of a 'keeper' hook should do the trick. This is just another big single hook with a large eye slipped on the first single and kept in place with silicone tubing. This practice is nothing new. The running treble, or 'commando' hook, is a long-established method of hooking those fish which come short to the lure.

Also available for adding to these lures is an amazing range of rubber skirts. You can dress your lure with different colours, with different amounts, and with different styles of skirt. It is rather like playing with your Barbie dolls! We all know of the tag of red wool on the treble of the much-maligned Colorado spoon. Very small amounts of different colours can make all the difference, as fly fishermen know very well. Most American lure makers produce a range of about thirty patterns and colours. I will look at lure colours separately but it is worth noting that the blades of the best spinner baits are also available in a variety of colours, just to add to the confusion.

It is fairly obvious from the names of these buzzer and spinner baits that they originated in America, once again primarily for bass-fishing enthusiasts. They have been used to great effect by a few of our more adventurous anglers. Vic and Martyn have used them in the States for bass and American pike with good results and they are firm believers in their effectiveness. Indeed, the strange thing about these lures is the instant effect they have on the pike. There are no taps or nibbles, just a positive take. Quite obviously these are 'reaction' lures.

Spinner baits are available in some very large sizes, including the double-willow-leaf No. 7. This has two 3-inch-long blades, which can cause an impressive commotion when reeled in. There are still only a few of these available in this country but I have listed the best of them along with the other lures.

20 FEET AND BELOW

Most of us in this country do not have regular access to waters with depths of 20–25 feet and more. Some gravel pits do have quite alarming depth changes, with drop-offs to over 40 feet, but these are a rarity. Of course, some of the really large waters which are of trolling size have depths well beyond the 40-foot mark. Generally speaking, lure fishing at these depths can be very difficult indeed from the bank and it is fair to say that the highly specialised sinking lures available really come into their own when fished from a boat. I am not very familiar with lures of this type. Obviously, spoon and spinner baits can be fished without too much trouble and apart from the fact that you are fishing at increased depth there really isn't much difference between them.

In fact, spinner baits can make very useful jigged lures, the blades revolving like helicopter rotors as the bait rises and falls through the water. The rubber skirt on the lure also dances enticingly, opening and closing as it is jigged up and down. This method of fishing these lures can also be used profitably where casting is restricted or among underwater obstructions. Indeed, all jigs and perks are designed for use where lateral movement of the bait is restricted. The lures which work best over great depths of water are the jigs and perks used in America and Scandinavia for ice fishing. Not only does fishing at these depths mean using a specialist type of bait, but also you are dealing with totally different fish behaviour. The fact that the fish are at these depths is interesting enough, but that they feed at these depths is even more so.

Most of us started our careers in lure fishing with the ever-popular mackerel spinners and Colorado spoons. Both of these lures are now objects of some derision, which is clearly unjustified. They wouldn't have been around for so long if they were not successful. We are far more used to the in-line spinner or bar spoon, such as the Mepps or the Voblex, than we are to these newly imported American lures. The ever-increasing popularity of the new lures has rather coloured our judgement of the tried and trusted favourites. It is always worth reassessing the success or worth of the lures in your box and I have found that the humble bar spoon is

of far more use than I would have anticipated. Similarly, the Colorado spoon has fallen into a period of redundancy, yet once it was extremely popular. The mackerel spinner, however, has never given me much confidence and I have put it aside while I experiment with the more sophisticated lure-angling techniques that can be employed with the greater range of contemporary lures.

One last innovation I have failed to mention is the introduction of the rubber worms, grubs and wobby tails to be found on many American lures. Once again, these additions have been developed for bass fishermen. One's immediate reaction is that they should be very attractive to perch, and that is indeed the case. They are also very effective for pike and we really need to keep an open mind when considering these and similar lure adornments. Vic uses wobble tails on his wobbled deadbaits. He cannot prove that it makes for a more attractive bait, but it doesn't put pike off – rather the contrary.

Generally speaking, these attachments are really an extension of the red wool tag which I mentioned earlier. The difference is that we now have a much wider choice of finishes to choose from. The smaller-sized muppets used by sea anglers are by far the easiest to try. Also available are rubber grubs (small worm-like creations with long flat tails) and I have used these as an additional attractor on spinner baits. They come in a variety of colours but I prefer the more conservative red, orange, green and black. I find that these four colours cover all my needs. It goes without saying that the Americans use hundreds of different colours and colour combinations along with rubber and plastic imitations of just about every creepy-crawly you could wish to meet at the waterside. Crayfish, worms, frogs and lizards are perhaps the creatures most often imitated, though a glance through any American angling magazine, such as *In-Fisherman*, will disclose a host of lures which are rarely seen or used over here. We have much to learn.

21

The Importance of Colour

I will now examine in detail the colours and colour patterns available to the lure angler. There are literally hundreds of them, and this is certainly a source of confusion to both the novice and the experienced lure angler alike. If just three or four lures were obtained in all the colours available, then the angler would be confronted with a collection well over 100.

When considering plugs it makes sense to keep the choice down to the following colour patterns:

1 perch
2 roach
3 chrome
4 black
5 hot tiger
6 white with red head
7 yellow with spots

I will try to explain briefly when and why I use each of them.

PERCH

Perch-scale lures are normally my first choice. In my opinion this is the most lifelike of all the colours generally available. However, I like the belly of these lures to be predominantly yellow with a pronounced red throat. I have no qualms in spraying them with paint until they conform exactly to my colour choice. The larger the lure, the more lifelike I prefer the finish. I believe that this is very important, because with the larger lures you are attempting to imitate nature. With the smaller ones you are using a caricature, accentuating certain fish characteristics – for example, big eyes, stripes on a perch, or a big head.

I have mentioned my preferences for colours such as red on my lures. The same applies for orange. The eyes of a predatory fish have a preference for the red end of the spectrum; research on perch has confirmed this. There can be no sense in flying in the face of such evidence and most of this is backed up by experience. It has become well known on Bewl Water that any lure used for trout which contains orange is very attractive to pike, as Vic discovered long ago with his orange wobbled baits. Orange appears to invoke aggressive instincts.

On bright sunny days, or any day when the light values are good, I would always recommend starting with a perch-pattern lure, and certainly when you are fishing clear water with good light penetration.

ROACH

Roach-scale lures are normally my second choice but on the duller days with the water slightly coloured I would make them my first. Once again a red throat should be painted on if not already on lures. The use of big eyes on lures has some justification in fact. The theory behind accentuating the eyes on lures is the strong fry-feeding instinct that predators are born with. All fry have much bigger eyes for their body size and this is believed to trigger a feeding response in young pike. Caricaturing this feature on your lures is intended to invoke this response, even in the older specimens. It really comes down to being confident in your lures. This sort of pseudo-science intrigues me, but I cannot vouch for other lure anglers.

(*Vic's theories on natural bait enhancement parallel Chris's thoughts on enhanced lures.*)

CHROME

Chrome-scale lures are always at their best in coloured water and when one is confronted with a heavy chop on the surface. Chrome lures have been very successful for me on windy days and I can only put this down to scattered light values. Light entering the water is broken and scattered in all directions so a bright lure such as a chrome or chrome-and-blue one must attract more light, presenting the pike with a more visible and stable target. Interestingly, in similar conditions I have done very well not only with brightly coloured lures, such as chrome, but also with those with a violent action. Once again, I can only presume that this is because not only is the light scattered but perhaps the lure vibrations are affected in the same way. A particular favourite that can be used in conditions such as these is a chrome-and-blue Heddon Magnum Clatter Tadpolly.

BLACK

I have found black lures a great change bait. I have caught pike on this colour at all times of the day and in all degrees of water clarity. I have heard that this is a very successful pattern for fishing for pike at night. I cannot comment from personal experience. I have to admit that I find night fishing a tiresome business. There are numerous reasons for this, but the deciding factor has been that it gets dark at night, which makes life very difficult as I can't see in the dark. I am not the sort of person to battle in the face of this sort of adversity so I will leave this fishing to those anglers who eat more carrots than I. I have, however, caught quite a few fish on black lures in the evening, and this seems to tie in quite nicely with the experiences of many sea-trout anglers, who find black flies and lures particularly killing at dusk. I have yet to buy a black lure; all of mine have resulted from a dose of spray paint.

HOT TIGER

These lures are a complete characterisation of a tiger's markings. They are basically striped in orange and chartreuse. As I have already mentioned, orange is a particular favourite of mine. Chartreuse (a fluorescent lime green) seems outrageous but it really does work. Stripes and scattered spots on lures definitely do have some effect on predators and are not applied just to catch the angler.

WHITE WITH RED HEAD

This is one of those strange colour combinations which seem to work for no apparent logical reason. White is at the opposite end of the achromatic scale from black, with a strong tonal contrast as well, so it is strange that it is also very effective as light values fall. In addition, I have found that this is a good choice of colour when one is confronted with cloudy or murky water. For some reason these colours are quite regularly employed on surface lures, a well-known example being the Heddon Lucky 13.

YELLOW WITH SPOTS

Such lures usually have either red or black spots, or a combination of each, and there seems to be no obvious reason why the colour combination should be so successful. There can be no denying, however, that the combination works extremely effectively and several very big fish were taken out of Bewl Bridge Reservoir when the pike culling operation first commenced.

I have been told that at some depth yellow appears as white, but this hardly explains the success. I have never been entirely convinced by the theory that colours change to different ones under water, but more of that later. This is a colour pattern which, though difficult to analyse, has proved to be a successful combination.

COLOUR IN SPOONS AND SPINNERS

Spoons and spinners are available in a variety of colours, but I must express my preference for the more traditional patterns. My favourites, in order of preference, are wholly copper; and copper on one side and silver, brass, or aluminium on the other. Painted spoons and spinners are available and I prefer those painted on one side with a metal finish on the other. The painted designs I favour are, again in order of preference, perch-scale, blue-perch-scale, zebra-striped on metal, zebra stripe with a yellow background, and, finally, plain red. Copper in particular is perhaps the single most popular spoon colour but it is difficult to ascertain accurately the reason for its effectiveness. It is probable that copper lures have been used far more often by anglers than other patterns but I have found that in practice copper spoons have produced more results for me than any others over a period of time.

(*Copper is a duller, cooler version of orange – Vic.*)

To a lesser extent spoons rely on their flash and wobbling action, which provide the stimulus that triggers a take from a pike. Spinners produce stronger vibrations, which flash as a secondary stimulus. A well made, well worked spoon should emit erratic light patterns caused by the bait wobbling and spinning on its own axis. The best way to imagine your spoon working properly is to try to make its movement resemble a turning fish which advertises, if only momentarily, its whereabouts, in much the same way as any fish betrays its presence when suddenly turning over or changing direction.

It is interesting that the erratic behaviour of fish is so often associated with a shoal actively feeding. This ties in with the specific feeding response mentioned earlier. Feeding fish are regarded by the predator as easier prey, as are those injured or dying.

A tremendous amount of work has been undertaken in the field of colour and fish response by our American friends. This research has led to the invention of a system called Color-C-Lector. However, before evaluating this I want to look at the way colours are seen under water and how this is affected by the degree of light penetration and the depth at which the lure is working. I cannot remember where I read the information that follows, but I consider it important.

Light when passed through water is broken down into separate wavelengths, perhaps best illustrated by the rainbow formed as light passes through raindrops. We all know the constitution of the rainbow, or at least the range of colours in the spectrum. The important thing for lure anglers to be aware of is how far each of these wavelengths penetrates water. Once their maximum penetration is reached the colours fade, becoming black, for colours cannot be perceived without light. It is important to remember that this applies to human vision, but fish have a totally different colour perception, which is governed by their eye construction. Predatory fish perceive the red end of the spectrum, which incidentally includes the infrareds, which are invisible to the human eye. Incredibly, the humble goldfish enjoys night vision which is unparalleled by many other creatures. Blues and greens are almost entirely non-perceptible, and this must be remembered when choosing lure colours. Each wavelength band is able to penetrate clear water up to a distance of 15 feet. The following table shows each spectrum colour and the depth of its penetration.

Colour	Band width	Depth
Red	15 feet	15 feet
Orange	15 feet	30 feet
Yellow	15 feet	45 feet
Green	15 feet	60 feet
Blue	15 feet	75 feet
Indigo/Violet	15 feet	90 feet

Colin Dyson spinning on a Dutch Lake.

You will notice that the last two colours have been considered as one, since it is difficult to distinguish between them.

It must be stressed that the table refers only to crystal-clear water in bright sunlight, and this can be a rare combination in this country. The light penetration is obviously cut down by the amount of suspended material in the water. Dull days and cloudy water would vastly reduce the depths at which colour changes could be effectively perceived.

The Color-C-Lector system has been designed to allow for these properties of light and there are now sets of lures available in the separate colours. The information provided by the Color-C-Lector system used in conjunction with fish finders and echo sounders should indicate which colour lure to use, taking into account water clarity, depth, and also the pH of the water.

Lures designed on these lines have had some modification; the blue lures have a black belly and the mauve lures have grey. I have no idea why this should be, but I can only presume that it is a consequence of the research that has been done.

22

Fishing the Lure

Anglers will always have their favourite lures, those that inspire confidence. Most lures will be found to have some of the various colours mentioned in the preceding chapter, either singly or in combination, and perhaps this is one reason for their success. It could always be argued that there is little point in using blue or purple on the grounds that you do not find blue or purple fish in our waters, but the system works and that is all we should worry about as lure anglers.

Light values can often dictate the type and size of lure to be selected. The choice may depend on the time of year, whether the water is still or running, and of course the depth of water you intend to fish.

The depth of water needs little explanation for it will dictate the lure type. If you only have

An angler sends a lure into the famous Thrope Park, scene of the national lure-fishing championship.

Large lures do not necessarily mean large pike.

3 feet of water then it would hardly make sense to use a fast-sinking lure which would immediately snag the bottom. The opposite is nearly always true, but there are occasions where a surface lure can be very effective over a good depth of water, especially in summer. The time of year is crucial: if you intend to concentrate on lure fishing there can be no doubt that you should start your lure-fishing career in the summer. The fish are more active and more inclined to chase after a lure.

RETRIEVE SPEEDS

Whilst on the subject of fish chasing lures, it is perhaps an opportune moment to talk about the retrieve speeds that average anglers use when lure fishing. You will notice that the experienced lure angler reels his or her lures back very slowly. In some cases the slower, the better. A good rule to remember is that you can hardly ever fish a lure too slowly. This is perhaps the most important lesson that we can learn about lure fishing and one that has taken me far too long to absorb. There are exceptions, of course. Some lures have very critical retrieve speeds, which must be adhered to if the lure is to work properly. Some of the surface lures fall into this category and need very specialised retrieve patterns in order to give their best performance. There are times, however, when we may need to fish a bait at some speed and there isn't an angler alive who could crank back a bait faster than a hungry summer pike could overhaul it.

As a general rule, when working a lure the old adage 'slow and deep' should be remembered. Perhaps trying to imitate a dying fish will be effective but, always remember that

Pike will fall to a wide variety of lures.

your bait constructed of metal, wood or plastic should represent a live creature, be it a fish, a reptile or mammal. I cannot stress the last sentence enough. It is one of the keys to success when fishing lures.

I have mentioned on several occasions summer pike and this is undoubtedly my favourite time of year for lure fishing, for then fish are that much more ready to chase a lure. The warmer weather and higher temperatures affect the behaviour of cold-blooded vertebrates to a far greater extent than mammals. Once the colder weather with its corresponding lower water temperature becomes stabilised the pike are less willing to respond to lures. There are those exceptional days when lure fishing can be very effective during the winter, but I would normally feel happier using natural baits at that time. Generally speaking, those few special

A good fish surfaces at the end of the fight.

Bert Rozemeijer with a superbly conditioned pike taken on a lure.

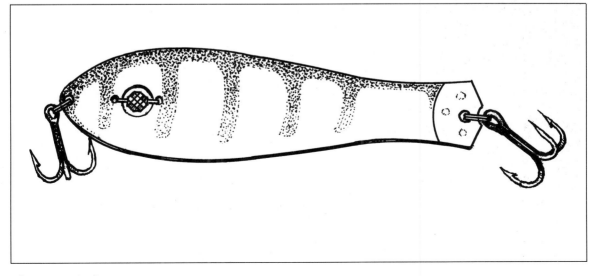

The Kuusamo Professor.

LURE TYPE GUIDANCE CHART					
	Depth range				
Make	0–2 feet	2–8 feet	8–15 feet	15–20 feet	20+ feet
PLUGS					
Arbogast	Jitterbug Sputterbuzz Hula Popper				Mudbug
Bagley's		B's no 1, 11, 111 Chatter B Small Fry Bass 'N' Shad Bang 'O' Bang 'O' B	Diving Smoo Diving Chatter B3 Super Deep Kill'r B1 Super Deep Kill'r B11 Diving B1, B11, B111	DB3 Magnum	DKB3 and DB3
Bill Norman			Deep Little N Reflect N 2JD and 3JD		DD22 Deep Diver
Bomber		Model A Long A	Model 7A and 8A Deep Runner–Long A	9A Magnum – Long 26A	400 and 600
Cotton Cordell		Rattlin' Shad Big 'O' Ripplin' Redfin	Wally Diver		Hellbender
Creek Chub	Injured Minnow Mouse	Pikie			
Helin		Flatfish			
Heddon	Crazy Crawler Meadow Mouse Lucky 13 Wood Vamp Zara Spook Torpedo Chugger Spook Dying Flutter	River Runt Tadpolly Timber Rattler Timber Minnow			
Kwikfish		Kwikfish			
Lazy Ike		Lazy Ike			
Manns			10+ and 15+	15+	20+ and 30+ Stretch 20+
Rapala		Shad Rap Fat Rap Minnows			
Rebel	Buzz 'N' Frog		Spoonbill Minnow Deep Wee Crawfish	Naturals	Sinking Deep Wee Crawfish
SINKING VIBRATORY LURES Bill Lewis Cotton Cordell Heddon Manns Storm					Rat-L-Trap Gay Blades Rattlin' Spot Sonar Leroy Brown Texas Shad

Make	Depth range				
	0–2 feet	2–8 feet	8–15 feet	15–20 feet	20+ feet
SPOONS					
ABU				Toby	
				Salmo	
				UTO	
				Atom	
Bill Norman	Weed Walker				
Buck Perry's				Spoonplug	
Creek Chub				Spoon	
Daredevils				Original	
Heddon		Moss Boss			
Johnson		Silver Minnow			
Kuusamo				Professor 00, 1 and 2	
Strike King		Timber King		Taiman	
				Rasanan	
				Rasanan Weedless	
BAR SPOONS					
ABU				Droppen	
				Morrum	
Kuusamo				Hauki-Lippa	
				Lippa	
Mepps				Musky Killer	
Yakima				Rooster Tails	
				Vibric Rooster Tails	
BUZZ BAITS					
Bill Norman		Triple Wing			
Blue Fox		Double Buzzer			
Bumble Bee		Bubble Buzz			
Strike King		Cackle Buzz			
SPINNER BAITS					
Bumble Bee				Chopper Rockerhead (twin spin)	
				Zee-Bee	
Mepps				Tandem Bass Killer	
Strike King				Diamond Leaf	
				Houston Model Magnum	

NOTES

0–2 feet   Many of the diving baits can, when fished very slowly, also be used in this topwater range. There are numerous other topwater minnow-type baits (Rapala, Rebel, Bagley's, etc.); the list is not exhaustive.

2–8 feet   By far the largest selection of lures is available to fish these depths. The list could be nearly endless, with most bait companies offering such lures.

8–15 feet   There are a few floating/diving lures which dive to these depths, although more are becoming available.

20 feet plus   There are a number of crayfish-type baits in most manufacturer's lists; only some of the more famous are listed. Spoons, spinnerbaits and bar spoons can, of course, be fished at many depths, as indicated, depending on speed of retrieve, how long the bait is allowed to sink before retrieving, etc. Beware, however, of retrieving too fast.

We would emphasise that this list is not exhaustive; it is intended to be a guide.

days in winter when lure fishing scores are also the days when any bait will be effective, as the pike are actively on the feed. Another problem with lure fishing in the winter is that the angler can lose body heat all too easily. Contrary to popular opinion, excessive movement causes heat loss.

The earlier the start to the season the better, and in the absence of a close season the months of April, May and June would be my first choice for lure fishing. As July progresses action slows and August is perhaps the worst month for any type of fishing. September and October share a brief resurgence before the frosts and rapidly falling water temperatures slow the pike's metabolism.

But don't take my word for it. Try it yourself. Pick up a lure rod, a selection of lures of various colour types, then consider carefully the depth of water, the time of year and the conditions. Decide on a lure, but be prepared to change several times, and fish with confidence, knowing that pike do fall victim to this form of artificial deception.

PART FIVE
WIDER HORIZONS

23

Boatcraft

A vast amount of pike angling is practised from the bank but almost inevitably it will be necessary at some stage to take to the water in order to get to the pike on a particular venue. Boats are the key to success on so many pike waters, providing the access and the means of location which would otherwise be denied. And yet for some reason so many anglers have reservations about boat fishing, particularly in winter. Admittedly, at times it is perhaps not advisable for the faint-hearted but, practised with a degree of common sense and care, fishing from a boat should prove safe and highly rewarding.

To fish on the Broads there is little option but to take to a boat. Otherwise hundreds upon hundreds of acres of potentially productive water would remain out of bounds. We therefore learned boatcraft at an early age. Even outside the Broadland area a boat will often prove an advantage – not only on the very large waters, where a boat is so essential, but even on smaller waters or rivers for the purpose of location or, again, for access to pike out of casting range.

Once you are afloat on a water no pike is out of reach; every inch of the water can be covered, and so much more knowledge that would otherwise be denied can now be gained. For instance, the water can be grid-searched by systematic swim changes or trailing or trolling techniques can be used. Long casting can be eliminated and so often fish can be caught when they are virtually under the boat. Inevitably, the end result will be that of a greater understanding of the quarry you are seeking and more fish caught.

ABOUT BOATS

Unfortunately, it is a fact of life that most hire boats are, at the best, poorly equipped for the pike angler and, at worst, positive safety hazards for the pike and/or the angler – old, poorly maintained boats, possibly rotten through in places with great nails and sharp edges protruding at strategic points from the bottom, which can catch and gouge boots, clothing and, even worse, a pristine freshly caught pike. Where such boats are encountered it is necessary to educate the boatyard, to show them the error of their ways and to convince them that they will have increased revenue if the quality of their boats improves.

Most boatyards will listen, but few will improve their boats to a fully acceptable standard. For instance, it is very rare to find good rope or anchors of sufficient quality on such boats. Nowadays most of the boats will be made of glass fibre, so at least rotten floorboards are eliminated and with them many of the protruding nails. Nevertheless, the bottom will still be rough and we are not aware of any boatyards which rectify this problem by supplying underlay or carpeting.

Obviously, it is necessary to be equipped with a few essential items of boat equipment in order to rectify the deficiencies of a hire boat on the day. If we were planning an outing at a new venue such items would include a good set of oars, our own 28lb metal anchors with long rope lengths, a spare pair of rowlocks, a seat cushion and, most important, a large piece of soft carpet or underlay to protect pike while they are unhooked. These are minimum essential items and may be supplemented by outriggers or boat rod rests, a graph recorder, and an outboard or electric outboard if allowed.

If you are fishing in a privately controlled water you are in the hands of the boatyard with regard to boat quality. If this is not the case it is obviously far better to use one's own boat. An owned boat can be kitted out exactly to meet your requirements, you will become used to the stability and its own peculiarities and after a while a fond attachment to that boat will grow. Thinking back to past encounters with fish which have fallen to the boat adds that little bit more to the whole appeal of boat fishing.

Ideally, having your own boat permanently moored at each venue saves hauling the boat from water to water on trailer or on the top of a car. But this can prove expensive unless several friends share the costs of acquiring several boats. The alternative is to tow the boat from place to place, ideally on a sound trailer, possibly even fitted with a winch to ease loading at the end of the day.

Choice of boat very much depends on the waters you fish. For instance, on most Broads a boat of 12–15 feet in length is ideal. Such a

Martyn uses an electric outboard to manoeuvre on shallow Broads waters.

Electric and petrol outboards are essential to the boat angler.

boat does not need to have a high freeboard, but obviously the more stable the better. On very large waters, however, a 12-foot shallow-sided boat would easily be swamped during high winds and would prove positively unsafe. For waters such as Lomond, more substantial boats are needed.

Stability is important. Clinker boats, being heavy by nature, tend to be fairly stable and make excellent pike boats. Flat-bottomed punts can be even better but absolute pigs to row. Nowadays, however, most boats tend to be fibreglass. This lighter material is far less stable, especially when the hull is almost V-shaped in design. When choosing a boat we look for as flat a U-shaped design as possible, but even then a fibreglass boat will heel quite violently to sudden moves. An incredible improvement can be obtained by the simple addition of floorboards. The extra weight provides stability and the flat bottom provided by the floorboards improves balance and safety.

Our ideal pike boat, therefore, is a fairly flat-bottomed fibreglass or clinker boat fitted with solid floorboards. The boat will then be provided with wall-to-wall carpeting or underlay. This is primarily with pike safety and care in mind but it serves a second function as it dampens sounds transmitted through the boat and assists where quietness may prove the key to success.

We have already mentioned the need for good anchors. So many boats are equipped with paint tins full of concrete. These are totally inefficient unless fitted with a set of long grapnel-type spikes which will dig into and grip the bottom. We prefer the metal 28lb anchors actually sold for the purpose. This may sound heavy and certainly at times this weight is something of an overkill, but we have known times when even these have been totally useless for keeping the boat in the required position. Indeed, on one occasion Martyn recalls literally bouncing down the River Waveney as the 28lb anchors, with ropes fully extended, proved insufficent to hold against a strong current with a wind blowing in the same direction.

Small boats mean a lack of space, so organisation is essential.

The anchor rope should also be chosen carefully. Most hire boats are kitted with an insufficient length of very coarse twisted rope. Such rope can provide an escape route, or possibly a death sentence, for pike. It is so easy for pike to dive at the last minute and for the line to catch in the lay of the rope, suffer abrasion and almost certainly part, allowing the pike to swim away with a mouthful of ironmongery. When fitting out your own boat this problem can be eliminated, for braided ropes are available from chandlers. These do not have the lay in which line will catch and therefore if a pike does dive round the anchor rope the chances of a breakage will be virtually eliminated. Such attention to detail at the outset is so important.

Finally, whilst on anchors our boats are fitted with grip-type cleats (again available from chandlers), which allow rope to be pulled through one way when the anchor is lifted but lock the rope when the right depth is found. This simple gadget is a vast improvement on a knot tied at the right depth, which has to be retied when you move to a swim of a different

It's always five degrees colder in a boat, but Roger Miller is wrapped up well enough to smile.

depth. Small fairleads or roller fairleads which assist in lifting and lowering the anchor are a further refinement.

Other improvements to the boat include attention to the rowlocks. So many boats are equipped with poorly fitting rowlocks which squeak, groan and broadcast loud shock waves to warn pike of your approach. Much of this noise can be eliminated with insulation tape fitted round the rowlock pin to dampen the sound and make for a more silent approach to the swim – the muffled-oars approach.

Once anglers and their luggage, rods, bait and other gear are aboard a small boat there is often little place left for unhooking. It is necessary to stow all this gear in an organised manner and take only as much tackle as is required. For instance, if you use a rucksack make sure that it is waterproof, as the bottom of the boat will quickly become flooded during a rainstorm. Tackle and cameras can soon be waterlogged if the rucksack becomes saturated. When a pike is caught chaos will reign if the boat is small and

there is no room for pike anglers, their tackle and the prize. If it really is too small the only answer is to take the pike to the bank and deal with it there, but this is most unsatisfactory unless the bank is very close. On one Dutch water we fish there is a nudist camp next to the bank which could make for some interesting photos if a fish is taken to that bank for unhooking and photography.

One improvement is the fitting of a removable centre thwart. As soon as the pike is caught the thwart is lifted out and stored away, providing a central working area for unhooking. However, any such conversion should be undertaken with care, since the centre thwart is usually an integral part of the boat, adding strength and serving load-bearing purposes.

Further improvements can be incorporated to suit individual requirements. The Americans have livebait wells fitted under the seats of their boats for keeping bait, but their boats are in an altogether different league, with swivel chairs and speedboat-style outboards fitted as norm. It suffices to say that if you are going to be confined to a boat for many hours and on many occasions the more refinements which can be made which improve comfort and efficiency, the more enjoyable the fishing will be.

ONCE AFLOAT

As you step into the boat you instantly become a far more efficient hunter. Mobility brings access, and with access the ability to search out your quarry. Yet we have seen experienced pike anglers, introduced to the fun of boat fishing for the first time, too scared to stand or hardly move in the boat, for fear of rocking and capsizing. Given time that fear diminishes but there is no need for apprehension in the first place. Provided one does not leap up and down with sudden movements there really is no

likelihood of the boat capsizing in normal conditions. It doesn't take long to get used to the rocking of the boat and to become aware of one's partner's movements. For example, if he is poised over the starboard side for a moment's relief (few boats are fitted with portaloos) it is obvious that one does not suddenly leap up, causing the boat to rock and your partner to do a belly-flop into the water. It happened to Vic and it was snowing at the time!

WIND EFFECTS
AND ANCHORING

Simple rules need to be adapted when using standard pike methods in boat fishing. There are almost no occasions on which baits should be legered. The chances of a pike running in towards you after taking the bait are relatively

A flat-bottomed punt makes an excellent fishing boat.

high and if runs are not noticed a deep-hooked pike could result. Static fishing from a boat should always be undertaken with a float as a bite indicator unless you are anchored with two poles and the boat itself is static and cannot be affected by the wind. Wind effect can prove a most unsettling problem.

First, wind will always cause an anchored boat to yaw, because wind does not blow at a constant rate all the time. As the wind strength falls, tension affects the boat less and the anchor ropes slacken, which causes the boat to yaw. If the wind increases the boat will swing back the other way. This constant swinging may even dislodge the anchors. A boat which constantly yaws will almost certainly move a legered bait, tending to bring it in towards you, so causing slack line, which reduces bite detection. A

float, however much the bait moves, will continue to show. Even if there is no wind, your own movement can rock the boat, to similar effect. Freelining can prove even more disastrous at anchor and yet so often we have seen legered baits cast out behind the boat to fish by themselves.

Wind will always be the boat angler's greatest problem, yet strong winds can result in good sport. One of our local waters is a classic example. Filby Broad fishes at its best in the very strongest winds and the fish tend to move about the Broad all day. Anchoring can then be a problem and very few anglers appear to appreciate the correct anchoring procedure in such conditions. When the wind is no more than moderate it is easy to anchor sideways on to the swim – simplicity itself. But when the

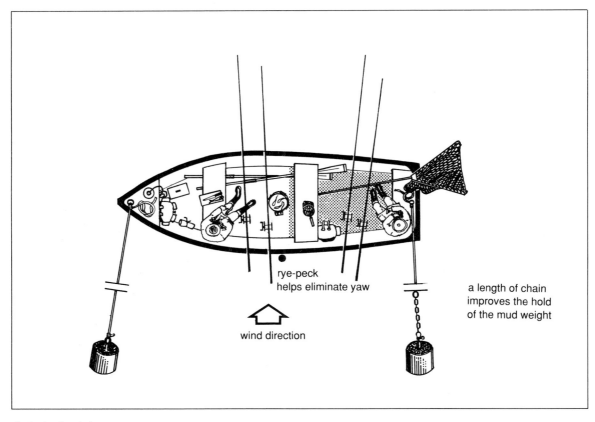

rye-peck
helps eliminate yaw

wind direction

a length of chain
improves the hold
of the mud weight

Anchoring in wind.

wind is strong it is not practical to anchor with the wind on the beam and some thought is required about how much anchor rope should be paid out. If the anchor rests on the bottom and directly under the bow it will not hold. Instead, the boat should lie bow into the wind. The front anchor is lowered and as much rope as possible it paid out. Finally the stern anchor is lowered. In exceptionally strong winds a second anchor at the bows may be needed. This emphasises the need for your own anchors and ropes so that if you are in a hire boat at least you are equipped with adequate gear. So often if the water is 8 feet deep and the anchor rope provided is only 8½ feet long it is impossible to moor up. Twenty feet of rope might be needed in such a situation.

We have mentioned poles. This is another very efficient form of mooring, provided the water is not too deep. Pushing two poles, often

Steve Harper proves that it is possible to get comfortable in a boat.

Mooring with rye-pecks.

called rye-pecks, firmly into the bottom so bow and stern can be secured to them eliminates wind swing or the boat dragging; it also provides a very firm fishing base. Where poles are provided they are usually thicker at one end. This is the end which should be pushed into the bottom, forming a wedge, which resists wind action better. Even so, on extremely windy days, in deeper swims where the full length of the pole is used and perhaps the pole is not quite as far in the bottom as desired, the poles may pull out, particularly when a pike is struck. Martyn can remember one or two occasions which on reflection now appear quite amusing but which at the time were not so funny. On one windy day several years ago as he struck into a fish a pole pulled free. As his companion, John Wilson, fought to control the boat and resecure the pole, Martyn tussled with the pike, which seemed to be constantly changing direction as the boat swung back and forth. He eventually managed to subdue a bewildered twenty, his first from that water. Poor John flaked exausted onto his seat, having finally secured control of the boat and their safety. On another occasion, on the same water and in the same swim, both poles pulled free and before Dave Humphries and Martyn could reel in, the boat as well as all the rods crashed into the tree-surrounded bank, rods bent at acute angles, lines snagging into branches. The boat spun the whole thing into one great tangled spider-webbed mess. On that occasion sanity almost left them and they merely chucked an anchor on the bank, got out of the boat and were last seen walking off into the surrounding marshes. Eventually, with composure regained, they returned to find that at least none of the rods was broken, though several hundred yards of line was totally and inextricably tangled.

Wind can be frustrating and it can cause problems. Our strongest message must be to make sure you are firmly anchored. Once this is achieved the other problems can be eliminated. For instance, preventing rods from being blown across the boat is relatively easy. We have used simple clip-on rod rests for years.

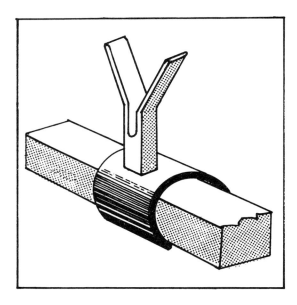

Marvic clip-on boat rod rest.

They can be made from rod-rest heads inserted into a length of strong flexible piping. The piping is cut along its length and can be clipped over the side of the boat. Outriggers are of course a more expensive alternative. Fortunately, running a tackle company has enabled us to make Marvic boat rests available to boat anglers through tackle shops.

Another wind problem is that of exposure. In a boat in the middle of a water the wind-chill factor will make it substantially colder. We would not recommend the use of umbrellas in a boat as they affect stability severely. Fitted canopies are a possibility but generally all one can do is ensure that you are equipped with enough clothing and a good one-piece suit. We emphasise a one-piece since in very strong cold winds one can get some protection from huddling down on the bottom of a boat, gaining shelter from the sides. The bottom will inevitably be damp, hence the need for proper waterproof protection. An additional advantage of the one-piece is that you can kneel down straddling a pike for unhooking and at the same time keep legs and knees dry.

On the smaller lakes and on rivers the wind

will prove too strong on very few occasions. This is not the case on big waters. There it is essential always to keep one eye on the weather. This is true even if the waters are relatively shallow. We have been caught crossing Hickling Broad with waves several feet high and water pouring into the boat as we have made for home. On those occasions a good outboard and the ability to keep the boat motoring straight into or with the wind, as opposed to allowing it to fetch beam on, have avoided the risk of capsizing. We have seen Horsey Mere lashed with such huge waves that under no circumstances would we have taken our small boat out onto the water, and Martyn has witnessed Lomond turn from relative tranquility and warm weather to a vicious gale of driving snow in a matter of minutes. On that occasion he was locked fast into a large Lomond pike and during the battle the nearby boats, having seen the forthcoming storm, all retreated for safety. As soon as John Watson slipped the net under a near-twenty the fish was quickly weighed and released and they both fled for the boatyard, even though the fish were feeding. It is better to live to fish another day.

On a large water, teamwork and walkie-talkies can help ensure that all enjoy sport.

APPROACHING THE SWIM

This is another practice which is perhaps not quite so easy in a boat. In bank fishing a relatively silent approach can always be guaranteed. Possibly some extra caution is needed if you wish to fish close in on a shallow water, but there are many places where your approach will not affect the pike. With boats this is different. Obviously, the shallower the water the more dramatic the effect, but there is no denying that the sound of an outboard motoring towards a swim is detected long before you arrive. We have even known instances on the shallow River Thurne when an outboard motor nearly half a mile away has been detected by our live-baits, making them agitated as soon as the drone of the outboard was noticeable. This has not happened once but on numerous occasions and obviously the fish have sensed the commotion. If a small roach can detect this, so too can a pike. It is also worth bearing in mind that the Thurne, like most Broadland waters, is used by motor cruisers and boats with outboards. One wonders what effect these engines would have on a water where they were not normally used.

It pays to cut the speed of the approach and in very shallow water to cut the outboard entirely. Rowing to the swim should prove quieter; certainly the rhythmic shock waves will not be present and any disturbance caused by the oars will not travel so far. We have already mentioned that rowlocks can be quietened. The approach can be made even more silent if one adopts Indian-style tactics and uses one oar as a paddle. This entails standing, and the angler's high-profile silhouette could prove off-putting to pike in extremely shallow clear water. In such circumstances mooring a little further away from a suspected holding swim could prove beneficial.

The Americans are far ahead of us when it comes to boat fishing. Their whole approach to manoeuvring a boat into a swim has been refined to cause the least disturbance. They may use their enormous outboards to speed across the water to the next swim (which may be 5 miles away) but as they approach the outboard is switched off and an electric outboard takes over. Those who have used an electric outboard will realise just how efficient these machines are. There is virtually no sound and minimum shock waves. The speed of approach can be controlled exactly and the boat can be manoeuvred almost on a sixpence. They are really quite incredible machines and, though they are rather expensive, we really cannot understand why more are not used by pike anglers today. In addition to this silent approach electric outboards have several other important uses in pike angling. For instance, in trolling an electric outboard will give a precise control over speed, which could not easily be obtained by the use of oars. In the United States, of course, electric outboards are readily available but even here one of the best models, marketed by Shakespeare, can be obtained from tackle shops.

It is essential not to ruin your quiet approach by throwing the anchors over the side, ripping the lid off a bait bucket, or generally preparing to cast out in a noisy fashion. Anchors should be gently lowered and clipped into their cleats, the lid of the bait bucket should have been loosened well before arrival and the rods should already be set up. Similarly, if the oars are to be stowed away this should be done as quietly as possible. If there has been no disturbance then any pike which was feeding in the area should still be there, unaware of your presence. The approach can be made even quieter if you are anchoring against the side, in particular a reedy margin, as instead of lowering anchors you can simply tie to a bankside branch or hitch the rope around a clump of reeds, so achieving silent mooring.

We cannot emphasise too strongly the need for care in developing silent boatcraft in pike fishing. It is not always needed – for example, on very deep large waters noise is likely to have

Sinking the rods in this way helps avoid problems with drifting weed and surface drag.

a minimal effect – but, if always practised, on the day it is most needed it will not let you down.

· On occasion, when you have fished a swim and no pike have been forthcoming, it can pay to dispense with the quiet approach altogether, even on very shallow waters. If you know pike are there but not feeding, keeping them unaware of your presence is hardly likely to change matters; if the pike are stirred up sport cannot get worse. The very fact that the pike have moved and been forced into activity can induce them to feed. Similarly, the pike may be lying inactive in a nearby weedy area or reed-bed and to enter that area in order to scare them out cannot cause your sport to deteriorate. It may be enough just to push them into an accessible area. Once moved they may, after being given time to settle, think of food. On one water, which Martyn is privileged to have fished, this disturbance method has become almost routine. On one of the first occasions he fished the water he did not realise that he was experiencing this situation. It was early morning during a club boat pike match. Martyn and his companion Dave were first to arrive in the small backwater which leads off the main broad. They had to approach through the narrow entrance, which, though less than 3 feet deep, was the deepest water available. They quietly eased through the entrance, knowing that it was reputedly the best spot, glided silently over the area and then mooored thirty yards away, with the intention of fishing back to the entrance. However, several other boats, also intent on coming into the backwater and not knowing about the entrance area's potential, paid less regard to their approach and rowed happily, and in some cases noisily, straight through the swim. When Dave and Martyn cast out they were fairly convinced that all the pike would have fled. however, this wasn't the case and two small fish quickly fell to livebaits. Martyn followed this up within ten minutes with a fish just two ounces under 25lb.

Since that time Martyn has evolved a particular approach to that water. In October and November there are occasions when the pike appear to force shoals of bream into the backwater and large numbers of pike then feed merrily throughout the day. On those occasions it is sufficient merely to cast out to catch pike. On other occasions, however, fewer pike are present, and once the early morning feeding spell (if it occurs) is over the water may appear fishless. At that stage anchors are lifted and the boat is punted Indian-style across the broad in search of pike. Most of the water is less than 3 feet deep but underneath lies some ten or more feet of soft silt. As soon as the boat approaches a pike it bolts away, creating a great surface disturbance and releasing a large cloud of silt. There are usually two or three pike together and as the water is so shallow the bow waves can be seen heading away. As the pike slow down the bow waves diminish and it is usually possible to identify the area to which these pike have moved. The baits are then cast around that spot and it is rarely more than a quarter of an hour before a run or two materialises. Unless a large number of pike have been disturbed, after one or two fish are caught the swim goes dead and so the whole process is repeated once again. Sometimes the pike are found in water which will barely cover their backs and, interestingly, it has been found that there are one or two spots on that silted broad where the bottom is relatively hard. These spots are very often the areas where the pike tend to be. They are also the places to which pike tend to return. After the whole water, which is not very large, has been disturbed and most of the pike have been forced to become active it is often productive to place the bait on the hard areas, so that when pike return they find a waiting morsel. Takes will then be forthcoming in those areas even though they were unproductive before the disturbance. Martyn usually fishes with Roger Miller on this water and together they have taken large numbers of double-figure pike. Fishing in this disturbance style proves unquestionably that at times the pike need activiting before they start feeding. Old-time Broads anglers used to send a dog in to the reeds in order to drive the pike into more open water – presumably not a little dog!

On some occasions you may arrive at a water to find a light covering of ice. The ice will not be so thick as to be unbreakable but will prevent fishing while it remains. Steve Harper and Martyn found these conditions on a water which had been fishing well. They decided to apply the disturbance method to this water and see if they could break the ice to provide an area of clear water, just in case the pike could be stimulated into feeding. They forced the boat through the ice into the swim and then spent more than an hour smashing ice with the oars and rowing round and round, forming a bigger and bigger area to fish in. Once it was cleared they could initially use only one rod each and the lines were constantly catching against the broken ice floes drifting in the free area. Within a few minutes the breeze had blown most of the ice rafts away to leave a small fishable area. Only ten minutes after they finished the ice clearance the first run materialised. They caught several fish from the area that day, to more than 18lb, in spite of the heavy disturbance and noisy ice-breaking.

The whole question of disturbance and the need for stealth and quietness at times requires complete reappraisal. Usually a cautious approach will pay dividends, but as can be seen from these examples that is not always the case. On occasions, sport has been quiet until a passing powerboat has disturbed the swim with a take following soon afterwards. Once Martyn retrieved a bait in order to allow the warden to row over for a chat and he did not bother recasting at that stage, merely allowing the bait to rest on the bottom beside the two boats. Seconds later a large pike took a liking to the bait. On another occasion Steve Brown caught a thirty in almost identical circumstances, having dropped his bait over the side while a boat was passing.

Another example where disturbance actually helped was at Haveringland Lake, which many years ago produced an English record pike. Martyn and friends had been fishing it all season and the pike, lying in clear, shallow water, had become fairly cautious. Quietly approaching along the dam in the morning, they could actually see the pike lying in close proximity to one another. One particular day Martyn lowered a bait among a shoal of some dozen pike and watched in amazement as all the pike circled the livebait, nosing it and nudging it, though not one grabbed the bait. Easing the bait away from the fish and changing it for one of the most lively in the bucket resulted in a very tentative take as one of the pike gently took the fresh livebait while the others watched, seemingly without interest. That pike then remained motionless with the bait lightly clamped in its mouth and it soon became obvious that it had no intention of turning or eating it. It could be seen that the hooks were outside the mouth and there was absolutely no point in striking. A stalemate existed for some ten minutes while the pike remained motionless. Gently pulling on the line produced no response and therefore, in desperation, Martyn picked up a large stone and tossed it in the air. As the stone hit the water a dozen pike bolted from the swim and in so doing one clamped firmly on its quarry, pausing momentarily to turn the bait, which ensured that the strike which followed was at last productive. Interestingly, within the next hour, seven more pike were caught in that area with no problems of tentative or uninterested takes.

BOAT TACKLE

Rods

Our preference is for 12-foot rods for boat fishing. Many anglers appear to believe that a shorter rod is necessary, but this is not the case. It is often believed that a long rod is more cumbersome when used in a boat, but of course the same amount of rod actually remains within the boat whatever its length and however much is outboard. A longer rod is a great help in playing fish, particularly when they are near to the

A 12-foot rod helps keep fish away from anchor ropes.

boat. If a pike dives for the anchor rope it can be more easily controlled. This is a very important advantage. There are others, such as greater line control, which is very useful when using floating lines and roaming or drifting livebaits, not to mention striking fish at a distance – though long casting is rarely needed.

As long casting with large deadbaits is unlikely to feature prominently in the majority of boat-fishing situations, a rod of about 2½lb test serves most purposes. On larger waters, for trolling, or to subdue hard-fighting loch pike, a more powerful rod may be necessary. Currently we consider that the ideal all-round boat pike rods are the 12-foot Daiwa Whisker of 2½ or 2¾lb test curve or the Tri-cast 2½lb rod.

Reels

Turning to reels, we embark on a subject on which there has been much debate – the use of multiplier reels for pike fishing. Martyn is a complete convert to these reels for boat fishing. Certainly, they have considerable advantages over standard fixed-spool reels. For example, heavy lines cause no problems on a multiplier, whereas most freshwater fixed-spool reels are simply incapable of effectively handling lines in

excess of 11lb BS. Coarser lines tend to spring off the fixed spool, causing coils and tangles.

The major advantage of the multiplier, however, is the free spool and clicker facility, where incorporated. Disengaging the spool and setting the clicker provides both an audible alarm and a check against the swing of the boat. When a boat is swinging heavily in the wind, a fixed-spool reel with the bail open requires the use of either an elastic band with the line clipped under it or a run clip. Inevitably, as the boat swings the line pulls free giving a false run. This does not happen with the multiplier. Similarly, if a take occurs whilst your eyes are not on the float – and no matter how vigilant you may be this is bound to occur at intervals – you are instantly alerted as the clicker sounds.

These reels have further advantages, particularly for trolling and lure fishing. There is, however, one main disadvantage: casting small baits any distance into the wind. Fortunately, distance is not often required, so there are few occasions where the multiplier is not a more efficient reel for boat fishing for pike than a fixed-spool.

Fortunately, some manufacturers have now listened to the constant requests for a fixed-spool with multiplier-type facilities. Firms such as Shimano and ABU have released free spool-type-reels predominantly for carp fishing, and are now incorporating clickers specifically for pike anglers. If you cannot afford the additional expense of a multiplier or cannot get used for fishing 'upside down and wrong-handed', one of this new breed of fixed-spool reels will eliminate many of the previous disadvantages.

RUN DETECTION

Most tackle, rigs and techniques mentioned elsewhere in the book can be applied to boat fishing, with the exception of specific bank-legering techniques. We have already emphasised the fact that most piking from a boat will require the use of a float. With livebaiting techniques one method which really does come

Martyn battens down the hatches in anticipation of a storm.

into its own is the use of a sunk float paternoster fished on a relatively tight line. This requires a positive means of bite detection other than the float, and again the clicker of a multiplier or a modern free-spool reel will prove far more efficient than a run clip. Even so, it is important to pay constant attention to the rods when you use a sunk float paternoster from a boat. This is because the yawing of the boat has a 'drawing in' effect, which causes the line to go slack periodically. If this is left a run may pass undetected, with the possibility of a deep-hooked fish. When the yaw causes such problems it will be necessary to tighten the line as often as necessary. In addition, a bomb of a reasonable size should be used on the paternoster link in order to ensure that positive indication results when a pike strikes towards the boat. The usual result in these circumstances is a short sharp burst of clicks from the reel and

then nothing as the bomb is dislodged and the line goes slack. With a fixed-spool reel and run clip all that may happen is that line pulls from the run clip, in much the same way as it does when the boat swings, and again this can often pass unnoticed. Alternatively, the line may have become jammed so tightly into the run clip that it does not pull out before the line goes slack. Again, the run is undetected. Quite clearly it can be seen that the use of a multiplier's clicker or free-spool-style reel has very positive run-detection capabilities which can help avoid deep-hooked fish.

ECHO SOUNDERS AND GRAPH RECORDERS

Before the advent of the graph recorder, echo sounders provided a means of obtaining some knowledge of the underwater terrain. They give an indication of depth, drop-offs and contours. Apart from that it is very difficult to use them for positive pike location. The echo sounder used to be of assistance in mapping a water, however a sense of watercraft coupled with an understanding of pike habits and habitat was an essential prerequisite in order to interpret the readings.

With the modern generation of graph recorders actual fish shoals and single large fish, such as pike, can be accurately located, in addition to the mapping of the bottom topography. At first it was said that the use of a graph recorder was unethical, and that it enabled the beginner to fish as effectively as the expert. Time has now proved that this is clearly nonsense. For instance, the graph recorder is of little use in shallow waters, as its beam will only detect fish directly under the boat, and these will often bolt away on sensing its approach. In very large waters, where there are significant drop-offs and great depths, the graph recorder has proved invaluable to those who are prepared to undertake the formidable task of location. Without the recorder years of research may be necessary to understand just one area of a great lake or loch. Even then one may spend all day fishing at the wrong depth. Life itself is too short to devote year upon year to coming to grips with truly large waters when there are so many and so much pike fishing to enjoy. The graph recorder eliminates some of this toil. Once the read-out can be interpreted correctly it provides a positive understanding of an area and what is happening on any one day. It greatly assists location and gives an accurate indication of the depth the pike are lying at. It doesn't catch the fish – you must still present the bait in the correct way – but it does help eliminate week upon week of fishing barren water. Surely there is nothing wrong with that. Indeed, we would suggest to those anglers wishing to fish the larger waters – such as the Scottish lochs, the large European lakes or the quite enormous lakes in America – that to forgo the use of a graph recorder on such waters would be a severe handicap, as much for an expert with many years of experience behind him as for a novice.

TO CONCLUDE

So gently now he eased the boat into the small reedy bay, not a sound as the anchors found their hold in the bottom silt. The oars slowly and methodically stowed away, all was ready. The small roach made its way towards the reeds, swimming against the pressure on the line, towards sanctuary and away from the open water. Too late the roach saw its fate and felt the great jaws clamp tight, drawing on its life's blood. 'A large fish, this,' thought our angler as the hooks were set. Indeed, within minutes a 20lb monster lay, subdued, in his giant net. Quickly the fish was hauled aboard, removed from the net and then placed on the rough floorboards. The pike thrashed, slamming its tail against the side, while the angler attempted to subdue its struggles. Despite his tackle, his initial expertise, he was not properly equipped; there was no soft cushioning on the bottom, no damp sack in which to wrap his capture, to quieten and protect this magnificent fish. With scales lost, sides scraped and bleeding, his pristine prize is now scarred for ever, evidence to all of his bad handling. Outwardly he disregards his damage, as the fish is unhooked, weighed and returned. It will not be such a prize for the next captor, bearing such battle scars. Surely, inwardly, our angler must know of the damage caused and the need for care and thought when handling pike in a boat.

Tranquillity returns and another roach makes its way towards the reedy sanctuary, but this time the roach remains untouched. Unknown to our careless angler, the sound of the thrashing of this previous prize against the side of the boat has signalled a warning and two much larger pike have drifted from the bay. They will not fill his net or his uncaring hands this day.

24

Conservation, Not Preservation

THE HELPING HAND OF THE PIKE ANGLERS' CLUB

The young lad had never seen or caught a pike before but some deep-rooted feeling – a primitive instinct – caused him to act intuitively. Time and time again he brought the rod rest down, viciously, on the fish's skull, sealing its fate still further with every blow, whilst at the same time jumping back, just in case by some remote chance the creature could fight back and catch him with its crocodile jaws.

That poor pike never had a chance. Martyn was but halfway round the lake on his dash to save the fish when the last gasp of life left the pike. Upon reaching the swim he was greeted by the glazed, staring eyes of the mutilated fish, firmly staked to the ground by the rod rest.

Later the lad understood. Never again would he be so afraid and soon that one boy would be on the road to becoming a pike angler. However, for every convert made at the waterside, through careful explanation and education, there will be countless others carrying on killing pike through fear and ignorance.

This is a never-ending uphill struggle, endeavouring to overcome the deep-rooted prejudice against pike, passed down from generation to generation. This alone explains the necessity for such an organisation as the Pike Anglers' Club of Great Britain (PAC) and other similar European organisations.

Martyn gently returns a magnificently conditioned fish.

When Martyn was first approached by Barry Rickards and Hugh Reynolds with a view to the second PAC committee becoming Norfolk-based, his natural reaction was to run and hide. Barry and company's reasoning for Norfolk was sound: there was a good nucleus of pike men from whom to form a committee. But who would be mad enough to volunteer? At the same time, although supporting the PAC, there was an apparent contradiction disturbing Martyn's mind which first needed resolving. The PAC promoted pike angling. With limited pike stocks and more anglers taking up pike fishing, who did not necessarily understand how to handle pike, this meant greater pressure on waters, more deaths from bad handling. Was the PAC self-defeating? Was it not far better to let pike angling take a back seat, with the resulting lower publicity, fewer pike anglers and hence less pressure, and better fishing? A policy of conservation by negative promotion?

These thoughts had been constantly turning over in Martyn's mind that morning when suddenly the young lad hooked into the pike and dragged the fish across the gravel bank in his effort to land it without an adequate landing net. This was followed by the sight of the rod rest silhouetted against the morning sun, battering down, driven through some misguided primitive instinct. Instantly the doubts vanished. Unquestionably there was a need for the PAC. Specialist angling was on the increase; so, inevitably, was pike fishing, with or without the PAC. This in turn meant there was a need for education, a need to teach the newcomers how to handle pike and how to return them in the condition they were caught. How else could the pike's right to remain alive, so as to continue performing the function that nature intended as both a quality and quantity controller, be protected?

The PAC policy and aims are not a contradiction. Perhaps one day it will not be needed except as a social club, but, then as now, it performed a vital role in the protection and conservation of what is probably our most important freshwater fish. After that, the first committee hand-over of the benevolent dictatorship known as the PAC from the hands of the founders (to whom all pike anglers will always be deeply indebted) is now history. Martyn found extremely willing volunteers in Vic and John Watson and the club continued to grow in strength and structure. Two more committees on, the PAC flourishes, with a larger membership, healthy balance sheet and, most important, respect from the angling world. Pike angling continues to increase in popularity, but the need for conservation is well voiced.

The PAC has naturally had its problems. Not always have members, or at times the committee, seen eye to eye. That is only to be expected in the growth and life of any organisation, but the cause will always reign supreme. Nowadays the PAC can reflect on many successes – such as reversals and prevention of livebait bans, influencing fishery management policies and the development of pike fisheries – and it is pleasing to note that during its existence it has had few wounds to lick.

We can all look at the PAC with pride but must never become complacent, for just round the corner some misguided individual may be ready to campaign for bans on livebaits or to promote senseless pike killing.

The aims and objectives of the PAC are therefore quite obvious. First, there is the promotion of pike angling, and coupled to this is education in correct pike-angling techniques, with the utmost regard to the care of the pike. These main aims form the reason why all caring pike anglers should join and support the cause. At the time of writing (September 1989) a new committee has taken over the PAC for the next four years. Full details about the club, membership subscriptions, and so on, can be obtained from Neville Fickling, Kilgarth, 27 Lodge Lane, Upton, Gainsborough, Lincolnshire.

Obviously we wholeheartedly endorse PAC policies which are based on sound common sense. At times, however, we hear of and see some very extreme attitudes being applied to

Past bad handling – shown by the state of the tail and the descaled flanks – detracted from Martyn's pleasure in the capture of this 25-pounder.

pike angling and we must question the wisdom of such extremism. We also question some current 'conservation' practices. We outline below our own opinions on the good handling and care of pike, highlighting those aspects which we find disturbing.

PIKE REMOVAL

It makes good sense to return all pike to the water in virtually all circumstances. Indeed, we can see no logical reason for removing and killing large pike. To remove such fish in any number from the water will almost certainly result in a future predator–prey imbalance and

an explosion of jack pike. To remove and kill such fish completely lacks sense. Quality fish are at a premium and would quickly be snapped up for stocking in managed pike fisheries. If large pike must be removed from a water because of some misguided fishery management policy then at least let them be saved and transferred to another water – provided it has adequate stocks of prey fish.

In contrast there are many occasions when small pike should be removed from a water. This does not necessarily mean killed, though it can often prove difficult to find a home for small pike. Pike anglers should not become too upset where a policy of removing small pike is carefully applied in a controlled manner to a water which is overrun with jack pike. Careful thinning of the stocks should improve the ultimate quality of the pike fishing and the fishery as a whole.

On an individual basis, it is well known that in the past pike were often taken for the pot or for setting up in a glass case. We do not particularly criticise the occasional small fish being taken for eating. Fortunately, this is not a common practice; the flavour is nothing special, with a distinctly muddy taste. We would not wish to encourage this practice and would frown on the t·'.ing of large pike for eating, but we would not become unduly upset if we heard of a small pike being taken for this purpose. In contrast, the killing of a good fish for setting up is a totally different matter. As already mentioned, the large fish help control the numbers of smaller predators in a balanced fishery. The removal of any large fish threatens this balance. As the glass-case specimen will inevitably be one of the water's better fish, the fishery will suffer as a result of one person's thoughtless action. If everyone were to take just one such glass-case specimen the effect of the removal of thousands of twenty-pound pike from our waters would clearly be quite disastrous. The recovery of our fisheries would take years. We can really see no justification for setting up a healthy specimen pike when it is so quick and easy to take a photograph.

PHOTOGRAPHY – AN ACCEPTABLE FORM OF PRESERVATION

Quite naturally we all want to preserve the memory of a particularly good fish. The camera really is the pike's saviour in this respect, capturing its portrait whilst the fish lives on.

There are, however, some very important ground rules which should carefully be practised with regard to fish photography, for the sake of the well-being of the fish. So often the result of taking a photograph is a badly damaged fish. Pike in particular can suffer at

this stage. They are big, long fish and at times can prove difficult to control, especially to those not experienced in handling them.

Let us assume you have just caught a large pike. In the first instance, if it really must be retained for any reason keep it only for the minimum amount of time and use one of the specialist pike sacks or tubes available nowadays – the larger the better. Keep the fish in the sack only while the camera equipment is being set up or until the light improves. Better still, carry a flash-gun and eliminate bad light as a reason for sacking fish.

When it comes to holding the fish, as with unhooking, do not be scared. It can do you little damage. First, ensure that the area where it is going to removed from the landing net, or sack, is soft damp grass, not brambles, stones or concrete. If the banks are hard, or you are boat

A giant fish lies on the soft carpeting of the boat.

fishing, take along some soft carpet, underlay or a specialist unhooking mat (available from most tackle shops).

If the fish has been in the sack remember that it will have had time to recover from its capture and will be considerably more lively and diffi-cult to control – another reason for taking photos quickly and returning the fish at once. If it has been retained it is sometimes best to stand for a minute holding the sack with the fish still inside, so allowing it to expend some of its energy in safety, where it can do little damage to itself, before it is removed for photography.

Resist at all costs the temptation of bag shots. Several pike together in a sack will cause damage to one another and as soon as you at-tempt to line up the fish on the ground inevi-tably damage will occur as one or the other thrashes or jumps.

Before removing the fish from the sack or landing net, prepare the area of bank where it is

We do not believe in bag shots but this catch of three twenties by Steve Harper is an exception – they were caught in the space of five minutes.

Modern retaining sacks should not be used to keep fish for long periods – only until the camera is made ready.

to be laid, then set up the camera so that the fish will be out of the water for a minimum period. If you are with a partner things are obviously easier, since he will be doing the focusing, framing and shooting while you hold the fish. If you often fish by yourself and want photos, other than of fish lying on the ground beside a pair of scales, it will be necessary to acquire a bulb release system and either an ex-pensive tripod or a bank stick with a camera adapter, which is much less expensive. All this must be set up before the fish is removed from the water. The camera should be focused at the spot where you will be holding the fish and, as a handy tip, if you insert a landing net pole at that spot, focus on the pole and frame the pic-ture around the pole. Then crouch next to the which the fish could kick out of your hands and fall to the ground.

The vertical format picture is the easier in this respect. It requires holding the fish either behind the jaw or actually using the inside of the jaw via the junction of the gill clefts as a handhold (in the same way as we later describe for unhooking). The fish is then held across your body while you crouch or kneel and the tail can even rest on the ground. Quite impressive photos can be obtained in this way yet the fish is never far from the ground and is supported by your body. If it does kick it can quickly be lowered to safety.

The horizontal format effectively involves holding the fish under, and to the back of the head with one hand whilst the other hand is placed under the fish around the anal fin, preferably with your arm also being used as a support behind the tail. In this way the fish is presented sideways on to the camera without its body sagging or the tail flipping round. If

A 23-pounder captured by Dave Humphries is carefully rested on a wet sack and damp grass . . .

pole in order to determine the correct framing of the picture so that your head, the fish's tail and snout are all included. Once set up and ready with the fish, the pole can quickly be removed and cast aside. With care a good picture can be taken in this way and after each picture the fish can be lowered to the ground and covered with the sack while the film is quickly wound on.

Holding the pike for photographing requires great care. There are two ways in which this can be achieved, one providing a horizontal and the other a vertical frame. Never hold pike far from the ground and certainly never stand up holding a fish, so that if the pike does begin to get out of control, twisting or kicking, it can be gently lowered to the ground without damage. There should be no circumstances in

. . . before being carefully supported for the camera.

you hold the fish in this way you can employ two positive alternatives if the fish kicks. As with the vertical method, the pike can be lowered gently to the ground, or it is easy to bring the hands round under the belly and grip the fish firmly, so smothering its kicks and preventing it from leaping from your hands.

Both methods become slighty more complicated in a boat. If you are wary of attempting to photograph a fish in a boat then you should make for the nearest bank, not towing the fish behind the boat in a sack but with the fish lying safely on the damp carpet or underlay in the bottom of the boat and well wrapped in a wet keepsack. In this way it will not be able to damage itself and you will be able to row quickly to the bank. Towing can cause damage to the fish; if it is towed for a considerable distance it could even be drowned by water passing through its gills in the reverse of the normal direction.

For photographing the fish in the boat the same principles apply. It is necessary to hold the fish firmly and confidently, not to be scared, and to be decisive when the fish kicks. Once again, do not stand with the fish in the boat; it causes instability. Preferably, sit on a seat and drape the fish across your body so that your body acts as a cushion. Again, this can be achieved both in the horizontal and vertical format. Boats tend to be small and therefore your partner may experience difficulty in framing the shot to get in both you and the pike. This is where a wide-angle lens is an essential asset and should always be carried if you wish to obtain good boat pictures of large pike.

Most pike fishing is undertaken in winter, in poor light. Flash is essential not only for night shots but also for fill-in flash, to enhance a picture during poor light and to enable a picture to be taken during early morning or late evening. As light values are often poor, try using a faster film in winter. At one time fast film produced very grainy pictures, particularly in black and white, but nowadays it is possible to use 400 ASA film and still obtain high-quality pictures with clear definition.

Beware of bright sunny days and shadows when taking pictures of pike. If you meter on a shaded area, there will be a danger of taking a false light reading, which could lead to an over-exposed picture, resulting in the body detail being burnt out and vice versa. In such circumstances shutting down the camera one stop will cut out more of the bright light, darken the back and protect the belly, often giving quite a stark contrast to the picture. It requires a little thought to ensure that you are not misled by the camera's light meter readings and it may pay to take a few shots at different settings around those indicated by the camera.

The modern 'do-it-all' cameras can give problems with fish photography, not only on bright days but also when a picture is being taken with water in the background. The light bouncing from the water can deceive the camera into giving a false reading. As the camera does not indicate the correct exposure you might find that the resulting picture is under-exposed and very dark. Again, it is worth taking several pictures at varied settings to overcome such problems. More expensive models, of course, have manual override. Even on fully automatic cameras, exposures can be bracketed: simply alter the film speed setting by one stop in either direction.

Good fish photography can be achieved only through constant practice and experimentation. If you have one of the modern auto-focus 35 mm cameras this becomes even more essential, otherwise all you will produce are mediocre pictures. Auto-focus cameras can, however, produce some tremendous action shots.

Simple tips, such as to meter and focus on the fish, are most important. Pike are long fish, and in winter when wide apertures may make depth of field short, if one is not careful not all of the fish will be in focus. This is particularly the case with vertically framed shots. In these instances focus on the middle of the fish so that there is a maximum chance of both head and tail being in focus. The lack of depth of field so often encountered in winter can be used to advantage to blur the background if only fish and angler are actually within the depth of field. The result will be that both angler and fish will be vividly accentuated against an out-of-focus background.

It is not our intention to give an A to Z of how to use a camera. Initially we would recommend careful study of this camera's manual. Our intention is to show that a little bit more thought is perhaps necessary with fish photography than more normal scenic shots. For instance, once you are experienced at the usual 'mug' shots, more unusual angles can be attempted and spectacular effects can be obtained through filters.

One of the most common mistakes in fish photography is the actual framing of the shot. Too much background seldom adds to the picture. Frame the shot to fill the picture with the subject. Make sure that horizons are level, in particular that the water horizon is not angled in such a way that it appears that the water is ready to pour downhill out of one side of the picture.

A little extra thought goes a long way to achieving better than average results. However, at all times it is essential to consider the welfare of the pike. Under no circumstances should a photograph session jeopardise the life of the fish in the slightest. Just apply basic ground rules. Prepare everything first, decide what shots you would like, only then get the fish out of the water and finally take the pictures as quickly as possible, handling the fish with care whilst denying her the sanctuary of water for as brief a period as possible.

TACKLE AND CONSERVATION

The care of pike, through good angling, commences long before a fish arrives on the bank.

It is necessary to consider carefully the tackle being used and to be sure that it can cope adequately with the situation, not just to ensure that the majority of hooked fish will be landed but to guarantee that they will *all* reach the net. We can see absolutely no justification for using light lines in pike fishing. At times one sees advocates of light-tackle pike fishing writing in the angling press. The articles usually highlight the sport and extra fight resulting from such light tackle but rarely do they mention fish lost through line breaking, or light wire parting. What happens to those fish, trailing terminal tackle, with a mouth full of hooks? In all honesty we would not recommend line under 11lb BS and we would only use such 'light' line in snag-free swims in conjunction with fixed-spool reels. Most of our fishing, however, is done with multipliers and in virtually all circumstances we use 15lb Sylcast. This is a line which has a bit of a 'tow-rope' reputation but that is precisely why we use it. It is strong, tough, abrasion-resistant and reliable.

Similarly, when it comes to wire traces there are many good-quality pike wires available nowadays, but for pike fishing we can see no reason to risk using wire of 15lb BS. Once a kink or a slight twist appears in the wire (which may happen unknown to the angler even as a result of livebait movement) it can be severely weakened. In most circumstances we use 20lb wire, but will upgrade this to 28lb BS in particularly snaggy waters on deep lakes or where exceptionally large pike may be encountered. We have sometimes seen it advocated that the lighter tackle will deceive more pike. We can honestly say that we have not found this to be the case and in any event the well-being of the pike must take prime consideration. What is the point in deceiving a pike to take your bait only to lose it, perhaps signing its death warrant?

Rods

With regard to conservation we have little to say about rods. Balanced tackle is important and thus it is obviously ludicrous to use a very powerful rod with a light line. For most of our pike fishing a rod of about 2½lb test curve is adequate. We have no room for bean-poles of

3½lb test curve, as are sometimes recommended. We can only see such rods leading to problems for the inexperienced pike angler when he strikes too hard, with the possibility of cracking off even on 11lb line. By using a rod of 2½/2¾lb test curve rod (the best we have found to date is the Daiwa Whisker) with 11–15lb line we are, if anything, erring towards an imbalance in favour of the line, which provides added security against line breaks.

Traces

Fine attention to detail is nowhere more essential than at the trace itself. Nowadays it is possible to purchase a number of specialist manufactured traces which are perfectly adequate, having been produced in consultation with experienced pike anglers. There is, however, atrocious tackle still on the market. Ideally, a trace should be at least 20 inches long. Too short a trace runs the risk that the line itself may encounter the pike's teeth, with the obvious results.

It is also important to consider the distance between hooks when using a standard tandem treble-hook rig (snap tackle). This distance should not be too great. For instance, never should one hook be in the tail of a deadbait and the other reach right to the head end. Obviously, some adustment for bait sizes is desirable but ideally from 1½ to 2 inches will cover most circumstances with average-sized baits. If the gap is too large and a pike picks up a bait and begins to swallow at once, inevitably one hook will soon be well down its throat and the pike deeply hooked.

Many anglers use a trace with an adjustable second treble hook. We are not in favour of such a system as if a hook can slide down the wire it will kink it badly, making for weakness. This could shorten the life of the trace and cause breakages. In addition, the sliding action can absorb the strike, leading to less efficient hooking. We prefer fixed hooks. The only disadvantage is that if you are constantly changing bait sizes it is necessary to have a supply of traces with slightly varied gaps between the hooks. A compromise can be achieved by allowing the second hook to slide. A crimp is threaded on the trace between the hooks and can be fixed at the desired distance. The second hook then rests against the crimp. This requires a special treble hook with a second eye along the shank. This treble cannot slide down the trace any farther once the crimp is fixed, so any possibility of kinking is eliminated. Such traces are marketed by Middy Floats Ltd.

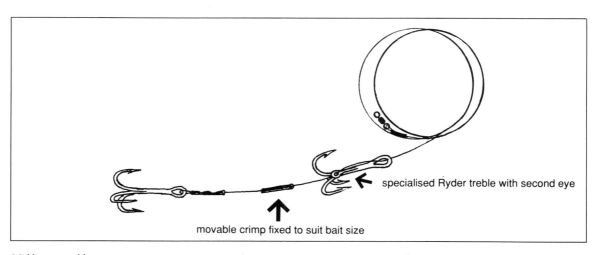

specialised Ryder treble with second eye

movable crimp fixed to suit bait size

Middy snap tackle.

Hooks

Looking back to the days of Alfred Jardine, his snap tackle now appears a crude object. Let us not forget, however, that it was made from products available at the time, when attitudes towards pike were different. Nowadays we are more enlightened. Or are we? A standard pike trace still consists of two treble hooks. That adds up to six prongs for hooking purposes. Admittedly two are used to retain the bait but in few other forms of fishing do we need so many hooks. Tradition dictates the use of a treble hook and English anglers are very loath to recognise improvements in this respect. For example, in Europe and America it was quickly realised that the double hook, designed by Vic, was sufficient in most circumstances. Fortunately, English anglers are converting to the use of the double hook and are beginning to appreciate that they hook just as many fish and unquestionably less damage occurs inside the pike's mouth, both in terms of hookholds and during unhooking.

There are circumstances when extra hooking power may be needed and, having recognised the reluctance of many anglers to switch completely to double hooks, Martyn spent

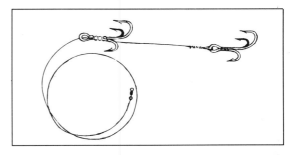

Pike trace incorporating Martyn's MP treble hooks.

some considerable time designing improvements to the old grapnel-style treble hook. His conclusions were that the baitholder did not need to be so large and the three prongs did not need an equal angle between them (120°). Reducing the angle of the two main hooking prongs to around 60° resulted in a hook in which the two hooking prongs stand prouder of the bait, which provides for more efficient hooking. In addition, because they are closer together it is obvious that if one hook prong is turned free from the flesh of the fish during unhooking the other, being more or less in line, will follow more easily. This has resulted in much easier unhooking. This MP Treble, marketed under the Marvic name, has proved

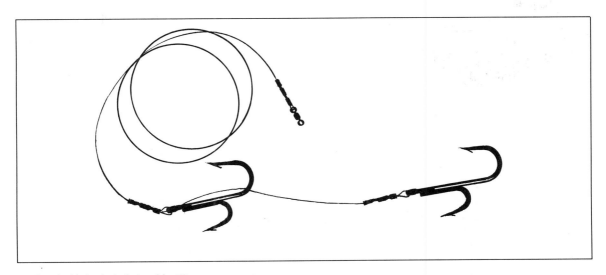

Modern double-hook rig designed by Vic.

to have the following qualities: better hooking, more efficient and quicker striking, and easier unhooking. For the conservation-minded pike angler there are now two choices of hook other than the standard treble, both of which go a very long way along the conservation road.

Hook sizes are also important. In America we were shown hooks large enough to land shark and were told that they were the standard musky and pike hooks – truly barbaric and unnecessary. Most modern lures, being imported from America, also contain hooks far too large, which will unquestionably cause damage to small pike twisting on the lure. Unfortunately, replacing them with smaller hooks may affect the action of the lure (this is discussed in Part Four). Modern live- and deadbaiting, however, can easily be practised with hooks of more sensible size. If you are using six prongs there is little point in using extra-large hooks. Surely one of those prongs will find a hold, even if the hooks are only size 8. Indeed, there are very few situations where hook sizes bigger than 6 are necessary, the ideal hooks being size 8 and 6, depending on bait size.

The question of barbless or barbed hooks has been much debated. First, we must say that we use hooks without barbs, except for the baitholder. We have fished barbless hooks or hooks with the barbs crushed for years and we cannot recall losing fish as a result. In addition, unhooking is certainly far easier and causes less damage than with barbed hooks. There is, however, one argument in favour of barbed hooks. We consider that far too many anglers use barbless hooks as a licence to delay the strike on the ground that if the hooks are easier to remove they can leave the take just a little longer and make sure they get the fish. This is totally misguided and as bad as the age-old concept of lighting and smoking a cigarette before striking. Under no circumstances should the strike be delayed just because the hooks are barbless. The easiest hook to remove from a pike is one in the front of its jaw, usually in the corner of its mouth, and it will do far less damage in this position than down its stomach.

A STRIKE AGAINST DEEP HOOKING

It is, of course, possible to strike too soon – for example, an instant strike may not set the hooks, when a very large bait is used. But it is nearly impossible to strike instantly in any event. Usually the take is indicated by a float or drop-off indicator and the time it takes to pick up the rod and tighten down to the fish is more than adequate. There is no need for a further ten-second delay, or the three or four minutes which we have seen some 'experienced' pike men wait before striking. The strike itself should not be violent or erratic. The line should be tightened until the fish is felt and then a good firm draw followed by maintained pressure is usually enough either to set the hooks or to allow them to sink deep as the pike reacts to line pressure ('kicking the hooks home'). There has been considerable debate as to when the hooks do eventually bite home. Some say it is not until the fish opens its mouth in an endeavour to eject the bait, and also that the hooks cannot be drawn home while the bait is clamped between the jaws. Others say this is nonsense. It probably varies greatly from fish to fish, depending on where and how the pike is holding the bait, how the hooks are positioned in the bait and whether one has been dislodged on the cast, or when the pike

Modern treble and double hooks.

grabs the bait, and many other factors. Sometimes the hook will go home immediately on striking, sometimes it may not take hold until later during the fight (whence the logic for always maintaining steady pressure on the fish). At other times the hook actually finds a hold when the pike itself strikes the bait. Whatever the circumstances, a firm, slow, but positive draw into the fish will do little harm and will avoid some of the break-offs we have seen from erratic hard striking.

HAIRS

Hair rigs appear to be in vogue with some pike anglers but personally we have not found an occasion where a hair rig has proved to be of particular value in pike fishing. We have tied eel sections direct to a hook, not for the specific purpose of using a hair rig but to ensure that the hook will pull straight from the light hair line as opposed to being embedded in a hard-skinned section of eel. In this way we have been able to fish single hooks with small eel sections. Our biggest fear with hair rigs for pike is the increased possibility of deep hooking. If hair rigs are used we suggest that there is no need for anything other than a single hook and we would maintain that the same philosophy of tightening down and striking as soon as a take is detected is even more critical. Certainly, the idea that 'it will take a little longer to get the hook in the mouth' is a recipe for deep hooking.

In other chapters we discuss the various rigs and highlight some of their deficiencies. We also discuss rigs designed to overcome bite-offs, which seem to be an old phenomenon, now reborn. We do not therefore propose to go into such rigs in any depth in this chapter. Needless to say, however, some thought should always be given to the rig or tackle being used and whether it can cause unnecssary harm to a pike. For instance, if you can't see a float because of poor light or wind, it should be changed to one you can see so that you can detect a take. It

certainly should not be fished blind. Merely waiting for the line to start peeling from the spool is foolhardy, for by then the pike may be hooked deeply. If you are constantly getting bite-offs or line breakages there is obviously something wrong and you should not continue fishing in such a way. Think the problem through and find a solution.

LANDING

When it comes to landing the fish, tradition handed down from generation to generation has advocated the use of a gaff. Nowadays, thankfully, such implements are few and far between, though only days before we wrote this Martyn witnessed the capture of a beautifully conditioned twenty marred only by an ugly great gash from an obviously recent bad gaffing attempt. Originally the gaff was not

Steve Harper displays the damaged jaw caused by some previously gaff-mad 'angler'.

thought particularly barbaric, because the fish was going to be killed quickly after landing. Nowadays, when pike are put back as quickly as possible, large knotless nets are the order of the day and in most circumstances these are perfectly adequate. On occasions, however, a pike will be drawn to the bank, or the boat, with loose flying trebles which have failed to find a hookhold. Sometimes it is possible to scoop a smaller pike out by hand by placing the fingers under the gill cover. The fish can then be unhooked with forceps as it is held over the water and returned without it ever having to come onto the bank or into the boat. With this procedure there is no danger of flying hooks catching in the net and causing damage to a twisting pike. But one must be wary as there is always a danger of the flying hooks becoming impaled in hand or arm if a pike suddenly twists or kicks. Lifting pike by hand is a method which requires not a little confidence and some degree of experience. If you are not confident in handling pike in this way or the fish is particularly large then by all means use the net. Do not lift the net in as soon as a fish is netted as inevitably the flying hooks will catch the netting. Instead, net the fish and then slowly draw the net up round the fish while attempting to keep the flying hooks away from the mesh until the fish is in the bottom. At least the pike will not end up dangling from the top of the net, suspended by an entrapped treble, as the net is lifted. It is not a perfect solution but at least a little care and thought minimises possible

Small pike can often be unhooked over the side of the boat.

damage. Beaching the fish may be an alternative but this should not be done on concrete reservoirs or gravel bottoms. The damage caused by dragging the fish along such surface is likely to be worse than any caused by a flying treble caught in the net.

Inevitably, in lure fishing, there will be flying trebles. Many lure anglers use large-mesh nets rather than the more popular smaller meshes. Unfortunately, they are usually of the knotted variety, but unquestionably they are less prone to problems from flying lure trebles. Perhaps one day we will see a net with a fine-mesh bottom and a very large but knotless mesh on the sides. Certainly, there is room for experimentation along these lines to see if improvements can be made. Incidentally, we have no particular recommendation with regard to triangular or round nets, though we slightly prefer triangular for pike and other long fish, where the head can be drawn right to the apex before netting, and round nets for more rounded, fat fish, such as carp.

GHOSTS BY THE RODS

Before considering the problem which causes perhaps the most concern to the less experienced pike angler, the question of unhooking, we must strongly criticise the practice which, although constantly condemned, never seems to change. This is the question of close attendance to the rods at all times. In a boat this problem doesn't arise, for you can't simply get up and go for a walk, unless you can walk on water or are kitted with an oxygen tank and wetsuit. So the rods are closely attended, no matter how many rods are fished, and there is little danger of a take going unheeded. On the other hand, on the bank there is a strong temptation to go for a wander, to talk to one's mates, when there hasn't been a take for an hour or so. The attitude appears to be that during the five-minute chat there can hardly be a take because there hasn't been one in the last hour. If the truth is known it is probably more

likley that one will occur but, take or not, such a practice is totally inexcusable. If your mate is only three yards away all well and good, but if he is a hundred yards down the bank there is absolutely no way you could get back to the rod before the pike has swallowed the bait. Such behaviour is tantamout to gorge baiting. The fact that one has a loud electronic bite indicator which will signal the take makes no difference. It is still necessary to get to the rod to make the strike.

Similarly, the practice of staggering rods along a hundred yards or more of bank is quite unacceptable. If it is considered necessary to have one bait a hundred yards along the bank from the other it can be achieved in two ways. One is to move to that swim. The other is to cast one bait into the other swim and then place that rod near to your other rod, so at least you can attend all the rods at all times.

If you wish to socialise without endangering the fish then fish close together. If there is any need to leave your rods for any reason, it will only be for a matter of seconds and they can be looked after by your friends. In all other circumstances baits should be reeled in and removed from the water.

On one occasion on the Thurne at Martham, Martyn saw the bank lined from Dungeon Corner to the Ferry with rods, but not one angler was in sight. No wonder several big pike have died in that system in recent years through deep hooking!

UNHOOKING

Just a Little Nick, or Two!

It was a very typical pikey day in October, the sort when pike feed hard for long periods. On this occasion, Vic and I couldn't fish, even though pike were being caught all over the Broad. We had agreed to be stewards for a boat pike-fishing match. I am not sure that such events should be promoted but this one was out of our hands and naturally the local PAC volunteered its services when asked, for the sake of the pike.

So on this particular day Vic and I rowed up and down the Broad, providing assistance as necessary, weighing fish, verifying captures and ensuring that the pike were returned unharmed.

By mid-afternoon a strong wind was blowing across the Broad and as we laboured once more against this wind we noticed a young lad hook into a fish. Being close at hand, we rowed over to offer assistance. The lad managed quite well, eventually subduing and landing a small pike. His father shared the boat and it was obvious he was no angler. It was also apparent that neither had any experience of unhooking pike. We arrived just in time to show them how it was done.

Our boat brushed alongside and Vic quickly offered his services while I stowed the oars. Now small pike are notorious for their antics and this one was no exception. The young lad and his father looked on in awe as Vic expertly guided his finger behind the gill cover and lifted the pike from the landing net. Vic made ready to demonstrate a quick unhooking, not so much to impress the young lad but to show him how easily it could and should be done. However, the best laid plans do not always work. At the critical moment the small pike kicked, managing to fly from Vic's finger, somersault, and then, with mouth open, land back on his finger, its teeth clamping hard and penetrating deeply.

It all happened in a matter of seconds. Father and son looked on in amazement, first shocked,

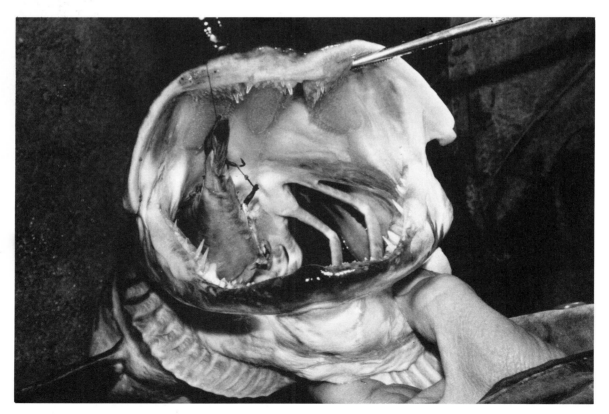

The jaws of a pike appear formidable to the inexperienced. Confidence is the key to efficient unhooking, though quick strikes will prevent deep hooking with all but the greediest of pike.

then horrified. Then the pike released its grip. Instantly a fountain of blood cascaded across the boat, spraying everything in sight. Vic was quick to react. He lifted his finger high into the air and waved it about frantically, reassuring the aghast anglers with such comments as 'No need to worry!' and 'It's just a little nick, it doesn't hurt.' Meanwhile, the blood fountain continued to leap across to the next boat, splattering the floor, tackle and anglers alike. The young lad's face turned snow-white and his dad's mouth gaped open at the sight of the ever-increasing carpet of blood. Vic continued to wave and spray! In order to stem the flow I passed a handkerchief to Vic, which he wrapped around his finger. Within seconds it turned from white to deep red. I doubt whether that young lad was ever allowed, or indeed had enough courage, to fish for pike again.

Accidents do happen; that is an inevitable fact of life. When handling pike one is unhooking a fish well endowed with razor-sharp teeth. Even if the fish were dead there would be a risk of sustaining a cut finger. But even a cut as deep as Vic incurred on that day is only a small wound, little payment for the enjoyment of pike fishing and the knowledge that the fish are carefully handled, properly unhooked and returned in good condition. A pike cut may bleed profusely for a few minutes, that is inevitable with a clean cut in cold conditions, but it is rare that a pike inflicts serious wounds during the course of unhooking. The majority of the cuts will indeed be little nicks or grazes.

The greatest cause of damage to pike and angler during the act of unhooking is the angler's own wariness of those teeth. If you are scared and hesitate at the start, problems may occur. There is nothing difficult about the operation. First, the pike is removed from the net and laid on soft damp ground, better an unhooking mat, or on the carpet or underlay on the bottom of the boat. The fish can be wrapped in a wet keepsack, with just the head exposed. This does help to quieten a lively fish. The pike can then be straddled with knees either side of its body to restrain its move-

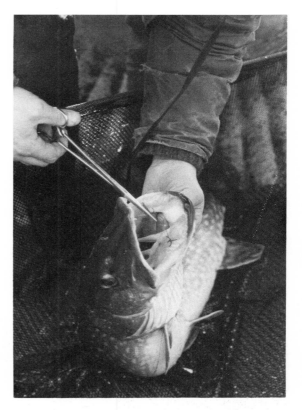

With the fish supported correctly, the hooks are easily and quickly removed.

ments. It is usually best to have the fish on its side or on its back. Then carefully insert a finger into the gill cover (Vic now uses a plastic finger stall) taking care not to touch the gill rakers until the V-bone of the bottom jaw is felt. This is very much like the bone at the bottom of your chin. Gentle upward pressure exerted at this point will cause the pike to open its mouth. Then, with a long pair of forceps, the hooks can usually be removed through the mouth.

Inevitably there will be odd occasions when a fish is more deeply hooked. The procedure for unhooking is much the same in this instance except that you will find it is easier to unhook the fish via the gill covers themselves. In this case the finger is used in the same way, but then the forceps are carefully inserted through the gill cover and between the gill rakers. Now

Correct unhooking procedure, with fish on soft protective matting.

the hooks can be reached with ease, even when far back in the throat, and, once free, they can be gently pulled out through the mouth. Alternatively, pull them carefully through the gill cover and detach the line from the trace to complete the operation. With the forceps clamped onto it, a hook can be turned upside down (reversed), which is a cleaner and neater method than pushing and pulling.

If the fish is very deeply hooked it can usually be unhooked if gentle pressure is applied to the line. Usually the flesh at the back of the throat and beginning of the stomach will fold out on itself exposing the hooks, which can then be released with forceps by the through-the-gill-cover method.

In the past the generally accepted unhooking tool was a gag, which forced the pike's mouth wide open, then the hooks were removed by a sharp-pointed black metal pike disgorger. We cannot condemn the use of such methods; they were all they had then. Nowadays, the metal disgorger has virtually disappeared and gags

have changed. The original gag had vicious spikes and a 'jaw-breaker' action. Many small pike must have had their jaw dislocated and the inside of the mouth badly mutilated by these instruments, but then most pike were killed. Today caring tackle shop proprietors sell a more humane version of the gag which does not have such spikes. We still do not recommend the use of any type of gag, as it is an inefficient instrument. By all means take the gag with you and, until you have established confidence with the correct method, use the gag only as a last resort. It is far better to use a gag than to leave hooks in a pike through fear or inability to unhook the fish. Nevertheless, we do think that even beginners should quickly acquaint themselves with the correct procedure. This will ensure quicker unhooking with fewer problems and less damage.

Some people use a glove on the unhooking hand in order to avoid cuts and grazes caused by the minor teeth at the back of the pike's upper jaw. It is true that a gloved hand does help avoid cuts, but an uncovered finger is more sensitive and less likely to cause accidental damage to the pike's gill rakers. Therefore we are not in favour of using a glove. An alternative is to use a finger stall, which are available from most chemists and offer more sensitivity than a gloved hand.

It is often recommended that if a fish kicks or jumps while your finger is inserted in the gill cover you should hang on at all costs. This is unwise. As soon as a fish starts to become uncontrollable your hand should be quickly removed. This will avoid damage. The fish cannot damage itself; it is on soft ground, it should be wrapped in the soft wet sack, and it is restrained between your knees. If, on the other hand, you hang on as the fish twists and thrashes, your fingers will take a battering. At the same time a great deal of pressure will be exerted on the pike's jawbone and severe damage could occur. We have seen people hanging on at all costs, even with fish lifted off the ground. This resulted in a tearing sound indicating jaw damage, followed by the fish

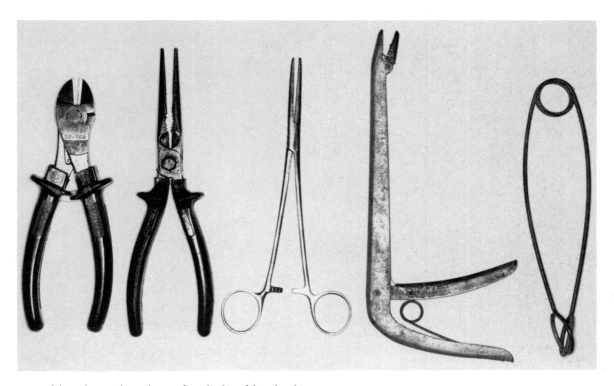

Some of the tools one pike angler uses for unhooking fish and making traces.

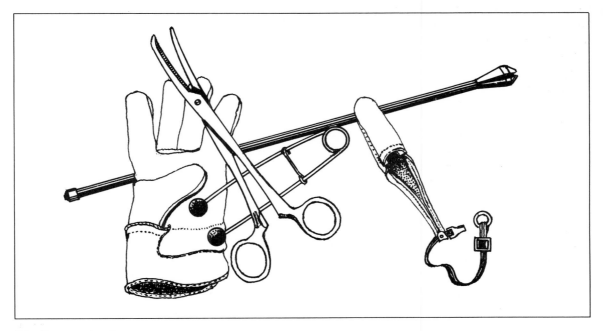

The pike surgeon's tools.

escaping the hold and falling to the ground, suffering further damage. We have seen this on several occasions and although we cannot be sure how much damage is caused when the tearing occurs it is obviously unacceptable. Such damage is more likely to occur if the fish is held off the ground without some support. This is particularly relevant when a fish is supported through the gill cover for photography. There should be some other support; for example, you can rest it along your body as you kneel down as described above. From this position it can quickly be lowered to the ground if it begins to twist.

Hooks can be removed more easily from a fish if the line is held taut while they are twisted free. This is easy when two anglers are involved, as one can hold the line while the other operates the forceps and holds the mouth open. If, however, you are by yourself the operation is slightly more complicated. If you hold the line or trace between your teeth you can usually apply enough tension and this leaves your two hands free.

Some people use a modern 'deep throat' pike disgorger to remove the hooks from deeply hooked pike. We have not found these to be any more efficient than the methods described, though anglers with limited pike-fishing experience might find them a useful additional unhooking tool. Those just taking up pike angling or those who feel relatively inexperienced at unhooking might feel more confident with this type of disgorger, provided this does not become an excuse for delaying the strike and relying on the instrument to remove deep-set hooks. The best cure for deep hooking is prevention of the problem in the first place, so strike quickly.

WEIGHING

Once it is unhooked, you may wish to weigh the pike, and perhaps take a photograph or two, before it is returned. Numerous good weigh slings made of soft nylon are available

Always use a purpose-made weigh sling; never hook the scales under the jaw.

nowadays. The sling should always be wetted before the fish is placed in it, in order to reduce any chance of slime or scale removal. Buy a large sling, capable of handling the largest pike you may catch. Unfortunately, we consider that very few of the designs available at present are suitable. We still use slings which were originally designed by John Watson and Martyn and once sold by the PAC, but these are no longer available. Possibly the best currently in production is the ET sling, which is of adequate size and slightly banana-shaped. It is best to avoid any sling which curls the fish up or bends its back in any way, so always lay the fish on its side rather than on its stomach or back. This will assist in avoiding undue stress. Remember that the fish is out of the water, out of its natural environment, so care is essential. Always use a weigh sling, regardless of the size of the fish. The practice of suspending fish with the scale hook inserted under the jaw does cause damage as the fish can so easily twist itself off. There is no excuse for this method today.

FREEDOM

Finally, when returning the fish, gently lower it into the water, allowing the pike to make its own way. On no account should a fish be tossed or thrown back. If the fish shows any signs of stress at this stage do not leave it but hold it gently upright until it recovers. It will usually quickly regain enough strength to swim away. However, if it is left and turns belly uppermost there is a danger that it will not survive. It seems that some instinct tells a fish that it is dying if it cannot turn upright.

We have laboured the point on conservation quite deliberately. Increased pressure on our pike stocks as pike angling increases in popularity can only be accommodated through the greater care of our fish. Without it the average size of pike in our fisheries will inevitably decline.

Fortunately, there is increasing evidence that things can be viewed optimistically. The incidence of repeat captures of big fish (Dora, the Thurne monster, for instance) shows that large fish, as well as small, do not particularly suffer through capture if handled by caring anglers. Remember, it is the big fish that are most likely to be damaged because more handling is involved. The fish will be weighed, photographed, and admired – and a twenty-pound fish gets heavy to hold after a while.

In addition, it is obvious that as angling pressure begins to affect any water it can lead to diminished returns. The result is that angling pressure then eases as anglers leave in search of new pastures and the latest 'in' water. With neglect the pike fishery thrives and within a few years the water will recover, perhaps ultimately to surpass its previous glory. Thus, to a degree, pike angling on a water is regulated by a balanced equation between pike anglers and pike stocks. However, we cannot become complacent because of this. As we have mentioned elsewhere in this book, England is only a small island and the upsurge in popularity in fishing will affect us all. Foreseeing this, the PAC has for many years encouraged the acquisition and management of fisheries for pike fishing; this is considered in the next chapter.

Martyn lovingly returns another big one.

25

Man-Made Pike Fisheries

Possibly 'man-made pike fishery' is something of a misnomer. A good pike fishery is virtually always a good general fishery. With careful management coupled with pike conservation all fisheries become managed pike fisheries. We can assist but we cannot create a pike fishery where there are no food fish. We can change the average weight of pike in a fishery, for better or worse. We can overfill a fishery with pike and enjoy superb sport in the short term and a rapid decline in the long term. Fishery management is a specialised practice. It should be undertaken with care, with an understanding of the biomass equations and of the pyramid theories on predator–prey relationships, and an appreciation that by tampering with any balance, on any water, unexpected results can arise.

The natural inclination when setting up a new pike fishery is to obtain as many fish, and preferably big ones, as possible, and then continue to fill the water with quality fish, expecting to create a brilliant pike fishery. In the short term this may work and sport may be hectic as hungry pike feed ravenously on anglers' baits. Inevitably, however, if not enough prey are available those pike will lose weight and the fishery will decline. Constantly topping up the fishery with extra-big fish, to maintain pike anglers' interest, is not the answer. Big fish are at a premium and badly needed in many fisheries which could support them. To put them into a fishery where they are not capable of maintaining their weight is clearly foolhardy.

We are not in favour of completely artificial pike fisheries. We prefer to dream of the unknown, the unexpected and the exciting possibility that a bigger fish may be just round the corner. In a totally artificial fishery all the fish will be known, from the biggest to the smallest. The dates and times of the last capture and their exact weight on each successive capture will be common knowledge. This may also be the case in a natural fishery subject to heavy angling pressure. Fortunately, in Norfok we are blessed with many virgin waters which have never seen a pike bait so our dreams remain intact. We quite appreciate that in parts of the country there is a need for more pike fisheries and the demand, understandably, is for quality fisheries which produce large pike. It becomes generally accepted that each fish is known and as such these 'artificial' managed fisheries do fulfil a function. Whether to fish these fisheries or travel to unknown pastures remains the prerogative of the angler.

How does one change a fishery into a managed pike fishery? First, it is necessary to know the water. We assume that you have gained control of the water and will follow all the formalities with regard to fish stocking. It is essential to gain a knowledge of fish stocks; the water authority may assist with this, or perhaps the local university may be interested in conducting a research project. You need to know something about the present predator populations. It may be necessary to remove substantial numbers of smaller pike in order to replace them with some larger pike. Do not forget, however, that little pike may be an important food source for their elders. It is essential to understand that only so many pike can be supported by the fishery. We make no apologies for labouring this point. No one likes catching underweight, poorly conditioned, emaciated pike. It may be necessary to adopt a policy of removing small pike and occasionally supplementing the stock of quality fish, as there will be some mortalities, as well as providing injections of prey fish as regular intervals. You could even top up with deadbaits if there is a prey deficiency, but this is an extreme policy, expensive and not really sustainable, though stocking with live prey fish does create sport for other anglers.

The fishery will need very strict conservation rules. We strongly recommend that no pike be retained at any time, particularly in the warmer summer and autumn months.

In Martyn and John's book *The Predator Becomes the Prey*, the pyramid theory is examined in order to show how one can find fisheries capable of sustaining extra-large pike. It is essential to appreciate the concept of the pyramid theory. At one time it was considered that a perfectly balanced fishery would have a head of pike of all sizes, but with a smaller number of larger pike. That is to say that there may be 100 small jack pike in a fishery, perhaps 50 fish in the 5–10lb range, 20 double-figure fish and only 2 or 3 over 20lb. A balanced fishery will only hold a head of pike of the total weight which that fishery is capable of supporting. If a few of the larger pike are removed nature's initial reaction is to protect the species, with a resulting increase in the numbers of smaller pike. In time some pike will grow through and the balance may be re-established, though it's rather like a politician's problem when juggling with economics – once out of balance it's almost impossible to return to equilibrium. Normally the total weight of pike the fishery can maintain will remain relatively stable. Cannibalistic predation can affect this slightly, as can any change in balance, such as a sudden fish kill in which large numbers of the prey fish are lost. If there are not outside influences, and if one can ascertain the total weight of pike in the fishery and therefore have some idea of the weight which can be maintained, removing x pounds of small fish and replacing them with the same aggregate weight of larger fish should preserve the natural balance and maintain the equilibrium of the fishery while the pike fishing improves.

Unfortunately, it is not always that easy. The fishery may be capable of sustaining large numbers of small pike by virtue of the size of prey in the water, or, indeed, the size of the water itself. The large pike may have difficulty in maintaining their weight as a result of the energy expended in having to catch large numbers of very small prey fish. It is necessary to work from a base and the theory of total sustainable weight is as good a starting-point as any.

Fishery mangement can be fun. Inevitably, involvement in the creation of a pike fishery soon ties you into the whole concept of running the fishery, with regard to all the species present. Unquestionably more and more man-assisted pike fisheries (for that is a more correct description) will be created to accommodate the continued growth of and interest in pike fishing. Their creation should be encouraged whether you can come to terms with the concept of artificial pike fisheries or not. Carp anglers long ago faced a similar problem with their fisheries. There is, however, something more wild, more rugged about pike fishing and we find it difficult to appreciate catching pike which have been stocked rather than those which are indigenous to a water. These are our personal thoughts but we are fortunate in having a large choice of natural fisheries available to us. Nevertheless, we firmly encourage the development of such fisheries as necessary to meet a growing need. But beware the possibility of things getting out of hand . . .

A DAY ON A 'PIKE FISHERY'

'Halt, where do you think you are going sonny?' a voice boomed out, breaking the tranquillity of the cold November morning.

'Just wandering over to have a look at the lake. I might try a few hours' pike fishing. It's a long time since I fished here,' I replied to the very authoritarian gentleman who had suddenly appeared, barring my path.

'Well, in that case go and join the queue

over at the entrance. You can't come in this way' was his response.

I made my way over in the direction he had pointed and eventually came to an official car park, a great gate and a kiosk, where a queue of some thirty or forty people waited patiently. Could this be the entrance he meant? Surely a lake could not be this popular. I joined the queue, my interest and curiosity now firmly aroused.

Some forty-five minutes later, having watched numbers of people leave and an equal number allowed into the complex, I arrived at the kiosk. The attendant looked at me questioningly and I stuttered and mumbled that I had come for a spot of pike fishing. She merely snapped that that was obvious – why else would I be standing there? But how much did I want? How long? Any preference of swim? One or two rods? I explained that I had just come for a few hours and did not have a particular length of time in mind. This idea was firmly cast from my mind. £10 per half-hour per rod. No one just came along for a few hours. I had to choose my time and my swim.

This fishery must have developed into something special since I was last here. I would give it an hour, I decided, and paid my £40 for the two rods. She gave me a ticket for swim number 98, apparently a good swim. I then said I would go and collect my rods, but that was met with the sharp reply that all tackle was provided at the swim; all I needed to do was go down to swim 98 at the appointed time and the previous person would reel in and leave the rods. I would take his place. I tried to mutter some objection about preferring my own tackle but she quickly left me with no doubt that I had no option. I then thought about bait and mentioned this. By now I was obviously being regarded as a troublemaker and without further breath she aimed me towards another kiosk. I hurried over. This whole day's fishing was turning into a complete farce.

The bait kiosk was all it purported to be. It contained every single form of deadbait I had ever encountered, in every different colour, plus countless exotic fish that I never knew existed. It was difficult to know where to start, so I opted for a few mackerel and herrings, working on the logic that all the exotics must have been well tried, so perhaps the old faithfuls would be effective. Grabbing a half-dozen of each and parting with another £20 note, I made my way to the lake. As I rounded a corner and saw the lake for the first time in years the adventure became much more of a horror story. There in front of me was a concrete bowl, more akin to a huge swimming pool than a pike lake. All the banks were concreted and the lake was totally uniform – not a tree, a bush or any form of natural vegetation in sight. At regular five-yard intervals a set of rod rests were cemented into the bank. Each held two rods with attendant angler sitting close by. This extended round the entire perimeter of the circular lake (I'm sure it wasn't shaped so in the past).

There were at least three hundred swims and I wandered slowly round looking for swim number 98. I could see that the fish were on the feed; the odd swirl studded the lake and a couple of anglers were playing fish.

I eventually arrived in my allotted swim as a bell tolled ten times and the previous angler packed up. It was exactly ten o'clock and now it was my turn. As he left the swim I asked if he had had any luck, to which he replied that he had lost one, a good fish. Apparently he had not seen anyone land a fish but plenty of people had been playing them and they were definitely on the feed.

With only an expensive hour to spare I quickly baited and cast out. I worked on the basis that as probably everybody cast out as far as possible, I would drop my baits short. Perhaps in this way I would get more takes. I thought it strange that there had been so may lost fish. The tackle seemed quite sensible: small double hooks, fairly strong line and a carbon-type rod. I say carbon-type because it seemed to have a better action than carbon and I thought that possibly it was constructed of some new space-age material. I concluded that the lost fish were caused by overfishing resulting in tackle shy pike.

I tried to disregard the unnatural appearance of the fishery and I had already resolved never to come again when the electronic drop-off sounded. I was quickly into a fish and it was obviously a big one. I had already decided it was more than twenty when, for no apparent reason, it slipped the hooks. What were these pike, some kind of super fish that could escape every angler's hooks? I reeled in, rebaited and recast, then sat back to contemplate the whole morning's events, the totally artificial nature of the fishing with everything laid on.

As I sat watching I saw that, over the next half hour, nearly every angler in each swim had a run, hooked a fish and duly lost it. Something didn't quite add up and I resolved that if I had another run during my allotted hour I would bully the fish as hard as possible, not giving it an inch, not allowing it to fight. I just wanted to see what was different, why these fish could not be landed.

There was five minutes left when at last my right-hand bait was taken. It was a slow run and from the instant I struck I gave no quarter. The fish was hauled protesting across the surface. It looked to be a mid-double and I gave it absolutely no chance. With landing net at the ready, the fish was brought to the edge. As it swirled just in front of the net, I caught sight of this 'pike' just before, once again, the hookhold gave. But now I knew. The glimpse had been just enough. It had been no living pike. It was some mechanical robotic man-made object designed to simulate a fish. That is why no one could land them; they weren't meant to be landed. That would shatter the pike-fishing illusion. I didn't even bother reeling in, just walked away in disgust. Storming in anger, as I passed the kiosk, I told all the waiting anglers what they were paying for. They just stared and looked at me as if I was some form of outcast and the burly security officer laughed and said:

'What's up with you? You must know that fishing for real fish has been banned for twenty

years. We offer the modern, socially acceptable alternative. Take it or leave it!'

I turned away in confusion, not knowing exactly what was happening to me. How could anglers have allowed such a thing to happen? Surely they must have presented a united front to preserve their sport? The whole thing had become one awful nightmare. The fishery bell rang loudly, signalling another shift.

I awoke, sweating. The alarm was ringing and I remembered that I was off to fish Martham Broad. It had been a nightmare after all, a nightmare which I trust will not come true. But then as I travelled towards the Broad I pondered yet again not only the dream but also the restrictions imposed on the water I was about to fish, some eighteen rules affecting the way in which I could fish for pike.

I can understand the need for some of these restrictions. Martham is a special case, but how many more special cases will be presented to the pike angler, or indeed to any angler in future years? To conserve pike and at the same time preserve our pike fishing we must resist bans, educate other anglers of the ecological value of pike in our waters and encourage all anglers to work together for the protection of angling and the conservation of all fish stocks. In addition, we need to ensure that man-made pike fisheries are created with care, not just crammed full of the biggest fish possible (creating artificial stock-pond environments). Finally, we all need to care for our pike and both their and our own environment. If not, my nightmare scenario may not be so far from reality.

26

Trout-Water Pike

Several years ago Martyn predicted the demise of the British pike record in the Pike Anglers' Club magazine. He suggested that it would fall at first to a Broadland pike but ultimately would be surpassed by an even greater fish from a trout reservoir. In the succeeding years these predictions have been fulfilled. First Neville Fickling landed the Thurne monster and subsequently he has been beaten several times by trout-water fish, including the Ardleigh fish and the more recent Welsh giants.

It is highly probable that the current pike record will be usurped by an even greater fish, which will in all probability be caught from a stillwater trout fishery. Only recently have pike anglers had access to just a handful of trout-only waters, due in part to continuous pressure applied by a few enterprising pike anglers on trout fishery authorities, and also due to a change in attitude by a few managers and administrators of such waters.

The skilful and protracted negotiations conducted by Bob Jones and friends eventually persuaded Welsh Water to allow pike fishing at Llandegfedd for a strictly limited period in October 1988. In view of the vociferous opposition from some local trout anglers, Bob should receive an accolade from all pike men, for not only were pike anglers allowed to fish but, unlike some authorities, Welsh Water agreed that any pike caught should be returned to the water. This latter decision was even more important than pike anglers' being given permission to fish.

The attitude to pike as a species by the great majority of game anglers is more readily understood when considered in its historical context. In the latter half of the last century and even when Vic was a young man, predators – furred, feathered or finned – were ruthlessly persecuted. This was a general and accepted policy pursued by riparian landowners, gamekeepers and river keepers in order to protect game stocks in an age when any creature that remotely threatened them was exterminated.

Even in those far-off days trout and salmon fishing commanded high rents and was to all intents and purposes exclusive to the wealthy. The best fisheries provided the largest revenue, so in an attempt to make fishing even better any fish, bird or mammal that so much as looked as if it might eat a fish was doomed. Otters were hunted; grebes, cormorants, herons and even ospreys were destroyed. River keepers waged total war on pike. They were netted, trapped, snared with wire loops and even shot. Small wonder, then, that the anti-pike attitude of some gamekeepers of the present generation remains as deep-rooted as ever. As enlightened pike anglers and conservationists we may deplore such views, but surely they are at least understandable. Today's game anglers are the sons of fathers who quite likely fished with their fathers, and fishing lore and traditions are prone to be handed down from one generation to the next.

Vic was no exception. He remembers his grandfather's view on these matters. Because he was an expert shot he was occasionally invited by King George V to help knock down the royal pheasants. (Martyn swears that when Vic is cut by a pike the ensuing blood is blue – perhaps a legacy from Vic's grandfather.) As an angler Vic's grandfather was a fly-only man, perhaps fishing for pike once a year, usually on a Boxing Day, and any he caught did not see water again, unless it was in the cooking pot.

Grandfather encouraged Vic to hunt, to shoot and to fish. At only thirteen Vic was allowed to use one of those fine 'royal' guns and he was encouraged to denude the neighbourhood of magpies, jays, rats, stoats and weasels, even hawks. He now shudders to think of it.

Perhaps the pike-killing attitude of game anglers is an inborn prejudice which only time can change. Strangely, past generations of coarse anglers, mainly drawn from the so-called working classes, held similar views to the game anglers; even today some still do. The coarse fisherman killed any pike he caught. If he did not wish to eat them they were left to rot on the bank. So pike were invariably killed, sometimes for food. (Although some will not agree, this can be tolerated, provided they are the smaller fish.) Others were killed through fear, or because the angler was too scared to even attempt to unhook the pike until it was dead. There was a further reason why pike were slaughtered: it was widely believed that they denuded the rivers of the roach and other fish which were the coarse anglers' traditional quarry. It says much for the resilence and fecundity of the species that it survived such an onslaught.

When pike anglers were first allowed to fish in the odd trout water it was on the understanding that any pike caught should be removed, and if this was not possible they had to be killed. In other words, the fishery managers were having their pike culled on the cheap. The Pike Anglers' Club quite rightly would not be party to such a practice. The fishery staff of trout waters seem to be totally ignorant of the vital role pike play in the ecology of any fishery, including trout waters. In order to quell the complaints of the equally misguided game fishermen themselves, they institute culls. Owners, managers, water authorities and administrators do not seem to comprehend that it is impossible to remove every pike from a water unless it is completely drained. Trying to eradicate pike by whatever means is an expensive folly that cannot possibly succeed. Not only trout anglers but coarse anglers too still lobby their committees to remove pike from their fisheries. Usually the most vociferous are those who know the least about any aspect of fishery management and even the simplest ecological truths. There may be some excuse for the latter, but not for those fishery managers who are, we hope, well educated and supposedly fully qualified in all aspects of fishery management.

In other countries the pike is considered a fine sporting fish and, unlike anglers here, fishermen do not differentiate between those fish with an adipose fin and those without. Because game fish were once fished for only by the upper classes, such fish came to be considered superior to all others. Good trout fishing is now available to anyone of whatever class or creed, and many coarse anglers take up trout fishing, if only to wet a line during the close season for coarse fishing. So at last the class barriers are crumbling, but prejudice is likely to remain on both sides for some time to come.

Vic was born into what were then called the upper middle classes. The only kind of fishing considered suitable for him was the pursuit of game fish. When it became known that he also enjoyed coarse fishing he was informed that it was altogether too plebeian – he would be forced to mix with common people below his station. In spite of such an attitude, quite unacceptable today, his family was enlightened enough not to put too many obstacles in his way, except to say, 'If you must, you must, but be it on your own head.' So he continued to go fishing and his game-fishing grandfather went out of his way to encourage him – on the sly!

We only mention Vic's past to show how easily prejudice can be passed on to succeeding generations, and is so deep-rooted that it has taken many, many years for such opinions to change. There are still those who consider that game fish are the only fish worth catching and that the only good pike are dead ones.

This untenable belief that pike are vermin must be understood in relation to past class values as well as in its historical context.

Trout anglers seem convinced that once pike

get into their waters they will proliferate to such an extent that eventually even the largest trout will be eaten. Erroneously, but again because of tradition, even non-anglers will have heard of monstrous pike whose capacity for fish and fowl is unlimited. Journalists revel in big-pike stories and you can be sure that they will lard their copy with such phrases as 'freshwater shark, jaws, ravening monster' and similar extravagances. So are myths perpetuated.

Trout anglers pay for their fishing, which helps pay for the rearing or purchase of fish for stocking their waters. They are most unlikely to approve of pike, which they think are forever chasing and devouring the trout they have paid through the nose for. If this were entirely the case we would share their unease, but scientific research proves otherwise. The pike is no more rapacious than any other freshwater predator inhabiting our waters. It eats because it needs to, and it only eats enough to sustain life and growth. Of course, if trout are also sharing its environment some will be taken, particularly recently stocked fish, but it is important to remember that the weaker fish are most likely to fall as prey, including those suffering from diseases such as eye fluke. So in this respect the pike is giving, if only partially, a beneficial service. At the same time all trout waters contain – or will, through natural stock-

ing – a variety of coarse fish. These too the pike will prey on; when it has had its fill of these it will not be taking trout.

Research at the Fresh Water Biological Associations' laboratory at Windermere indicates that a pike can remain healthy and retain its body weight with an annual intake of food equal to its own weight plus 40 per cent. A 10lb pike can therefore exist on 14lb of fish per annum. But pike grow, and in order to achieve this they consume more. Experiments indicate that pike are quite capable of maintaining a steady rate of growth with an intake of food of 3½ times their own weight. Even so, this could hardly be considered rapacious. What percentage of food trout would comprise can only be surmised. The calorific and protein value of trout is high, so in all probability pike would need rather less of them than other species, apart from eels, whose calorific value is even higher. Even if a pike fed exclusively on trout, which is highly unlikely, it could put on weight by consuming less than the intake percentage quoted by the fishery biologists because of the calorific value of the food it was eating.

If nature is not interfered with an ecological balance is maintained. If pike are present in a trout water of reasonable size and are not persecuted the water will not become overrun with the species. It will contain a relatively few large pike, slightly more weighing between 10 and 20lb, and smaller fish will also be present, but they will be subject to predation by the larger ones. The pike themselves will limit their own proliferation. The pyramid theory mentioned elsewhere will apply.

All the pike in a trout water will consume some trout, particularly those unwary recently stocked fish. As they are introduced to the water these fish tend to remain shoaled as they explore their new and strange environment. At this stage stock trout are at their most vulnerable, and will suffer pike predation. But they soon disperse and the majority survive. Naturally, the areas where the trout are released – usually around the trout pens – are often hotspots for the pike angler.

Most trout fishery staff carry out a continuous campaign in an attempt to eradicate the pike from their waters. The pike are even gill-netted on their spawning grounds. Fish are killed and sent to the market or, as an appeasement to the growing pike angling lobby, are transported elsewhere. It is a completely fruitless exercise incapable of any degree of success and a total waste of money. Scientific papers are available to prove that a policy of pike removal always results in an equal, or initially increased, tonnage of pike remaining. Instead of a few large pike with a scattering of medium-sized ones there are now pike everywhere and they are all small fish. This inevitable result of pike-culling campaigns occurs not just in this country but wherever a cull has been conducted throughout the whole global range of this species.

So trout anglers who pester a fishery manager to cull the pike will find that retribution is at hand, for they will have pike trouble as never before. Little pike which once skulked in cover in order to avoid being eaten by the few larger ones now rule the roost. They can spread far and wide and take kindly to the trout anglers' lures. Where before only the odd pike took a fly, it now becomes a commonplace occurrence. Expensive lures are bitten off leaders, no doubt leading to yet another demand for an increase in pike culling activity. Such crass stupidity is hardly believable, but if trout anglers are unaware of the consequences of pike removal, as indeed are most fishery managers, they cannot be entirely blamed for trying, however misguided their actions may be. However, we do blame them for not recognising the inevitable result of their culling policies, which are plain for all to see, and also for not bothering to carry out any research themselves or attempting to study the many reports on the effects of pike removal which are freely available.

One such report was compiled by the Irish Inland Fisheries Trust. In an attempt to improve Irish trout fishing, an ongoing and vigorous campaign to remove pike had been conducted for many years. Sensibly, the Irish have kept meticulous records and these show that not only is it quite impossible to get rid of pike but all the culls have achieved is to kill off the really good pike fishing which would have attracted overseas pike anglers, not to mention the revenue that they would have generated as tourists. Now the pike are smaller and there are many more of them. The Irish have come to realise that the game is not worth the candle, as well as being a waste of public money.

We have tried to explain why game anglers hold such strong views on the undesirability of pike in their waters. Perhaps more than some, we can understand and sympathise with their attitudes. For instance, if Vic had not enjoyed catching any fish and coarse fish in particular, he might have shared their views. Tradition dies hard and his forebears, apart from one eccentric cleric, were game fishers to a man.

Trout anglers are possibly quite unaware that the best policy to adopt when pike are present in their waters is to leave them well alone, or at least only cull a percentage of fish under 10lb. Because they talk and fish with those of similar interests, the trout men have no inkling of the arguments that have been presented in this chapter. They are in the main unlikely to read books or periodicals other than those devoted to their particular angling interests. As for their own books and magazines, it is highly unlikely that many articles will appear in them extolling the virtue of pike. To change deep-seated attitudes takes time and some – however scientific the facts, or however authoritive the argument – will not be persuaded. We have to admit to a lack of tolerance for either bigots or fanatics, religious or otherwise, as such people will not listen to reason and can best be totally ignored. But the great majority of ignorant trout anglers, ignorant in the nicest possible sense, if given facts and figures, presented politely, will at least consider the merits of any case put to them. Surely they can be persuaded that hordes of little pike in their waters can in no way be to their advantage. Once they understand that the root cause of this problem is pike culls, they will not be undertaken so readily. If eventually some of the trout anglers themselves start to question pike removal it will carry far more weight with those who manage the fisheries than any amount of lobbying from pike anglers.

It is now beginning to be realised that pike play an important ecological role in any fishery and contribute to maintaining a healthy natural balance. No longer recognised as a liability, and even tolerated today, in the years ahead pike will be welcome as an important asset to be safeguarded. The pike has an important role in the disposing of diseased and damaged fish and by its cannibalistic nature controls overpopulation by its own species. In a trout fishery, pike will predate unwanted species to an extent, though not entirely, but at least every time a pike makes a meal of a roach or perch one trout lives longer and trout anglers don't want such species in their waters either. There are only three species of coarse fish in these islands capable of growing to heavy weights: pike, carp and catfish. A 40lb pike is enormous, but they can grow even heavier, and when accepted for the magnificent sporting fish it undoubtedly is, and encouraged to thrive in all waters, game and coarse, we can predict with confidence that the 50lb barrier will be broken.

However, the strongest argument, the one above all others which will ensure that pike and pike anglers will eventually be accepted in and on game fisheries, is financial. Good pike fishing commands good money. Pike anglers will travel far, and pay well, to fish a fine pike water. Today there are game fisheries which close in October and do not open until the spring. Yet during that time stock has to be bought or reared, the fishery and its buildings have to be maintained, boats and outboards serviced or replaced, salaries and wages paid – and not a trout fisherman with a full wallet in sight! So, instead of spending even more on the annual early-spring gill-netting operation which is actually destroying a valuable resource, all this expenditure could be offset by revenue obtained from pike anglers, by exploiting the very asset that the managers have been endeavour-

ing to destroy. Indeed, the income from pike fishing on such waters would pay for not a few extra trout to be stocked and those the pike might eat as well.

Llandegfedd opened for a trial period of two weeks and it is estimated that the sale of day tickets and boat-hire charges produced a revenue of over £11,000. A water such as Llandegfedd would not be crawling with pike unless continuous culls have been implemented, and then pike anglers would not be interested in the hordes of jack pike. It would be sensible not to open trout waters to pike anglers for the whole of the trout close season. This would put intolerable pressure on the relatively few large pike and the quality of the pike fishing would deteriorate. Inevitably, the result would be less interest on the part of pike anglers. It would be more sensible if such waters were opened for limited periods, perhaps for one week a month, or for two or three two-week periods between October and March. The pike fishing would be superb and the revenue large enough to interest the most unadventurous management.

There is a worry that if pike fishing in trout waters came to be generally accepted management staff would be tempted to open their waters throughout the winter in anticipation of even greater revenue. The law of diminishing returns would soon apply, with a diminishing number of pike anglers visiting such waters.

As more game waters open such privileges will entail obligations on the part of pike anglers. At first many restrictions will be imposed by management, primarily to protect overwintering trout. It would be very sensible that most restrictions, even if they seem unwarranted and even ridiculous, as some will no doubt be, are strictly adhered to. As managers come to appreciate the value of new customers, sensible negotiations would enable pike anglers to have the more unjustifiable restrictions rescinded. What will do great harm and harden the attitudes of both trout anglers and management is if rule bending becomes rife. There are a very few individuals in the specimen-hunting

Charlie Beane has every right to look pleased with this mean-looking 22lb specimen.

world, which includes the pike anglers, who are dishonest and unscrupulous. Their quite unacceptable behaviour, both here and abroad, has tarnished the reputations of thousands of law-abiding anglers. So do not be surprised if trout fishery staff view pike anglers with suspicion at first. Those who do break the rules should be denied access to such waters. What we fear is that their actions could also involve those who obey the rules, however restrictive they may be considered. At worst, a water recently opened could be closed again and the hard work and effort ruined for a decade.

It cannot happen overnight but inevitably more and more trout waters will be open to pike anglers. The Pike Anglers' Club has changed attitudes, most pike caught are now returned and we have better pike fishing and larger fish in more waters than in the past. As for the future, if the game anglers and pike anglers can share a trout water in harmony, and management come to realise that the pike in their waters are an asset rather than a liability, we should be able to enjoy some of the best pike fishing in Europe.

27

Past, Present and Future

In this chapter Vic outlines a number of his thoughts relating to pike angling and angling in general, opinions with which Martyn is in total agreement.

I had intended to spend my remaining years, after attaining almost three score years and ten, painting, writing, fishing and birdwatching. I looked forward to those activities which have enabled me to ignore an increasingly violent and turbulent world by finding quiet peace and relaxation. But the best laid schemes . . . I find myself working harder than ever, there seems little time even for fishing, and 16 June is like any other day, not special as it used to be. Designing fishing tackle is mentally rewarding, but material rewards come harder when the product has to be sold in a competitive market where many others compete for their share of the business.

So, instead of relaxing at the waterside, I have to type and answer letters and that infernal device the telephone rings at the most inopportune moments. As for painting, not a hope! Fine sable brushes are neglected while oil paint hardens in the tube. Art is confined to graphics: packages have to be designed and publicity material and advertisements prepared, as well as stands for international trade fairs. Perhaps I am mad to contemplate yet another demanding career when I could so easily sit quietly by some tranquil lake and

Vic on location during the filming of the video Primeval Pike *(Malthouse Productions).*

cease to worry that mankind is hell-bent on destroying its environment.

I must be a glutton for work, for apart from taking on a more than a full time job I became involved in planning and writing this book with Martyn.

So much work is entirely my own fault. I make no excuses, nor do I seek sympathy. No doubt if the years could be peeled back and I was about to retire I should make exactly the same hare-brained decisions. Quiet rustication remains a dream. I relish new challenges; it is part of my make-up. Starting a competitive business from scratch, never having been involved in such a venture before, was like being reborn in a strange and alien world. But it has been vibrant, exciting and immensely stimulating. It either succeeds or I am put under the daisies rather sooner than I would hope. I have no intention of occupying the six-foot plot yet if I can possibly avoid it, for I am a great believer in the often quoted adage that hard work never killed anyone. However, stress and frustration, those insidious evils, have at times come perilously close. And that is the time, however urgent the tasks undone, to go fishing.

As I write, sitting in the conservatory in the late spring sunshine, I look at the garden where there is so much to do, and beyond down the Waveney valley. The winding river, like so many but a shadow of what it once was not so long ago, still holds some crafty chub. The great roach have been replaced by shoals of lesser fish, odd tench idle the summer away in the quiet deeper holes, and carp, escapees from Waveney Valley lakes, share such pools too.

At the first hint of rain the mill owners open the sluices so that the river becomes a turbid torrent, effectively sweeping the tiny fry downstream. If any survive they will only do so until agricultural or pesticide pollution ensures their demise. What is so poignant is that as I gaze across the valley it looks much as it always has done, perhaps for centuries.

In winter the large gaggle of Canada geese which roost on nearby Homersfield Lake sweep low over the cottage just after dawn on their way to graze the day away in the water meadows. Their exhilarating sonorous calls remind me nostalgically of my youth, when I lived beside the desolate, beautiful saltings that fringe the north Norfolk coast. I spent days and nights of gales and frost and snow sheltering in the creeks, listening to the high-pitched fluting whistle of the drake wigeon and the garrulous chorus of the wild brent geese which flighted in on the tide to feed on the even then diminishing beds of eel-grass. That has long gone, perhaps another warning of how man is polluting the sea. The duck and geese still arrive each autumn, riding the jet stream from Novaya Zemlya, the Taimyr Peninsula and even Kamchatka, while the pinkfeet make the shorter journey from Iceland. The fact that the wildfowl still arrive each year as they have always done through countless aeons long before *Homo sapiens* evolved is immensely reassuring.

Nature is resilient, given time; if man regains his senses, his depredations will be rectified. Species in the main are adaptable. With the eel-grass virtually extinct the duck and geese have been forced to exploit other food sources. The wigeon graze on the sea aster seeds and both they and the brent, both marine birds, browse the fresh marshes and will fly inland to obtain the succulent shoots of winter wheat. Playing a great fish is exhilarating, a heavy mix of intense excitement and trepidation, but although I have enjoyed the experience many times I have been fortunate to have been close to and undetected by wild geese by night, listening to their intimate conversations as the clouds race across the face of a winter moon. That, too, is an exhilarating experience.

I have also been privileged and sometimes saddened to witness how angling and, indeed, the attitudes of anglers have changed in this century. When I fished as a boy, fishing tackle had changed little or if at all from that used by our Victorian forebears. The rods were constructed of greenheart, heavy as lead, or bamboo or Tonkin cane, with lancewood top sections, while the wealthy fished with split cane. Gut for coarse fishing was sold in lengths called 'yard gut bottoms' and had to be well soaked before knotting. I kept mine, as well as hooks to gut, sandwiched between two wet pads of felt which fitted into a round tobacco tin. Lines were of flax or braided silk and needed endless care. They had to be preserved with grease such as Mucilin, but this was expensive, so my lines were liberally rubbed down with beef or mutton fat. If the line was left on the reel and not wound on a line dryer at the end of a day's fishing it rotted.

Specimen groups were unheard of. There were just three types of angler: game, sea and coarse. The trout and salmon men were interested only in fish with adipose fins and the coarse anglers – I wonder who gave them that derogatory title – were divided into two; the match men and the rest. I was one of the rest, never having been interested in the competitive side of angling, then or since, though I admire the match anglers' skills and acknowledge the contribution they have made to the design of modern-day tackle.

I went fishing because I liked sitting by water, because I enjoyed the sparkle of sunlight dancing from ripple to ripple, and the play of light on the waterside plants as they trembled in the breeze. I revelled in the soporific drone of numerous insects, the insistent cooing of woodpigeons and the wild creatures that tolerated my intrusion. I went fishing because above anything else in life I had a strange innate desire to catch fish. Then nearly every angler was a pleasure fisherman. We all fished in much the same way – quill float, light line and tiny hooks. Baits were simple. The most popular were worms or bread in many forms, including paste. Maggots, politely called gentles, were hard to come by for a country lad but could be obtained by surreptitiously purloining raw meat or liver from the kitchen (my mother was always complaining that her butcher sold her short weight). The meat was secreted well away from the house and provided fine fat gentles.

It did not occur to any of us to try to catch the larger fish by design. We just hoped that a big fish would take our bait now and again, which they did, but it took great skill, plus a large measure of luck, if such fish were not to snap the line like cotton. There was also the more insuperable difficulty of landing a larger-than-average fish with little nets which were quite inadequate.

But, as Isaak Walton once stated, all fishermen are brothers of the angle. Perhaps we were in my youth; I wish it were so today. Once anglers were happy to share a swim and what secrets they knew were frequently passed on to anyone who cared to ask.

When I was about eight years old I was fishing a pond set in the 'Walks' at Kings Lynn. I was hoping to catch some little roach with a knob of bread paste on my one and only tiny 16 hook tied to a few inches of real gut. This was suspended under a twopenny float fixed to a yard or two of flax line tied to the tip of a garden cane. Impatience, the prerogative of small boys, made me keep lifting the bait out of the water to make sure it was still on the hook. An ancient angler was fishing close by. Perhaps he was on the right side of thirty but he looked very old to me. Turning, he spoke kindly: 'Son, you'll never catch a fish unless your bait is *in* the water.' That was the best piece of angling advice I had ever received and it has stood me in good stead through the years.

A decade or so ago I was pike fishing. It was one of those boring occasions when the static deadbaits had been ignored for hours, apart from an adventurous jack which had been foolish enough to attempt to sneak off with a bait nearly as large as itself. I began to feel sure that I would be better employed elsewhere and had started to stow away some of the gear prior to leaving. Then I remembered those timely words. I had a whole mackerel lying nicely at the base of a drop-off, my bait was in the water, and there I decided it should stay.

As I suspected, the mackerel remained untouched. The darkness was near and as a chill mist drifted over the rods I stowed one away, then bent down to lift the second from the rests. At that exact moment the indicator fell and the line trickled through the rings. That fish weighed a fraction over 32½lb. I only had a hand in its catching; someone, perhaps long dead, should surely receive some of the credit.

When I started to fish in earnest, waters received little angling pressure. The rivers may have been in decline but had not deteriorated to the parlous state they are in today. Fishing was free, or available for the odd shilling, or two or could be obtained by asking politely (it still can be if you know how). Secrecy and competition, except in match angling circles, was unheard of. Yet in spite of our woefully inadequate tackle I and my friends managed to land a good fish or two (that very first two-pound roach from Rockland Dyke – what a joy!). Big fish were not the reason for our enthusiasm. We went fishing for pure enjoyment, to revel in the quiet of beautiful countryside; to catch fish certainly, but that was not all important. Comradeship with a kindred spirit iced the cake. Watching a scarlet-tipped float reflected in green water, wondering if it would sink from sight; the smell of crushed water-mint – such things made me an angler. They still do. Of course it is exciting to add to such pleasures the capture of a large and crafty fish, but if I fail it really does not matter one iota.

Nowadays a successful angler is lionised in the weekly press, and his expertise is judged solely by the number of twenties he has caught. I won't mention names, but there are those who plan and scheme and strive to catch more twenties or even thirties in a season, or even a lifetime, than any other angler. I feel profoundly sorry for them. What a terrible burden it must become! Endless time and expense for what! Adulation from fellow anglers, perhaps, but today jealousy is a more likely reaction. Fishing can of course be serious, but it should also be fun, not an imposition, not so fiercely competitive that in realising an ambition knowledge is withheld from friends, waters poached, rules ignored and furtive secrecy indulged in. It cannot be right that this obsession, the desire to catch more and larger fish than anyone else, can turn a normal sane individual into a crashing bore, and even make him behave with arrogant selfishness and cause him to set aside decent civilised behaviour at the waterside. I have seen this unacceptable side of specimen hunting develop over the years and want no part of it.

Alas, young anglers are influenced by some of these 'heroes'. In our affluent society the youngster can equip himself with the latest high-technology gear, he can purchase superb baits and if he baits up a swim with buckets of the stuff he will, if he is patient enough, catch a fine fish. It is all too easy. Within a week or two his foot is on the first rung of the 'twenty' ladder. Small fish or fish of a species other than that he intends to catch are despised. Soon this youngster is on the treadmill. He may eventually knock up a whole series of big fish, so perhaps he could be called an angler of sorts.

However, I would not deny anyone such a doubtful pleasure. It is still a free country. If an angler is besotted with large fish only, or fish of one species, he is free to indulge his whim. It is sad that the spirit, the mystique, the real joys of this most delicate and gentle art of angling may never be his. Scarlet-spotted little trout from a Scottish burn, working a fly down a sea-trout pool when the fish are crashing on the surface and the darkness is Stygian, winkling a chub out of a fastness of tree roots, trotting the current for grayling, wobbling a deadbait past the nose of a large pike you can clearly see, deceiving a wily old trout with a perfect cast and a home-tied imitation of the flies he is taking – are all these magic moments never to be enjoyed by the 'modern' angler? I too like catching big fish. I have been involved with specimen groups and angling politics when president of the PAC. Regrettably, politics and angling are now irreversibly entwined, more's the pity, but it is necessary if angling is to survive. But, strange as it will seem to some, I am still happy to while away an hour or two fishing a village pond for gudgeon or anything else that fancies a maggot or a little worm, as happy as when I am fishing for huge pike in Holland. There is rather more to angling than a tally of twenties.

One inevitable trend which is becoming increasingly prevalent is the proliferation of syndicate waters. Waters once available on a day-ticket basis are now controlled by a handful of anglers who are prepared to pay through the nose for their fishing. I still keep an open mind on syndicates since there are strong arguments both for and against. If a syndicate fishery is well run the fishing is preserved and possibly improved. With vegetation only minimally controlled to keep swims fishable the environment becomes a wildlife haven. All well and good. But perhaps the privileged members should remember that local anglers, pensioners and youngsters in particular, have a fishery denied them. Some pensioners and certainly the very young may well lack transport, and if an angler has been able to fish a water near home all his life and then suddenly finds it far beyond his means he is naturally aggrieved.

I have to admit that I cannot understand why it seems to have become standard practice to introduce carp into as many waters as possible. Carp may well do untold harm. God forbid that one day every water should become a carp fishery! Make no mistake, I love carp, but the popularity of carp fishing has spread from angler to angler like a contagious disease. As with any revolution, the old order has been swept aside and angling in this country has changed dramatically and will continue to change. Certainly this has brought great benefits. Carp anglers have pioneered advances in tackle design, the trade has responded and European anglers have followed hard on the heels of their British counterparts. The export of specialist tackle increases yearly and the nation gains. It is already apparent that pike angling, constantly gaining in popularity, will develop along similar lines.

I too enjoy carp fishing, for I love angling in all its forms; but my attitude, as in my pike angling, is more experimental and adventurous than stereotyped. Bivvies and boilies are not for me.

It has been fascinating to see how angling has changed during a lifetime since I first held a fishing rod in my hand. As for anglers, the majority are still truly brothers of the angle. Alas, a minority have tarnished this gentle art by their churlish unacceptable behaviour. But as the attitudes of society have changed and anglers are part of that society there are bound to be individuals within angling who reflect every type of human behaviour, from the best to the worst.

I have attempted, inadequately I suspect, to hint at my philosophy as an angler. The following I have quoted in another book, but I make no apology for repetition, for it describes so succinctly my angling career over the years.

Edward Hewitt, an American describing the phases an angler passes through in his lifetime said: 'First he wants to catch the most fish, then the largest, finally he wants to catch the most difficult fish regardless of size.'

To hell with the twenties!

I left this chapter until the script of this book was virtually complete, and now only a few sentences remain to be written. I feel a great sense of relief. Now I have a few moments to watch the albino sparrow, for all the world like a snow-white canary, which visits my garden every day for his ration of wholemeal breadcrumb and birdseed.

I remember some of the great fish that I have caught, but they are relatively unimportant – perhaps red-letter days among all the others, but nothing more. I remember, too, a dace taken on a minute dry fly from a crystal stream hardly twelve inches deep. Edward Hewitt would have understood. The valley shimmers in the heat of an early summer's day and, to quote from, Ecclesiastes, 'Truly the light is sweet, and a pleasant thing it is for the eyes to behold the sun.'

I wish I were fishing.

28

The Straitjacket –
A Social Comment

From the beginning, man has been a hunter, dependent on success for food, for survival.

One cannot change habits of a lifetime, yet alone instincts bred into humanity. But, here in the 1990s, bans follow bans, frustration leading ultimately to violence as more and more constraints imposes a straitjacket on those evolved instincts.

Conservation in today's world is a necessity which can be carried to extremes by the well-meaning. We need to protect what is left of our environment. Man has already destroyed and raped so much of the natural world but we cannot, and should not, attempt to destroy or restrict man's natural instinct for hunting. Inevitably this would then be unleashed on football terraces, in Wild West shoot-outs in the streets as frustration causes the straitjacket to snap. But what has this to do with pike angling?

Quite simply, fishing is a hunting sport, but with its own sensible self-constraining conservation rules. Pike fishing is the coarse angler's greatest release for the hunting instinct. What better way than to stalk another hunter? Angling performs an extremely important role in society; it provides man with the ability to hunt without harming the environment or other human beings. With its policies of fish protection and careful handling and return it even protects its quarry. It is the perfect outlet for an instinctive desire of man the carnivore.

Within angling, pike fishing often sits outcast, supported only by pike anglers and a minority of more enlightened anglers. This clearly should not be the case. It is necessary for all anglers to close ranks to protect angling from extremists and self-righteous movements which do not comprehend that in a modern

Martyn with a fine fish from Decoy Broad, so often a heartbreak water.

society a straitjacket of restrictions cannot stop man being a hunter, or that to cast out such forms of passive hunting will only result in the suppressed instinct eventually unleashing itself in other, perhaps undesirable ways.

Surely, therefore, angling should feature prominently as a sport to be encouraged within our schools – far better than hooliganism on the terraces or boredom and violence on the streets. Angling itself is said to be the largest participatory sport in this country. Is it not time we as a body were totally united in an effort to protect our rights and our instincts, and to promote the benefits of angling in society? This includes the rewarding pursuit of pike angling, the greatest release for man the hunter. Perhaps this will never happen, because, having released some of our natural desires in pursuit of our pastime, we are pacifists with no socially unacceptable instincts to unleash. Perhaps, therefore, we will always remain apathetic!

PART SIX
OVERSEAS AND FAR AWAY

29

On Dutch Waters

by Bert Rozemeijer

I suppose I must have rewritten this chapter some four times before I decided to limit myself to a description of our larger waters only. A pity, for there is a wealth of fishing in Holland. Pike inhabit all the drains in the Polders and I would need another chapter to write of the peat bogs. These bogs consist of a lake system hidden in a forest of reeds and surrounded by woodlands, composed mainly of birch, willow, alders and oaks. A day's catch of twenty pike is not uncommon and some fish grow large. Every year 30lb pike are reported in the papers. I have never caught one so large from the peat bogs but I have witnessed such an event on quite a few occasions.

The pike fishing in the canals can be good.

Bert Rozemeijer with a magnificent near 44lb Dutch pike.

Some are deep and wide and bank fishing is possible. Visitors fishing in these canals should not expect to catch pike in numbers but the average size is high, good-sized doubles, and there is always the chance of a really good fish. However, as in English waters, the pike are not evenly spread. Location is the key to success.

The lakes in Holland are man-made, but for every angler hoping to contact an exceptional fish it would be wise to concentrate on them. These large lakes are gravel pits formed by the extraction of aggregate needed for the massive road- and house-building projects begun soon after the war. The lakes have one thing in common: they are very deep; depths of 100 feet or even more than 200 feet can be found. The average size of such waters is 2 square kilometres (about 80 acres) but some are more than three or four times as large. The pike fishing can only be described as fantastic – not for the same numbers of fish as can be caught in the peat bogs but because these pike grow to immense proportions. I must try to curb my enthusiasm when describing such waters and the great pike that inhabit them, but with a little luck every angler should manage to catch at least a twenty.

Bank fishing is possible in a few places, but very often the pike are out of casting range, so the use of a boat is crucial if these waters are to be fished efficiently. Some boats can be hired, but it would be advisable for any visitor to bring his own as there are launching ramps at many points. While a depth finder is helpful – it will indicate the shoals of prey fish, which will give some indication that a pike or two will be in the vicinity – a graph recorder is perhaps more important.

Before I discuss how to fish these large deep waters, it might be as well to mention the tackle we use in Holland. As you know, pike can be caught by many methods. Deadbaiting can be superb in autumn and winter, livebaits always work and lure fishing, which can be difficult at times, seems to be really effective in Holland and in some conditions even better than live- or deadbaiting. The large American

Bert Rozemeijer, probably Holland's most knowledgeable pike angler, deep in concentration as he watches the graph recorder.

bucktail lures seem especially deadly when used by weedbeds and plenty of pike succumb to flies. Because we have had fish on all these methods our fishing is always full of interest.

There are many spinning rods on the market. The lightest just cannot handle a good pike, but I sometimes have three spinning rods in the boat. The lightest, just 7 feet long, will handle light plugs and spinners. I use these spinning rods when fishing the shallows, not more than 10 feet deep. I prefer stiff-actioned rods with a sensitive tip, for the key to successful lure fishing is sensitivity. Jan Schreiner, one of our better angling writers, once wrote that a spinning rod should resemble an open nerve; every movement of the lure should be transmitted by the rod to the hand so even the most delicate take can be felt, not only from pike but from other predators such as perch and zander. Fish do not always hit the lure savagely. Sometimes the take is so gentle as to be hardly discernible, and these can be missed when the rod is not sensitive enough and the tackle unbalanced. An unbalanced outfit would fail to hook many fish and that makes for inefficient angling.

One rod will cast a certain weight better than another. I use one that works best with a lure weighing 15 grams. Such a lure can be cast a long distance but is not so easy to hook fish at long ranges, so I prefer to use shorter casts covering every inch of the water. This allows me to use lighter lures, about half the weight the rod can handle; then the full sensitivity of the rod can be utilised. A Shakespeare Big S weighs about 15 grams but its heavy resistance on the retrieve bends the rod tip, sensitivity is reduced, and those light takes are not even felt.

The shallows can be lure-fished up to mid-November, then the pike have to be sought in deeper water and fishing becomes more difficult. It is a hard job indeed to locate pike in a huge expanse of deep and open water.

However, in the early morning the big pike often hunt at the surface. During full daylight while fishing open water we have to rely on pike being attracted to the lures, often from a distance. Because the pike sense the lures by vibration and water disturbance, small plugs, spoons and spinners are not that effective. Even if a little lure is detected, the pike may well not give chase as it will have to use more energy than it would obtain if such a morsel were a fish to be consumed. We use much larger lures, ones that set up a real commotion, and rods to measure, heavy enough to handle lures in the weight range of 30–60 grams. However, the vibration of the lures should be transmitted by the rod so that the angler is aware of how it is performing. If it is worked too fast, there is too much pressure on the rod tip; if too slow, perhaps none at all.

When using these heavier rods I am much happier with a multiplying reel because it gives

Trolling on a very special Dutch water over pike of 40lb plus.

me ultimate control in casting them. I have found that casting a jointed plug with a fixed-spool reel all too often results in the hooks snagging the wire trace, a rarity with multipliers. When fishing the open water early in the morning, I begin by using plugs that dive only some 6 feet down. Favourites are Rapala Magnums Nos 14–18. Weighted spinners such as the Mepps Giant Killer or Vibrox Nos 5 or 6 do equally as well. When using spoons we always fish with the thin-bladed types, 3–5 inches long. Pako spoons have become very popular in Holland, and no wonder, for they have accounted for pike up to 30lb.

When I fish either shallow or deeper water I anchor the boat with nothing more than a lead-filled can fitted with an eye to take the anchor line. Then we (I seldom fish alone) fish all round the boat, each concentrating on his half of the water. It never takes more than ten or fifteen minutes to cover the area thoroughly. Then we move some fifty yards and start again. Because our casts reach the limit of previous casts no water is missed. If one of us does connect with a large pike the other hauls up the anchor as quickly as possible and takes up the oars. Until we started to carry out this procedure more than one big fish fouled the anchor rope.

We also troll lures. It is not difficult but does require both energy and skill in boat handling. In most of the Dutch lakes the use of an outboard for trolling is forbidden, so there is no alternative but to row. However, plenty of lures work well at a normal rowing speed. I always use floating plugs or those that sink very slowly. Good trolling plugs are the Rapala Silvers, both the 30 and 20 gram. These sink, but if the heavy split rings are changed for a lighter variety they become floaters. Kwikfish are excellent for trolling, and in particular the jointed variety has a most vigorous action, with the added advantage that it can be trolled very slowly. When using Kwikfish I incorporate a lead sinker rigged in a special manner. I use two lengths of line of the same breaking strain as the reel line. One length equals the rod length, the other is a foot shorter. A three-way swivel is joined to the reel line, the shorter length of line is secured to the middle eye and the longest to the remaining eye. This latter length takes the plug and trace and a bomb is knotted to the shorter length. The bomb can be quite small, just heavy enough to sink the plug. The reason for the variation in length between the lead link and the plug link should be obvious: it prevents the trebles on the plugs fouling the lead link. This cannot happen with the rig described.

We let the rig sink beside the boat then row away until enough line is paid out. Even when anglers are not using a graph recorder the depth can be ascertained with reasonably accuracy. Once the plug starts to fish it is most important to note the angle of the line between rod tip and water surface. If the angle steepens the plug is fishing deep; conversely, when the angle decreases and the line rises the plug is working more shallowly. In this way you can control the fishing depth with some degree of accuracy.

Trolling spools can also be very effective, certainly on warm days when many pike remain in the upper layer of water just under the surface. We prefer to use long wide-bladed spoons as these have a tendency to rise in the water if we row faster but sink slowly as we decrease speed. Depth control using spoons can best be achieved if they are not fished too far behind the boat. Normally, we do not exceed a line length of more than 50 feet. We vary the depth by noting the angle of the line, so by controlling the boat's speed we can control the fishing depth. Even so, trolling is even more efficient with a graph recorder, for the bottom contours are continuously displayed, which enables the boat's speed to be altered to compensate for depth changes as they occur.

All this is very fine for the angler holding his rod but the one rowing has to leave his rod fishing for itself, which means that any pike that takes his line cannot be hit at once but has to hook itself. A fast tip-actioned rod certainly helps and only some 20 inches of the rod tip

Outriggers and graph recorders, tools of the large-water troller.

should project over the boat's side. The butt is held by a tackle box or some similar weight, such as the graph recorder battery. When a pike strikes the lure only the fast-action tip bends. Even so, the rod must be grabbed immediately and the fish struck. We have found that this technique hooks pike just as effectively as the angler who holds the rod in his hand.

In many of our big waters we find pike in shallow and very weedy areas. The growth is so thick that plugs or any form of lure cannot be used. Livebaits are just as useless as they quickly bury themselves in the undergrowth. There are, of course, many so-called weedless lures available. After many trials I am convinced that they are not only weedless but pikeless as well. By far the best way of tackling these weed-strewn shallows is to use a large bucktail fly. With a kink in the hook shank they swim point uppermost and the stiff bucktail fibres mask the point so they skip through the weed cleanly.

An outrigger and a line-release device for trolling.

A great deal of fly fishing for pike is practised in Holland. Most anglers use the fly in the Polders; indeed, only a few specialist anglers tackle the great lakes at all. For eight years the only method I used for pike was fly fishing, and even now if it was ordained that I was only allowed to use one method I would happily settle for my fly rod. The method is so versatile that provided I could have a variety of floating and sinking fly lines I could tackle any water.

We fix a short leader of 15–20lb to the fly line, which should be heavy, size 8 weight-forward for preference, and a shooting head rather than a double-taper line which requires more false casting to obtain distance. False casting has yet a further disadvantage in that it dries the fly and a dry fly does not sink well. I also use a rather special size of rod and after many trials have found that this short, stiff rod seems to give better results than a more normal type. A slight drawback is that such a rod is not too easy to cast a fly with, but practice makes perfect. However, once mastered it will drive the hook into a pike's jaw far better than the more normal softer-actioned weapons. When the pike takes the fly it grips hard and the stiffer rod ensures a high proportion of hook sets. A normal fly reel that will accommodate an extra 50 yards of backing and a short wire trace is all that is needed to complete this simple outfit. The wire, of course, is vital; some anglers rely on the 20lb nylon but they soon discover that any pike, large or small, can slice through it as a knife cuts butter.

The technique of fly casting for pike is really quite simple but as the water is often crystal-clear and shallow the approach must be cautious. Any noise when anchoring or any unnecessary movement can so easily spook the fish. The amount of line needed is pulled from the reel and with just one false cast the bucktail is dropped in the water and dragged through until it is thoroughly wet. Then, with no more than three or four more false casts, the bucktail can be dropped where you will. Let the fly sink, then strip the fly back with a series of slow pulls varied by short fast jerks. Nearly always

you can watch the action of the fly and at the same time see any pike that takes. Such an exciting and heart-stopping event can so easily lead to a hurried strike and a missed fish. It is much better to wait for the odd second until a pull is felt; then and only then should a hard strike be made. Small pike can be played by stripping in line by hand but bigger fish should be played from the reel. If a large pike decides to depart at speed and begins a long run, loose line lying on the floorboards can so easily snag in the odds and ends that we all strew around. Luckily, most big pike head for open water and if the anchor is lifted the boat can follow the fish. Perhaps fly fishing is not easy for an angler unused to the technique, but it can soon be learnt, and if you hook a 20lb fish in such shallow water you will never forget it.

So lure fishing for pike can be excellent in Dutch waters. Pike can be caught on lures throughout the season but at the end of September we switch to using live- and deadbaits. The water has started to cool and the pike become more lethargic and less inclined to chase fast-moving baits. Static lures do not appeal and those moving very slowly snag the bottom, so you are forced to use fish baits. Static deadbaiting will take fish but all too often the bait may be lying in an area devoid of pike. However, before describing our methods we will discuss pike behaviour at this time of the year.

The water temperature drops steadily as the autumn progresses. By mid-September the warm surface layer may be 20 feet deep, only 12 a month later and less than 6 in November. It all depends on air temperature. If the weather is mild the warm-water layer may well extend deeper for a longer period. Similarly, if the weather turns cold the top warmer layer will diminish rapidly.

Pike do not like cold water as much as many of us believe, which is exactly the opposite of what is believed in America, as Vic and Martyn mention in Chapter 31. Inactive fish are often suspended in cold water, but inactive fish are of no interest to us. What we seek are those active fish more likely to feed. These fish will always be in the warm-water layer and this dictates the depth at which the bait is presented. The best chance of contacting one of our huge Dutch pike is in October and early November because the warm water layer is thinner and the active pike more concentrated. I know that in some respects this is theory, but by capitalising on the theory I and my companions have enjoyed some superb pike fishing.

We do not use complicated rigs and when fishing for pike I think it nonsensical to use other than the simplest of tackle. We have naturally tried out a number of rigs and found through experience that just two seem to work more efficiently than all the others. We use live- and deadbaits and every year either I or a friend takes a 25lb fish. Even so, although I have caught pike to over 43lb, my rod is comparatively light. It is a three-piece 14-footer with a test curve of 1¾lb. It is far too light to cast the large baits we favour but very handy for controlling a large fish as it is drawn near the boat. When trailing, boat casting is unnecesary; we just lower the baits and row away from the floats. With two in the boat we vary not only the depth the bait is fished at but also the distance it trails behind. Rods project so more water is covered. The bankside floats support the bait at a depth of about 12 feet while the lakeside bait is set to trail 6 or 9 feet deeper. One float follows close behind the boat, perhaps 20 feet astern; the other at 30 feet.

At first we had problems holding the bait down when rowing into a head wind as the floats worked down the line towards the baits. Nowadays we use a trolling lock – a curved length of plastic tubing to the middle of which is attached a link swivel for attachment to the bottom of the float. The line passes through the tube and, when any pressure is on the line, it locks on, but can slide when the line is slack. When, with a fish in play, the float reaches the tip ring it slides down the line quite easily. It is still necessary to use a bead and a stop knot in the normal way. I use a 15-gram weight riding on the line and resting against the trace swivel to hold the large baits down.

Trolling lock.

The trailing rig comprises a Marvic double or VB hook for lip-hooking followed by two trebles attached to a 25-inch 28lb test wire trace. The double hook is free to slide but is held fast with a length of silicone tubing which covers the whole shank, and the trebles are crimped. The middle treble is set at the base of the bait's pectoral fin the other at the rear of the dorsal fin. I never use small hooks or barbless ones either.

[Bert uses much larger hooks than are fashionable here. Seeing and using his large baits both alive and dead we quickly followed his examples – VB and MP.]

This simple rig is designed so that the hooks can be set with a hard strike immediately after the float sinks. It is very seldom that a pike fails to be hooked unless it is very small. Little pike manage to grab the bait between the two trebles, but as we are fishing for the really large fish it is of little consequence.

Perhaps is all sounds too easy, but catching our big pike is quite as difficult as anywhere else. By far the most important factor, which is essential for success, is skill in boat handling. The man on the oars can make or break the day. It would take pages to explain the intricacies, for each boat has its own characteristics and one may have to be handled differently from another. Then, of course, there is wind, and we do have winds in Holland that can blow a boat off line or drive you towards the bank, making it impossible to fish effectively. Only long experience can cope with such adverse conditions and we have had to learn the hard way. But the big pike are there, and such difficulties we have learnt to overcome. Only a gale and four-foot waves prevent us going afloat!

*

After years of exploring Dutch waters with the aid of a graph recorder Bert Rozemeijer has acquired an extensive knowledge of the depth band that large pike favour in every month of the year. His findings relate to the deep clearwater lakes of Holland, but undoubtedly they are relevant to similar waters elsewhere. Perhaps his most surprising discovery is that big pike spend much of their time suspended high in the water just above or *below* the thermocline. For those who have not read Richard Walker's classic *Stillwater Angling*, the thermocline is the point of separation between the upper layer of warmer water and the deeper cold water. It remains at a constant 4°C at all times.

The depth of the thermocline varies with the seasons. It is shallower in the colder months and at its deepest in late summer. Like the pike, the prey fish, including vast shoals of bream, also use the upper layers. If a pike needs to feed it will hunt in the same depth band as its intended prey. Reinforcing this theory are the catches that Colin Dyson and Archie Braddock have made using buoyant deadbaits presented at half-depth or even higher in water some 18 feet deep.

After feeding a pike will retire to what we call the digestive lies. In Holland a replete pike will hang just above or below the thermocline. This behaviour has evolved over millions of years, so that a pike can rest without expenditure of energy and digest its food at the slowest possible rate, so obtaining maximum benefit.

To clarify where resting pike have been plotted, we include a copy of Bert's graph, which depicts the cross-section of a large deep lake. The dots just above or below the line represent pike resting in the vicinity of the thermocline at differing months of the year.

Bert Rozemeijer's researches have begun to unravel the complexities of pike location in deep waters. Those of us who fish such waters would be wise to take his findings seriously.

Vic and Martyn have both fished in Holland and indeed Vic has now been travelling abroad for several years. The following thoughts are his.

I agree with all that Bert has said. Fly fishing for pike is fascinating and I try to describe what fun Colin Dyson and I have had fishing the peat bogs in Chapter 30.

Deep, clear and often windswept, the great lakes of Holland are a challenge. They pose difficult enough problems for the Dutch anglers who can fish when fishing seems propitious. As for visitors hoping to tangle with a megapike, success depends far more on luck than on angling skills – the luck that some big fish will be feeding when you are afloat, and that during the short feeding spell your boat is in the vicinity. And luck with the weather too, which can make boat fishing difficult and at times impossible. I have fished these lakes on occasions, usually with Bert but also with Martyn and two separate weeks with Colin. Colin has had a week at the best time of year for the last three years. The time before last it seemed that the wind never ceased blowing a steady gale force 8 gusting to 10. The racing, lowering clouds appeared to have collected most of the Atlantic Ocean, as well as the North Sea, and deposited that little lot on top of us.

In all my visits, my best Dutch pike to date

depth in metres

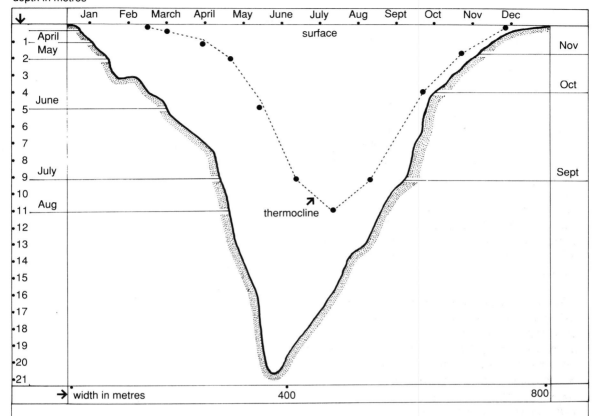

Cross-section of a large Dutch lake.

The graph shows Bert Rozemeijer's studies of resting, inactive pike. The larger dots indicate such pike positioned on or just below the thermocline.

As can be seen, both pike and thermocline are close to the surface until the water starts to warm in March–April. The pike lie deep during the summer months, but will rise to the surface for short feeding spells, usually in the early morning.

weighed a shade over 19lb and the less said about Colin's efforts the better. But Colin is an experienced pike angler; he was just defeated by the elements. It is debatable whether he or I am the Jonah! He nearly cracked it once. Just as our three floats moved closer to each other, as Bert angled the boat to cope with the wind, Colin's float sank. We had just noted a very large active pike on the graph recorder display and undoubtedly it was this fish that had taken

Colin's bream livebait. Normally, when the float disappears it stays down but on this occasion it bobbed up to the surface and lay flat. It did little else, so Colin had to no option but to tighten down and strike. For some reason the pike must have ejected the bait, but what a sorry mangled mess of a bream was disconsolately retrieved. It had been taken by a very big pike. The evidence was irrefutable. Earlier Bert had caught a thirty-five, netted by Colin

A large Dutch pike which was not put off by a Gazette bung.

and unhooked by me, so we each claimed a pound or two.

On another occasion I was in at the kill in more ways than one. Bert was playing a good fish which subsequently weighed 25lb. I sunk the net and waited. As Bert drew the fish over the net a flying treble snagged in the spreader cord, so I was left with a large pike securely fixed to the net and lying beyond it. This was a pretty pickle, to be sure. Very delicately, and not too sure if it was a sensible thing to do, I eased the net to the side of the boat. I then leant far over the gunwale and managed to grasp the pike with both hands, securing a hold at the junction of the gill covers where they meet at the back of the chin. That pike did not take too kindly to this unexpected assault. I was aware of being blinded by spray and I collapsed

into a heap at the bottom of the boat along with the pike and net. It was sheer good fortune that the flying treble did not embed itself in some part of my anatomy. Bert uses big trebles, at least size 2. It would not have been a pleasant experience.

Not only do the pike in these deep lakes grow large, they are long fish with massive tails, and they fight far harder than any pike I have tangled with in our own waters. Once a twelve-pounder, fighting some 30 feet directly below the boat, slammed my rod down so hard that it smacked against the gunwale with alaring force.

Bert has mentioned inactive pike. I have seen plenty of those lying suspended in deep water. The huge arched signal on the graph recorder that denoted their presence would

Vic looks overawed as he cradles a 35lb Dutch monster caught by Bert Rozemeijer.

cause a gasp from the most stoical of anglers. Once Colin and I passed over three of them lying close together, strangely enough in much the same area where Bert had taken his 43lb fish. Although we trailed our big baits just over their heads at least three times they would have nothing to do with them. Those who think the use of graph recorders is unethical might well change their views. All the recorder told us was that the fish were there; it did not help in their catching. If it is possible to anchor accurately in deep water, in spite of the undertow, and position paternoster baits close to such fish, they might be stirred into activity – a technique I hope to try one day. But then inactive pike are not that easy.

When Martyn and I were fishing we had seen quite a few fish lying very deep. I tried

bumping a fair-sized smelt deadbait along the bottom, which would, I hoped, interest a large zander even if the pike were not attracted. No zander materialised and I caught pike, small 3 or 4lb fish which were hauled up from 40 or 50 feet, and when released swam down again apparently none the worse for their experience. I mentioned this to Bert that evening and he said that bottom fishing usually resulted in catching little pike for that was the only place they could hide, below their larger relatives who would make a meal of them given the chance.

Just after dawn on two successive June mornings Martyn and I saw shoals of large bream swimming with their glistening dark backs out of the water as though they were intent upon travelling in a straight line to some distant part of the lake. On both occasions these shoals were attacked by very large pike indeed. Seeing the commotion, we rowed frantically to within range and cast large plugs at the bream shoal. But we always managed to arrive too late; the pike had fed and retired to the deeps while our plugs searched the water in vain.

Those great pike would take float-suspended live- or deadbaits, as Bert has described. A huge herring or mackerel with balsa rods or foam inserted via the vent so it trails along horizontally as though swimming normally seems nearly as effective as a roach or bream livebait. Bert considers that one of the most attractive baits for these pike is a fair-sized perch. It would be unthinkable to use such baits at home, but Dutch waters are crawling with fish. Perch abound and baits of all sizes can be obtained from professional fishermen. When I can obtain such big perch I have no compunction whatever in using them for bait in the huge lakes of Holland.

As I have mentioned elsewhere, I am not overconcerned about chasing round the country searching for big fish; there is so much more to fishing than that. But I have to admit that there is always a feeling of suppressed excitement and anticipation when afloat in Holland. When the float stabs under and you pick up the

Vic strains at the weight of a large Dutch fish.

rod, in the second before striking you cannot help wondering 'Will it be 5 or 50lb?' It would be nice to catch a Dutch twenty but if I don't I have still enjoyed some superb fishing in excellent company. What more could an angler ask for?

30

Lost in a Peat Bog –
A Case for the Fly

The late October day was unusually calm for Holland, where so often the wind can scythe through the polders, seemingly for ever. Then the waves surge across the larger waters so that boat fishing becomes difficult and even hazardous. But on this day, after dawn, a slight mist dispersed to reveal a sky of deepening blue, the sun shone warmly and I sensed that it was likely to be a shirtsleeve day.

At the entrance to the first small lake –

perhaps 'broad' would decribe it more accurately – I felt at home but strangely detached, for surely this was how the Norfolk Broads must have looked a century ago. The lake was one of many, interconnected by canals and drains, some so narrow and overgrown that the boat could be pulled along only with difficulty. Phragmites reed stems, 10 feet tall and topped with feathery seed heads, brushed against the hull, and our passing released the tang of sweet-

These are timeless waters, a fenland wilderness, unchanged in character in centuries.

scented water-mint, which mingled with the primeval smell of ancient silt and decaying water lilies.

These Dutch peat-bog lakes were dug as were the Norfolk Broads, but unlike the latter they have remained inviolate from pollution and powered boats. This maze of waters, each encompassed by reeds and sedges, through which thrust dense thickets of hazel, willow and alder, are dotted with matted islands of bulrush and reedmace. Grotesque water lily rhizomes, like giant brussels sprout stems, pineapple-patterned, float on the surface of the water, which is so translucent, so crystal-clear that every variation of the algae-strewn bottom can be discerned in minute detail. Spiky water soliders contrast with rotten waterlogged tree branches and the dying lily leaves are limp, ragged and blotched.

These lakes are shallow, at most three or four feet deep. When the boat slides clear of the drain and noses towards open water, unseen pike create heaving bow waves as they seek cover deep in the lily beds. Also sheltering under this jungle canopy are perch, roach, rudd, bream and tench.

These are timeless waters, a fenland wilderness, unchanged in character for centuries. A coypu trap and the odd notice declaring that powerboats are *verboten* are the only visible signs that man has penetrated such sanctuaries. But for such incongruities I could have been lost in a time warp; time was irrelevant, it could have been 1788 or 1888. Only by glancing at my carbon rod and modern reel could I return, perhaps reluctantly, to reality.

In October the dense lily beds start to die back, the underwater jungle thins imperceptibly and the leaves change colour as they decay. At the onset of winter the lilies no longer provide food and shelter, and the fish shoals move to the margins and lie beneath a canopy of overhanging tree branches. The pike follow. It is then that the Dutch angler guides his livebait close by the bank and under the trees, for he knows the open water is barren. Most English pike anglers, untutored in the ways of pike in such waters, would fare badly. The splash of a deadbait cast into such clear, shallow water would create a disastrous disturbance, then it would become enveloped in a cocoon of filamentous weed before sinking deep into glutinous ooze. Any attempt to add buoyancy would be of little help for the bait would be lost in the impenetrable tangle of lily stems. But, in spite of all the hazards, there is a way such peat bog lakes can be fished – fished as an American angler would fish the 'stick-ups' and reedbeds for large-mouthed bass, working weedless lures or surface baits, snapping a plastic worm or casting bucktail flies as we did, Colin Dyson and Remco in one boat, Bert Rozemeijer and I in another, letting the boat drift, or with a barely perceptible pull on the oars moving cautiously within casting range of an island, the shallow margins or a dense lily bed.

Our rods were like wands, fitted with small

A Dutch angler secures his pike fly.

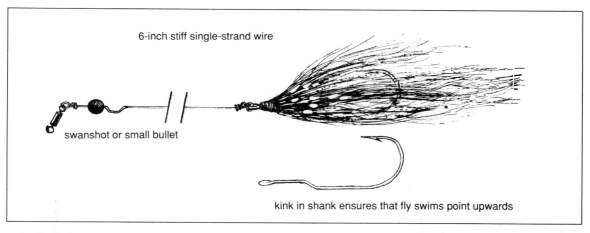

6-inch stiff single-strand wire

swanshot or small bullet

kink in shank ensures that fly swims point upwards

Bucktail pike fly.

fixed-spool reels. The bucktails – yellow, orange, black or white – could be tipped with a Mr Twister worm if need be. The fly is simply dressed on a large silver hook whose shank is bent into a right-angled step to ensure that it can be retrieved with point and bend uppermost. With a fly attached to some 5 or 6 inches of stiff single-strand wire holding a swanshot or a little bullet, and with the bucktail fibres masking the hook point, it can be cast into and drawn through a veritable jungle of weed and yet emerge pristine and weedless. Very rarely did the hook foul a lily leaf stem. When it did a sharp snap with the rod would usually jerk it free.

Such large flies are easily held back by air resistance and even a heavy weight-forward fly line is little help, but they could be cast with ease using our light fixed-spool outfits.

The sky stayed blue, the sun shone, we spent the whole day moving from one lake to another, penetrating even deeper into the wilderness. Even with my normal sure sense of direction I became totally disoriented. I was happy that I was not alone.

On that one day the pike were disinclined to sample our flies. Even the odd angler livebaiting under the trees had nothing to show for his efforts. We cast and cast again, dropping the fly inches from the bank, alongside the clump of

reedmace, into the heart of the lily beds, then skipping it over the leaves or letting it sink enticingly in the clear patches before twitching it back.

It was intensely quiet. Not a ripple disturbed the surface; every tree, every reed stem, was reflected as a perfect mirrored image of itself.

This fish fell to a pike fly with a commando-style hook extension.

Occasionally the trance was broken as Remco and Bert called across to each other, discussing tactics in incomprehensible Dutch. I would join in, bantering Colin for his lack of success, which was on an exact par with mine.

A flash, a boil of disturbed water, caused me to look round quickly – just in time to catch a glimpse of barred flanks and vivid vermilion ventral fins, as Bert drew a splendid perch alongside the boat. But of pike not a sign! Normally six or seven fish can be expected. That had happened to Bert and Remco the last time they had fished the lakes, only a week or so before our visit. It was the old, old story so often told to anglers – 'You should have been here last week' or 'It's looking good for tomorrow.'

Yellowing leaves fluttered down, patterning the surface with golden rafts. The sun continued to shine and we fished on, watching our flies, looking for all the world like little darting fish, as we worked them right up to the boat, ready for yet another cast. To us they looked irresistible. How many pike saw them too we shall never know, but after a thousand casts and as the sun was low over the horizon we disturbed a heavy fish. We watched its progress, the impressive humping bow wave which

Fly fishing for pike is rarely practised in England, but it can prove most rewarding.

moved away before subsiding. Stealthily we followed but, although we covered the area where we were sure the giant fish was lying, we need not have bothered. In such clear waters spooked fish are rarely caught. A little later a smaller pike boiled at Bert's fly. It missed but was more successful at its second attempt after Bert had cast again. I slid my hand down the line so that I could hold the hook shank and twist it free. At that moment the pike spun round and one of its larger teeth lacerated the tip of my finger. Perhaps honours were even. Remco also caught a small pike, while Colin and I remained fishless. But what matter? It had been a good day, a great day, one of the best day's pike fishing that I have enjoyed for years. Practice makes perfect. Talking afterwards, Colin and I agreed that as the day progressed our casting accuracy improved, so that dropping a fly within inches of the target became second nature.

Fly fishing for pike is a subtle technique, demanding accuracy of casting and delicate variation of retrieve. Weedy and snag-ridden waters can be tackled with confidence and I shall fly-fish such waters in the future. My one regret is that I did not discover the potential of such a fascinating form of fishing until recently. But you *can* teach an old dog new tricks. So perhaps one day I shall hook a really large pike deep among the lilies. Now that would be spectacular indeed!

A pike resigned in defeat.

31

By Way of Contrast, the United States

'With a surface area of 186 thousand acres' and, describing a smaller lake, 'offers about 200 miles of shoreline to the angler' – these quotes from that excellent American magazine *In-Fisherman* emphasises the vast difference between so many of their waters and our own. Apart from Loch Lomond and some of the larger Irish loughs our fisheries are minuscule farm ponds in comparison. Such huge expanses of water – not to mention the Great Lakes, which are inland seas – help explain the difference in fishing techniques used by American and European anglers. They also explain why the Americans have developed specialised sport-fishing boats and sophisticated fish-finding devices. Without them such waters cannot be fished efficiently. Imagine taking a rowing boat on a lake where the opposite shore line is invisible, far below the horizon, and a good swim is 10 miles away!

Towards the close of the 1989 season we spent two Sundays fishing a Broadland water of some 800 acres, which is large by our standards. It is owned by a water company and power-boats are forbidden, including the non-polluting electric outboards. You may not launch your own craft so in order to fish at all it is necessary to obtain a boat from one of the three boat hirers. With such a monopoly they have little incentive to modernise their equipment. If you want to fish you use their boats, take it or leave it. A few fibreglass boats are available, but the majority are ancient and constructed of wood. Some are patched with the odd plank. These are older boats and have less freeboard than the modern ones, and because they are flat-bottomed and of reasonable beam

they are easier to row and more stable. Our particular boat had a gaping hole just below the gunwale on one quarter, which did not inspire confidence. The rowlocks wobbled in their sockets, making for some difficulty in rowing, and we considered it necessary to shift position with delicacy just in case a foot went clean through the bottom of this ludicrous contraption.

The concrete blocks which served as anchors were not heavy enough to hold the boat in a wind, nor did the mooring ropes prove adequate. They were knotted, too thin to handle, and too short to reach the bottom in deeper water. As a former navy man Vic thought the whole outfit was a bosun's nightmare. We had to pay for the privilege of fishing from this inadequate boat as well!

American boats are safe, fast and comfortable. At the time of writing a bass boat would set you back $18,000 and some cost even more, but what a difference from the boat we have just described! It may be constructed of glass or aluminium and powered by an outboard capable of planing the boat at 25 or 30 knots, which is essential for getting to distant fish-holding areas. Once there, the silent electric outboards, such as our Shakespeare model, are fixed to the bow and perhaps another at the stern. Both are operated by foot controls, which enables the angler to move the boat ahead, astern, diagonally or beam on and fish at the same time. Quite why more pike anglers do not invest in electric outboards continues to baffle us. They are such an asset when pike fishing from a boat.

Apart from the essential graph recorder, a

American sophistication – walleye boat carpeted throughout and equipped with graph recorder, depth finder, battery gauge, bow and stern electric outboards, two main outboards, bait well and padded swivel chairs.

pH meter enables readings to be obtained at any depth, and another electronic gadget indicates water temperature. The built-in fish well through which fresh water is circulated will hold livebaits, as well as any trophy fish, and maintains them in exellent condition. As for the seats, these are padded, support the back and are swivelled so that you can turn to face any direction and cast from a sitting position. Buoyancy tanks are fitted (there were none on our Broadland craft) and there are also lockers to stow gear, while the inside of these American boats is fully carpeted right up to the gunwale. The Americans can fish in five star comfort. As for our hired boats, we would be ashamed to ask an American angler to fish from one. The expression on his face would be wonderful to see. Putting his trust in God, he might be persuaded to go afloat but Americans are polite when guests and perhaps the only comment likely to be passed would be 'How quaint'!

We are also a technological nation. Boats such as the Americans use could be manufactured here. Indeed, we are in the forefront of offshore powerboat design. But there are so few waters where they could be used that it would not be economically viable to produce such boats for British freshwater anglers. And, with the 'no power' rule (which for some inexplicable reason applies to electric outboards as well), we shall have to continue using rowing boats on many of our local Broadland waters for the foreseeable future. At least it is good exercise.

At the moment Vic is acting as consultant to a friend who manufactures components made from fibreglass. It is hoped to market a small boat capable of seating two anglers in comfort yet which can be launched or recovered by one man with ease. It will be extremely stable and seaworthy. It won't be in the same league as American boats but it will be a vast improvement on the ones we have to suffer now.

OF AMERICAN PIKE

What the Americans call northern pike are almost certainly the same species, both in appearance and genetically, as our *Esox lucius*. The pike is distributed throughout every country in the Northern Hemisphere bordering the Pole. It is indigenous in the USSR, Canada, Alaska, the United States, the British Isles, Continental Europe and Scandinavia. It is present in Northern Spain, Italy and the Balkans. In some southern and western states of the United States pike have been introduced as well.

Pike are a cool-water species capable of reaching weights of over 70lb. With so many huge and varied waters in the United States and Canada one would expect that pike could reach their full growth potential in at least a few of them. Strangely, it seems that they don't. As we have paid only one fishing visit to America we are hardly qualified to hazard an explanation as to the reason, but we do read American books and the *In-Fisherman* magazine. Doug Stange, executive editor, has kindly given us permission to quote from his publication's book on pike, and what follows has been gleaned from that and other sources.

The American record pike list records only one 40lb pike. That superb specimen weighed 46lb 2oz and was captured in New York State in 1940. Only a dozen fish of 30lb or over are listed, all caught during the last two decades with the exception of one in 1952. In Canada a huge 49lb fish was caught in 1890, three forty-twos from 1946 to 1977 and a good thirty – 37lb 8oz – in 1974. It may well be that pike do not receive so much angling pressure from American anglers as their cousin the muskie.

In Canada pike are fished for professionally and the crop sold commercially. Canada has a wealth of waters, some huge, some only accessible by float plane. There must be some so remote that netting would be uneconomic. Such waters, if rarely disturbed, and provided that prey fish of an adequate size were available to pike, might harbour some huge specimens. But in such a harsh climate with ice-free water available for only a relatively short period the conditions might inhibit continuous and steady growth. Certainly, with so many waters in North America and so few in the British Isles in

comparision, it is an enigma why far more large pike are captured over here. We can only theorise and précis what little research has been done in the United States and note the findings of American anglers and professional guides. What is becoming clear is that European pike and North American pike appear to have totally different behaviour patterns during the warm summer months.

In Canada and the more northern American states winters are cold but the summers can be very hot. Our summers are more temperate; only every 10–15 years do we have high temperatures for days on end. Indeed, at times it seems our seasons are merging into one long continuous 'nothing'. The differing climates may in part affect pike behaviour on either side of the Atlantic.

Apart from reservoirs and the odd large gravel pit our waters are shallow, and pike in large deep waters behave differently from those confined in very shallow lakes and Broads. Perhaps our deep reservoirs bear some similarity in temperature and structure to the American waters, as do the larger lakes in Holland. Our pike can be caught in such waters in summer and the pike are in fine condition and obviously feeding. In America pike retire to the deeps where the water is cooler and appear to feed rarely or not at all. We admit that we cannot even hint at the reasons for this obvious difference in behaviour, but we shall return to this problem later. Perhaps temperature is the key; the hotter the summer, the less pike feed.

If, as the Americans have found, pike move deep in order to find water temperatures in which they feel comfortable, there are only relatively few waters here where they can do so in this country. On the Broads, where most of the water does not exceed a depth of 10 feet, and much averages 3–5 feet, there is no cool water for the pike in the warmer months, apart from the odd spring. Yet pike will feed and continue to put on weight. Admittedly, feeding occurs in the cool of the morning and evening and certainly during the dark hours. With no deep water pike will utilise lily beds, bottom weed and reedbeds for shade in the heat of the day. Pike may prefer cooler water, but with none available they have to adapt, whatever the temperature.

It is possible that through natural selection over countless generations our pike have successfully adapted to a shallow-water environment, but this theory does not hold good for the Dutch gravel-pit pike, which can live at depths of 40, 50 or 60 feet if they choose, as we know they are wont to do.

We are lucky that in this country and on the Continent the pike can find prey to suit every stage of their growth. A pike will grow and consequently put on weight if it can obtain prey of suitable size with less expenditure of energy than the prey replenishes when digested. If a large pike has to be forever chasing little fish it burns up more energy than can be replaced, so its condition will deteriorate and it will lose weight.

If prey fish in a water do not grow big enough to satisfy a large pike's requirements, the pike are liable to stop growing, remaining at the size at which they can best utilise the available food supply. Both here and in Europe we have roach and rudd, little ones to satisfy little pike and much larger ones to supply the needs of pike in double figures. Both these species can grow to weights of 2 or 3lb. So can perch. As pike grow even larger there are bream of 3, 4 and 5lb, tench, smaller pike, carp, and, in trout reservoirs, rainbows and browns. In the lochs of Scotland sea trout, salmon and powan also provide pike with fodder.

Eels are a particularly rich food. Most waters hold them. Their calorific value is as high as prime beef and eels are available to pike not just in summer, as many believe, but in winter too.

It is, however, unlikely that a 20lb-plus pike will feed exclusively on larger fish. It will take small ones provided it requires little energy to capture them. Very large pike will swim through shoals of fish fry, mouths open, scooping them in as a basking shark engulfs plankton. Plenty of very large pike have been caught on little 3-inch gudgeon or sprats of similar size,

while herring or mackerel halves have accounted for hundreds of large pike. Such baits may not be the size that large pike prefer but they are taken because they are easy to obtain and readily available and little energy need be expended in taking them. It seems possible that the reason north American pike do not appear to grow as large as their European counterparts is not because of their environment but because of the lack of prey of varying sizes in their habitat. To quote from the *In-Fisherman* book, 'if pike are to obtain their maximum growth potential it is apparent that the food source not only has to be the right type and right size, but must also be available in corresponding different lake zones pike use as they grow from one size to another'.

THE EFFECT OF WATER TEMPERATURE ON PIKE LOCATION

The *In-Fisherman* book devotes much argument to prove that pike are a cool water fish, or, as they aptly say, 'the coolest of the cool'. In spring when cool water is evenly distributed, pike will shoal in shallow water near to their spawning areas and may remain in these areas after spawning until the water begins to warm. Again in autumn cooling water encourages the pike to seek shallower water. Whilst the smaller pike will tolerate warm water and feed during the summer, once water temperatures reach the high sixties Fahrenheit the larger pike are rarely caught, and in very warm water they appear to suffer stress and stop feeding altogether. They search for the coolest water they can find and even penetrate below the thermocline if a minimum amount of oxygen is present to sustain life and the pH value is suitable. In Canada, where temperatures remain lower, perhaps 50°F in the main body of water rather than in the shallows, pike will feed during the summer months. Evidence from both anglers and biologists indicates that not only do Canadian pike feed in cool water but they can grow in winter when the lake surface is heavily iced over. It has also been noted that even in high summer the very cold streams entering the northern Mississippi attract pike, and they will take baits in such places, likewise where cool water wells up from springs. In such areas the water temperature is some 30° cooler than the main river. In the Great Lakes anglers trolling for salmon with lures set to run at 60 feet on a downrigger occasionally hook pike. At this depth the water temperature is some 52°F, much as in most of the Canadian lakes.

The Americans know where the large pike are to be found in summer. Over here, location is the key to the catching of large pike, summer or winter, as it is on the Continent. Yet even with this knowledge American pike seem difficult or impossible to catch in summer. Biologists have used trawls to capture deepwater pike in summer. Included in the net were the prey fish, high-fat-content species like ciscoes. This proves that predator and prey were present in the same depth band. Some of the pike trawled up were large fish and all had shrunken V-shaped bellies, denoting that they had fasted for a lengthy period.

This evidence contrasts with the behaviour of deepwater summer pike in the large Dutch lakes. Here much of the water is over 40 feet deep and even deeper, with areas where the graph recorder indicates 100 feet or more. In both summer and autumn very large pike can hang or lie close to the bottom at a depth of 40 or 50 feet. We have seen the impressive hook-shaped signals on our graph recorder, which not only recorded the depth but also gave an indication of the immense size of the fish.

In June we both saw very big Dutch pike actively feeding, striking at their prey right on the surface, even though there was more than 100 feet of water below them. Obviously the water temperature is high at the surface, yet the pike leave the cooler more comfortable deep water in order to feed. Prey fish – including zander, perch and little pike – will be available to the pike in deeper water, yet they are prepared to tolerate the warm surface layers even when food is available where it is cooler. We do not feel we can offer an explanation, only record the facts.

Bert Rozemeijer, his angling friend Remco, and others catch the big pike of these deep waters in summer. They troll deep-diving plugs running at depths from 10 to 20 or 25 feet. All the pike caught are in good condition, which indicates that they are feeding normally. In fact, they are feeding in the pattern common to pike in this country: feeding is at its heaviest after spawning, heavy in May, slightly less in June, and decreases monthly until winter, when food intake is at its lowest, ceasing only for the period of active procreation.

All this evidence of the willingness of large pike to feed regularly in summer in Britian, Ireland and on the Continent of Europe but not, it appears, in the United States, has intrigued us greatly. Pike have changed little over 60 million years of evolution, as we know from fossil records. The ancient types were remarkably similar to *Esox lucius* and had similar feeding habitats. The pike of today has changed little genetically, if at all, for over a million years, which demonstrates that the species reached a peak of efficiency as a predator countless aeons ago. We think that during this vast period of time even if the pike has not changed genetically some may well have evolved different behavioural traits influenced by environmental and geographical factors, allied to the size and type of prey available in their particular habitat. There are many examples of the species having to adapt to suit a special set of circumstances in order to survive. We also know that a species, even in a similar or confined locality, can develop dissimilar behaviour patterns. Galapagos finches are an example.

Evidence from many sources – biologists, professional guides and anglers – certainly indicates that in the United States large pike are very difficult to catch in summer except in localised areas where the water temperature is much lower than the main body of water. Belief can so easily become angling legend. If

American guides and anglers are convinced that it is virtually impossible to catch the bigger pike in the summer they are unlikely to waste much time fishing for them. A great many who fish for pike in the United States are lure-oriented and a pike lying in the gloom of deep water, feeding perhaps only rarely, is most unlikely to take a moving lure which is within striking range for only a second or two and probably invisible. Luminous lures are, of course, available. Neither of us has any experience of them, though we have been led to believe that they can be effective.

More enterprising are those such as the *In-Fisherman* staff who use a wide range of angling methods – including, more recently, our own European styles. Pike have been located deep down and fished for with jigs, lures and suspended livebaits presented at the depth the pike were lying at. In their own words, it was all to no avail. We find it difficult to accept that American pike should behave in so totally different a way from European ones. Certainly such lethargic fish, with metabolism virtually inert, would be difficult to tempt. We have encountered much the same phenomenon, but unlike the American pike our semi-hibernating fish (for want of a better term) can be caught.

We know that in winter very large pike can remain in shallow water whence their prey have all departed for more comfortable quarters. These pike have little to feed on and seem to be able to exist without loss of weight, which indicates a considerable metabolic reduction. The only differences are that the American pike are lying deep, ours shallow, and the time of year varies. The effect of these factors, if any, is impossible to determine.

We also feel that the type of prey available to American fish may have some bearing on the problem. The bait fish available to these deep-water predators are shad, smelt and cisco, a worthwhile meal to a medium-sized pike. However, the larger fish would have to use up energy in finding a shoal, which might mean moving some distance even before they could chase individual members. A big pike would

need to feed frequently in order to obtain nourishment equal to or greater than its energy requirements.

In Europe large pike have a more advantageous environment, with larger prey available in relative abundance. They can obtain food without undue energy expenditure in order to maintain a steady rate of growth. We know that fish can exist without eating for exceptionally long periods, so it is no surprise to us that American pike should cease to feed for some months. What is more difficult is to comprehend the reason.

In all probability this behaviour results from the unavailability of prey of suitable size. In such a situation big pike would be forever hunting, thus expending a geat deal of energy, which could only be replaced by the ingestion of large quantities of the smaller bait fish. In other words, a pike would have to expend maximum energy for a minimal return. No wild creature could operate so inefficiently.

If this hypothesis is anywhere near the mark, we think that nature would have made the best of a unique set of circumstances by the evolution of a specially adapted behaviour pattern – in this case not feeding at certain times of the year, because the game is not worth the candle. If that is so, water temperatures may have little bearing on the matter.

American pike are considered difficult to catch no doubt because fishing for fasting pike is believed to be a waste of time – a reasonable enough supposition. We are not so arrogant as to say that we could catch them either. From our own experience we know that even the most lethargic pike can be induced to take a bait, even when they are replete and inactive during periods of digestion, though such an occurrence is rare. If the same criteria are applied to American somnolent non-feeding fish with reduced metabolic activity, it might be possible to discover a way to tempt them.

The pike is an extra-efficient predator and by far its strongest instinct is to hunt for food. The instincts which cause it to fast, to slow down its metabolism, are never likley to be stronger than its primary drive. Put in human terms, a pike will eat occasionally despite itself – provided that food can be obtained with little or no expenditure of energy. Fish are an instinctive and not a thinking life form. The only way we can catch them by angling is to present a lure or bait that triggers an instinctive response.

A parallel can be drawn from the conduct of Atlantic salmon. Once they get into fresh water they cease to feed, yet the feeding instinct remains so strong that they will grab at flies and lures. This instinct even overrides temporarily the urge to forge onwards to the spawning redds.

One further factor needs consideration – the aggressive instinct. Pike can develop territorial habits and show aggression towards an intruder. Both lures and natural baits can invoke an attack. In chasing off an interloper the primary instinct must also be activated for bait-sized fish baits are liable to be eaten as an end result of an aggressvie response to intrusion. It seems logical that it might be possible to stimulate these fasting pike by exploiting both responses. Of the two the stimulation of the primary feeding instinct would in our opinion be more likely to succeed. According to American research,

pike like to lie over cool sediment on the lake bottom where the water tends to cloudiness. It might be that deadbaits fished in these areas might just do the trick. That is one method we would employ to try to catch those elusive pike, and we would keep at it long enough to obtain evidence one way or the other. An alternative would be to fish a paternostered live-bait literally within a foot or two of the snouts of the pike – not easy in deep water. This opinion being based on our own experience as pike anglers – though not, of course, of pike angling in America – we are inclined to suspect that such pike are catchable. We might be barking up the wrong tree entirely but we have always worked on the premiss that once located, pike are catchable.

Vic has reached a stage in his life when catching easy fish, even if they are lunkers, is not quite so appealing as it once was. But difficult fish, whatever their size, are a different matter. And if a difficult fish is large, well, that is icing on the cake. We would both like to spend time coming to terms with American pike. We are certain that the odds would be stacked in their favour: they would not be thick on the ground and location would be none too easy – but what a challenge!

32

A Great Pike and Other Things – Vic's Story

When I was demobbed from the navy in 1946 the government, in a rare burst of generosity and no doubt wary of letting me loose improperly dressed in a land fit for heroes, sent me home via Norwich. There I was presented with some trousers, one pair of socks, a choice of black or brown shoes, a shirt and a dreadful tie that clashed with the very reasonable jacket that was also thrust upon me. No doubt the powers that be had decided that the weather was set fair for the years ahead; no raincoat materialised. I rather fancied a flat hat, but none was forthcoming, so I had to choose between a trilby and a pork pie. I chose the latter, wore it once then stuck some ancient salmon flies into it. At least it might impress other anglers. Barely recovering from the shock of this largesse, I was ushered into another room where I was presented with a Post Office savings book containing a credit entry for £76 and the odd shilling or two. I presumed this was considered ample compensation for having spent nearly five years desperately trying to avoid any proximity to very nasty things that had a habit of exploding. (On more than one occasion I failed to succeed in that laudable aim.)

In those far-off days £76 was a tidy sum. It would purchase an excellent second-hand car and twice as much would buy a house. In celebration of this auspicious start in civilian life I booked in at the Maid's Head, enjoyed a tolerable evening meal, upset the waiter with that excruciating tie and downed a whole bottle of superb claret. Life felt good. I had little idea what career I intended to pursue, had vague aspirations of becoming a painter and so toyed with the idea of enrolling as an art student. I did, but many years later.

After a succession of jobs which I loathed I was immensely relieved when the navy informed me that something had brewed up in Korea and my outdated knowledge of underwater weapons might be useful. Such decisions by their Lordships at the Admiralty have always amazed me. However much I had fancied myself as an artist, there was little scope to indulge in such activities at sea but just once my artistic capabilities, or lack of them, were given full rein. During my first spell in the navy I was serving in one of HM ships engaged on convoy escort duties. As we were in dock three weeks for boiler cleaning and sundry repairs due to the attentions of hostile aircraft, I suggested to the first lieutenant that our camouflage, which in my opinion left much to be desired, should be reconsidered. I presented him with a set of coloured drawings, explaining that my design would, I was certain, confuse the enemy. This was of particular importance to me as that ship, either through bad luck or design, always appeared to attract very unfriendly aircraft, E-boats and, once or twice, sneaky submarines. Where that ship went I had to go, so I had a vested interest in its remaining afloat.

'Jimmy the one', lower-deck slang for lesser gods like first lieutenants, seemed impressed. 'Good show Bellars, I think the captain might like to look at these,' he said, as he inspected my efforts. I was quite flattered, as well as being secretly rather proud of my design. I had arranged matters so that if the ship was seen from either beam it would appear to be steaming faster than it really was. Even better, it would

also seem to be steering some 20 degrees off its actual course. This in theory would make the enemy calculations inaccurate and any torpedo launched at us should pass harmlessly ahead. It was good to think of causing discomfort and perplexity to enemy commanders. I even fantasised further, imagining delicate instruments being sent back to the manufacturers as unreliable, causing chaos in the German navy.

The very next day I was summoned to Jimmy the one's cabin. He had my drawings spread around and my service record open. 'Stand at ease. I have shown these to the captain and as we are about to paint ship he thinks your ideas are worth a try.' Glancing at my records he said, 'I see you have already been recomended for officer training. I shall amend your record further in that direction.'

'Aye, aye, Sir' I replied, which is the safest thing for a junior rating to say when conversing with the high and mighty in the service.

'Such initiative will stand you in good stead if you gain your commission. That's all. You may carry on.' So saying, Jimmy dismissed me.

My elation was somewhat deflated soon after, when a further message from the first lieutenant sent me to the bosun's mate. The 'buffer' eyed me. I detected a hint of scorn in his remarks.

'Well, lad', he said, 'I hear you are going to paint the bleedin' ship.'

Before I could explain I was burdened with brushes, paint kettles, and a number of wire brushes and drums of paint, one containing the notorious Admiralty grey known universally as pusser's crabfat. I had by then risen to the exalted rank of leading seaman and was detailed to take charge of a painting party overseen by a petty officer.

I did little painting. I pulled rank on that one, and following my design drew lines all over the hull and upper works, numbering the shapes these produced with black paint. The numbers corresponded to a host of receptacles containing the colours I mixed – gallons and gallons of white, light and dark blues and greens, off-whites and suitably doctored crabfat. The odd splodge of very dark-toned paint, even black at times, put the finishing touches to over a week's work. To my eyes the result was spectacular; even the funnel appeared half its height. I was not popular with my painters, demanding accuracy, and more than once insisting that a section be repainted. The rest of the lower deck were highly amused, thought I was some kind of nut case and promptly christened me Dazzle. The officers seemed happy enough with their ship, now unlike any other of our consorts, but one thought the aesthetic sleek line of the hull had been somewhat impaired. I wanted to tell him that that was one of the objects of the exercise but thought it better not to start an argument with someone of far higher rank. I was even more flattered when over a period of time other ships of our flotilla sprouted imitiations of our unique pattern.

Some months later we were hit by not one but two torpedoes, and sank like a stone. The survivors went to considerable lengths to inform me that I was solely responsible for the loss not only of the ship but of their personal belongings as well. This I considered grossly unfair as it was pitch black when we were clobbered, and our camouflage played no part in our misfortune. Their belief was unshakable and no logical argument would alter their attitude one iota. Perhaps their lordships took the same view. Service personnel were recompensed for inventions put into practice; I never heard from them, but must have been forgiven as I eventually sported a fair amount of gold braid.

By now you may well be wondering just what place such reminiscence has in a book concerned with pike. Well, it has, even if the relevance may seem slighty obscure. At least it informs those who do not know me personally that I must be a little long in the tooth, perhaps even hints at my character. In recalling some of the more hilarious episodes of my youth, so nearly lost in the mists of time, memory is sharpened. My brief involvement with the world of camouflage and the receipt of £76 at my demobilisation both in their respective ways profoundly affected my attitude to fishing. Without the cash I could not have afforded some reasonable tackle so quickly, and, as for my 'skills' in the art of camouflage, they have played an important part in my life as an angler ever since. By relating such episodes I have been able to recall with clarity other half-forgotten events which happened at much the same time. Without that £76 I would have not hooked a pike the like of which I shall probably never tangle with again.

Soon I was hovering outside the window display of Browne's tackle shop, which was then tucked away towards the top of Timber Hill, in Norwich. I gazed awestruck at beautiful split-cane rods with a whipping every inch, as well as greenheart and Tonkin cane rods, the latter mottled and shiny, fly boxes, baskets and a bewildering display of brightly painted floats. I spent an hour in that shop and when I dragged myself away I owned one of the most expensive rods on display, a hexagonal split-cane gem, a 9-foot salmon spinning rod made by Hardy. I had been assured that such a weapon would tame any pike that swam. As I held the slim cork handle and the assistant obligingly pulled the tip down I felt a gradual build-up of power and I was convinced, so a fortune left my pocket and was swallowed by the till, which immediately snapped shut in what appeared to be a very self-congratulatory manner. Spending that £14 was an extravagance I worried about for days afterwards. I still needed a reel. There were some beautifully engineered models available then. Perhaps the most suitable for my purpose would have been an Allcock's Ariel. I had to drag my eyes away from those, the Mallochs and Silexes too, eventually settling for a cheap but adequate star-backed wooden centrepin which in today's currency would cost about 25 pence. Line was a problem. Good lines were oil-dressed, looking like but a little thinner in diameter than a plasticised fly line. Also of less diameter, and a

The famous Allcock's Aerial reel, c. 1915, with accessories.

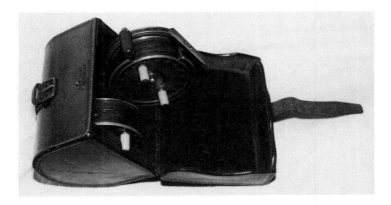

A Hardy Silex casting reel with spare spool in a rare leather carrying case, c. 1920.

little cheaper, was plaited silk. Down-market flax line was available and for the needy, and I counted myself in that category, there was also a sea-fishing monstrosity called cuttyhunk. This absorbed water like a sponge, swelled abominably and had a propensity to rot overnight.

I compromised, purchasing 25 yards of best silk line of 12lb breaking strain and 100 yards of flax of the same strength for backing. As for pike floats, the choice was simple. There was only one, the *Fishing Gazette* bung. I chose one of medium size, but even so it was so huge I doubted if any pike could pull it down. The choice of pike tackles was just as limited: Jardine snaps, size 4 or 2 treble hooks whipped to 6 inches of strong gimp, some to wire. A few Jardine leads, pilot floats and a gaff head completed my outfit. I was probably as well equipped as any pike angler of the time, and possibly better than most.

I was now all set to catch a large pike but, with deadbaits undreamed of, except for spinning, there was an unforeseen snag. I had no gear to catch livebaits with. I learnt all too soon that acquiring one set of tackle usually necessitated buying another, and this I could not afford. I sorted this problem out with little expenditure or reduction of my meagre resources. I acquired a cheap boy's reel for a few old pence, some split shot at tuppence a tin, a few size 16 hooks to yard gut bottoms, a couple of quill floats and 25 yards of 2lb flax line.

Using my pike rod I could now catch baits, albeit with difficulty. Once I had enough baits in the bucket I reassembled my rod for pike fishing. It was another two years before I owned a proper roach or bottom rod.

I had settled in the Waveney Valley and started fishing for pike in that charming river, usually the stretch between Bungay and Ellingham Mill. I did well considering my inexperience. Within days I caught my very first double. As I gazed down on yellow-dappled flanks as it lay on the grass, I was convinced I had caught a twenty. My borrowed, rusty and no doubt inadequate spring balance claimed otherwise; the pointer hovered just over the 12lb mark. Even so, it was a fine fish from the river and lucky too, for any pike caught then were inevitably killed. Until it fancied my little dace it must have lived a charmed life. Its luck held. I slipped it back into the river, watching fascinated as with a flick of its blotched tail it faded from sight.

Later, while enjoying an afternoon spinning in early September, I encountered another angler earnestly engaged in the same occupation. It is not always the case today but at that time brothers of the angle greeted each other with courtesy and always stopped to chat and even offer each other advice. My fellow angler was a sporting parson in every sense. It turned out that he was my local vicar and we soon became firm friends, spending hour after hour fishing together, even for the then supposedly un-catchable carp. While waiting for one of our floats to sink below the surface we would become involved in deep and lengthy discussions on a wide-ranging variety of topics. Even today I can remember some of the gems; apart from religion, music and art, we tackled such diverse subjects as the amazing intuition and perversity of women, the sad decline in the taste and content of post-war sausages, the respective merits of Indian and China teas, and – all too often – the reason why our floats remained motionless. Halcyon days indeed!

That reverend gentleman, for gentleman he undoubtedly was, was as fanatical an angler as any I have ever met in a lifetime's fishing. When he had to officiate at a baptism, wedding or a burial he would fish on to the last possible moment before rushing off to church in his ancient Vauxhall car, which with unfailing regularity never started unless vigorous use was made of the starting handle. He was at times a little absent-minded, for he was getting on in years, and I was told by one of his parishioners that he once conducted a wedding service with muddy wellington boots peeping out from under his vestments. He often said that fonts would provide an excellent livebait storage facility, but even he, though he must have been sorely tempted, never as far as I know put that idea into practice.

Country parsons are often given access to private waters denied lesser mortals, so through his intercession with the head of an aristocratic family which owned a vast estate I was allowed to fish a large and very private water reputed to hold monster pike. I was always offered a lift in the parson's decrepit car whenever he fished that water, usually on the strict understanding that I would be responsible for getting the engine running. It was a perverse brute, steadfastly refusing to fire, and at times it even reduced that impatient vicar to use ungodly language. On cold and frosty mornings I used to crank its handle for up to ten minutes without avail. Then I had to push the wretched thing until we reached a slope in the vicarage

drive where it could usually be persuaded to start. When parochial duties curtailed the parson's fishing, I could at least catch a bus, which deposited me within easy walking distance of the lake.

My treasured new rod was soon dealing with pike far larger than my 12lb Waveney fish. One memorable day at September's close I landed what turned out to be my largest pike for a decade. It weighed 26¾lb on the manor house scales, which were hastily rushed down to the lakeside in a wheelbarrow. No keepnet then made would have housed such a fish, but the large livebait cage, which the generous owner kept stocked for the use of his guests, was at hand. To their consternation, a score or two or roach and skimmer bream had to share their confined space with that huge pike until those mammoth scales arrived.

I was sorely tempted to give that superb fish a new home in a glass case but, realising that this was far beyond my means, perhaps a little reluctantly I carried the pike to the water and as it faded away into the depths I knew I had done the right thing. Such a beautiful creature deserved her freedom.

Throughout my life any good luck has nearly always been swiftly followed by the reverse. If I have occasionally been fortunate enough to receive an unexpected financial windfall, as sure as God makes little apples within a day or two the car would break down, needing expensive repairs, or a horrendous rates demand would arrive. Elated though I was at having caught a pike larger than many an angler far more experienced than myself had ever caught in a lifetime's fishing, my elation was tempered by the thought of retribution to come. During the next week I dreaded the rattle of the letterbox but miraculously no summons, rude letter from the bank or even a demand for payment of an overdue account materialised. I didn't break my rod, fall in the river or have to be rushed to hospital. I began to have a cheery word with the postman and as the days passed I thought that just for once my luck would hold. But no, I was soon to be sadly disillusioned. The fates had granted me, a novice angler, a magnificent fish but during the next week I had to pay the price. Perhaps rightly so, for if I had caught another even larger pike so soon after I might well have become insufferable, pontificating on the catching of pike to far better anglers than myself.

On the days following my great success I began to question standard pike tackle. Although I was a raw beginner, I had soon become dissatisfied with the terminal pike tackle then in almost universal use. I felt it was sadly in need of modification. Not only pike tackle, either. I began experimenting, trying to make all kinds of improvements, and even constructed a pike-sized landing net from the rim of a bicycle wheel. How to make such a net had only just begun to formulate in my mind on my next and perhaps most momentous pike-fishing day. However, I had modified my tackle, a little. I could see that snap tackles on 6 inches of wire terminating in a loop to which the line was knotted were courting disaster. All 6 inches could be engulfed by even a moderately sized fish, resulting in the line being severed by those razor-sharp teeth. This little problem I cured easily enough. I bought a few quite large swivels of the type used by sea anglers. I passed the loop of the snap tackle through the eye of the swivel and over the other eye and pulled taut. To the free eye I twisted on a 12-inch length of single-strand 20lb BS alasticum wire, which terminated in another swivel. To this swivel I could knot the line, which was far superior to tying it to the wire loop. Perhaps this was the very first anti-bite-off rig.

A following weekday, warm grey and still, when not even a breath of wind stirred the yellowing leaves of late October, I rowed across the lake towards a large reed-fringed bay. The lack of wind made rowing effortless as I watched the vortices gently swirling where each oar had dipped. Their dwindling ripples mingled with the wake, then, as they faded, the lake surface stilled again to leave no trace of my passing. Reaching the entrance to the bay I

nosed the bow into the reeds, positioning the boat some 20 yards inside the eastern point. Hitching the bow line round a bundle of reed stems, I moved to the stern and lowered a mud weight so that the boat projected at right angles to the line of the shore. So moored I was able to cast a bait close to the reed edge on either side, while a semicircle of inviting water lay beyond the stern. Just outside the reeds the depth hardly reached 3 feet, five or six yards further out it had deepened to 5, then the bottom gradually sloped until with a last little dip it levelled off at an average depth of 11 feet. So within a few yards of the boat's stern was a drop off, but I knew nothing of them or their fish-holding propensities at that time.

I assembled the rod, passed the line through the rings and then through the central hole of two pilot floats, making sure their bright-red halves faced the rod tip. Knotting the line to the trace swivel I then slipped it into the groove of the bung and held it in place with the tapered wooden peg. This huge bung was set some 6 inches above the trace and I pegged the lower pilot float 12 inches above it, letting the second run free. Last of all I secured a Jardine lead close to the trace swivel. Nasty things, Jardine leads – elongated ovals, grooved to take the line, which is then twisted into a spiralled wire at each end to secure it. Jardines fell off fairly regularly.

I knew little of sliding floats and at that time none was available, so the depth a bait could be fished at was dictated by the length of rod. Casting out this Christmas tree of tackle to any distance needed some ingenuity. For those owning free-running Aerials and the like there was little problem, but my wooden Nottingham was near-useless in this respect. By far the easiest way that I could cast was to strip line from the reel and let it lie on the deckboards. Usually this would run out without snagging. For longer casts the coils had to be reversed or an impressive tangle could ensue. Such a performance must seem incredible but, in spite of such vagaries and having to use tackle hardly changed since Victorian times, we learnt not only to master our difficulties but catch fine fish as well.

A small roach was quickly hooked on the snap tackle and then swung away to splash down just off the reeds by the point. The flotilla of floats settled, the bung giving an odd half-hearted bob, soon subsiding into immobility, for it was far too huge for the little roach to tow around. I had chosen a small bait so that I could fish as close to the reeds as possible. A larger one would almost certainly have sought sanctuary in the tangle of underwater stems. The trap was set. Now all I needed to do was to savour the beauty of the lake with its thatched boathouse, magnificent bankside trees and abundant wildfowl.

The coots, which had scurried deep into the fastness of reeds when I arrived, started to venture out. After some tentative and furtive slipping in and out of cover they gained courage and were soon dotted over the surface of the bay. Having perhaps decided that I posed little threat, they behaved like all coots, either diving for weed or continuously quarrelling.

The bung lay undisturbed, appearing twice its size due to reflection. The smaller pilot floats lay one close and the other some feet away from that strident red-topped egg, looking for all the world as though with nothing better to do it had spawned a set of twins. I reeled the whole conglomeration a little nearer, stirring the small roach into a moment's lethargic activity before all lay still again. A heron flapped lazily towards the bay, shanks trailing, and banked sharply as it saw me, informing the world of my presence by one short staccato cry. Then, wheeling away, it attempted to land on the very topmost branches of a Scots fir which grew near the lakeside some two hundred yards away. With arched neck and wildly flapping wings that great angular bird teetered back and forth until at last it secured a firm foothold. Then, with fully extended neck, it no doubt cogitated on whether it was far enough away from my boat for safety. Fascinated by the heron's antics I had forgotten the floats. Hastily glancing in their direction, I saw them, three scarlet beacons, as immobile as ever.

Rebaiting, I searched the reed edge to the other side of the boat and, although the bay was still occupied by a horde of coots – which did not augur well, for any sensible coot will make itself scarce when a huge pike is on the prowl – I had a feeling impossible to describe that I should not try pastures new.

Another hour passed, enlivened for a few

Looking for all the world as though with nothing better to do it had spawned a set of twins . . .

moments by the sight of what I then thought were whitefronted geese, whose sonorous calls were held and enclosed between one tree-lined bank and the other. They passed over, perhaps making a first reconnaissance of their winter feeding grounds after their long journey from the northern tundras. They were far more probably the rarer bean geese which still winter in the Yare Valley. I was surprised by their early arrival, but not for long; 1946/47 was one of the severest winters for generations. Even the sea froze along the coast and thick snow mantled Norfolk until April.

Common sense told me to move, but still that inner voice conselled me to stay. I compromised and promised myself a further half an hour fishing the bay. If nothing transpired, move I would. Repositioning the bung so that I could present a bait deeper, I decided to fish the open water. I selected my largest bait, a near-half-pound roach, and, although the two pilot floats were touching the tip ring and the bait hung by the rod handle, I managed to project them all at least 25 yards. The bung bobbed nicely as the bait towed it hither and thither. I unscrewed the flask, poured some coffee and placed the mug on the thwart beside me. I watched the float. It appeared to be moving to some purpose, then, before I realised the significance of the increased speed, the float actually created a wake and in a flash it was gone. The fixed pilot float disappeared down the same hole and the curve in the well greased line straightened while the second free-running pilot float wobbled and gyrated. As I grabbed the rod, the coffee mug clattered on the floorboards. I hardly noticed. The line tightened to the rod tip. Holding the reel firmly, I swept the rod up and back. That rod bent and bent full circle. It actually creaked, but made no impression on what I instinctively knew was a fish far, far larger than the 26-pounder I had caught not two weeks before. How can I describe the awesome power of that fish? Imagine being snagged in a waterlogged sack of potatoes, a sack of potatoes that moved slowly and inexorably out of the bay. I was forced to yield line,

grudgingly, a yard at a time, and as each yard left the reel the noisy check screamed in protest. I slammed the rod over, first to one side then to the other. I need not have bothered. That pike did not change direction, did not increase speed. It just moved ever onward. I applied the maximum pressure that my 12lb line would stand, to no avail whatsoever.

A kaleidoscope of impressions of those hectic moments has remained in my memory, as sharp today as they were all those years ago. My mind was in a turmoil of elation, excitement, fear and downright despair. As each second passed, and yard after yard of line left the reel, passed through the tip ring and disappeared into the lake, realisation dawned that retribution was at hand. I instinctively knew now that I was not destined to catch that fish, but even so I tried. My only hope was somehow to unhitch the bow line and then, one-handed, haul up the mud weight. I succeeded with the first. The boat yawed sideways, its bow swinging round until it was pointing towards the open water. While I was trying to break the weight free from the glutinous sucking mud I felt two juddering thumps which snatched the rod tip viciously downwards, then nothing. The floats bobbed to the surface, followed by an immense and turbulent disturbance of the surface, for all the world as if a great bubble of gas had erupted. As the surface calmed I reeled in to discover that the wire of the snap tackle had been severed. I have never encountered a pike capable of biting through wire, so how could it have broken? Always I make absolutely sure that my wire does not have even the hint of a kink, and besides, had it been kinked, it would not have stood up to such a sustained pressure for so long. I decided that somehow the trace had become snagged on some obstruction.

I retackled, moved to a new swim and fished on in a desultory manner for some twenty minutes. I had to know if it was a snag that had caused the loss of that pike. So I rowed back to the boathouse, collected the grapnel and spent perhaps an hour scouring the lake bed in the vicinity of where that great fish had been lost. I

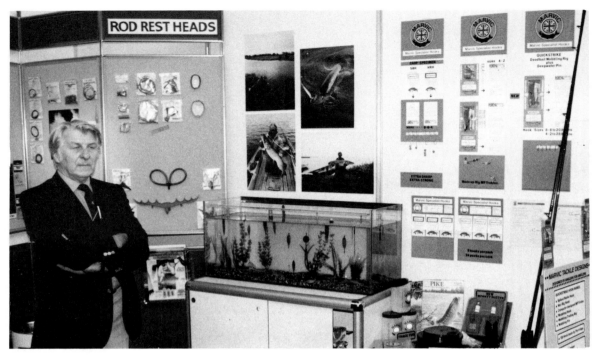

Vic at work.

found nothing. Perhaps I had missed a few inches of metal or wooden stake protruding vertically from the bottom; I shall never know.

With the greyness beginning to deepen I rowed back to the shore, secured the boat, broke down my rod, put the unused baits back in the cage, shouldered my haversack and walked towards the house and the entrance to the estate. I had walked on a few steps when I came face to face with the owner.

'How have you got on?' he asked, indicating one of the wooden seats by the lakeside.

I had forgotten that every evening he took a walk round part of the estate in company with his inseparable companion, a flaxen-coated yellow labrador bitch called Nits. We sat down and I told him all that had happened. He expressed his sympathy, but did not seem surprised.

'Yes,' he said, 'there is a huge pike in my lake. What's more, I have actually seen it. So, young man, you have managed to do what so many others have tried to do but failed. You have hooked that fish.' He paused, his eyes wandering over the lake until he was looking directly at the bay. 'Over there, you say? Some good pike have come from that spot over the years.'

I asked him to tell me about the time he had seen the great pike.

'Well,' he said, 'I like to take out a boat when the pike are by the reeds at spawning time. There is one place they particularly favour, the reedy shallows down the far end. I just let the boat drift. I have seen some whoppers, thirty pounds or more. Last spring I saw what I can only describe as a huge log of a fish. It dwarfed the rest, and there were some big pike present. It made those look like jacks in comparison.' He paused, scratched Nits behind the ears and continued. 'It must have been as long as this.' Holding his walking stick horizontally, he held his other hand at least two feet beyond the free end.

Perhaps I missed a few inches of metal or a wooden stake . . .

'But that's over five feet long,' I said. 'That's incredible.'

He continued: 'What's more, that pike was as broad across the back as Nits.'

Hearing her name Nits looked up expectantly, thumped her tail on the ground, then, realising that her master wasn't about to leave, put her muzzle between her paws and went back to sleep.

Because my companion was not an angler, who are sometimes prone to exaggeration, but a naturalist used to accurate observation of wildlife, I had no grounds to disbelieve his story. We chatted a while and watched a tree-creeper scuttling mouse-like on the trunk of an ancient oak and the huge flocks of wood-pigeons circling the woods before roosting for the night. Then he stood up and called to Nits, 'Time to go home, old girl.' Turning to me, he said, 'That was most interesting. I hope you will come and try for that pike gain.'

I thanked him and we walked to where the path forked, where I headed for one of the estate's entrance gates. As I reached it one of the keepers, also homeward bound, called out, 'Any luck?' As briefly as I could, I related yet again all that had occurred. He looked at me and, glancing at my rod, now disjointed and in two lengths, sucked his teeth. Then, in the broadest Norfolk dialect, he spoke the words I shall ever remember: 'Aah – thar's big 'ole poike in thar, bor, but yew' ont catch 'em.'

His prediction has proved entirely accurate to this very day.

Epilogue

Tension caused the line to sing in the wind as it cut through the water. A huge bow wave made purposely towards the reedbeds. The hunter reluctantly gave quarter to his quarry as the line was wrested from his reel. Two adversaries respectively locked in battle, one for his prize and the other for her freedom. Minutes passed, an eternity for our angler. There was seemingly no end to this great pike's power. Lost in the lonely little bay on the far corner of this great water, the troubles of the angler's world forgotten, the search for more food no longer of importance to the pike. Both hunters totally preoccupied in their epic struggle. Suddenly the pike sensed freedom, turned and swam through a great weedbed. Turning several times, she left the line firmly entangled and the angler's concern mounted with every tortuous grating as it reluctantly passed through both weed and coarse reed roots. Then all movement ceased. The line held fast but had, in its passage, lassoed the great body of this freshwater shark. With each struggle the line drew tighter, cut deeper into her flanks. Freedom was now out of the question. Caught by line, reed and roots, each instinctive futile struggle tightened the noose.

Our angler could not pull harder, for fear of a breakage. His line was strong but the pike was too firmly snagged. Carefully, he lifted the anchors of his small wooden boat and eased himself towards the bank and the offending reeds. As he stared, searching into the depths, in the dying embers of this bitter winter's day, at last he caught sight of his quarry, firmly trapped but beyond reach. For a second the eyes of these two hunters clashed. One full of desire and ambition, the other uncomprehending of her plight, perhaps pleading for release.

Our hunter grabbed the line between his hands, and, leaning over the side, pulled from several angles in his attempt to free the pike and land his captive.

Minutes passed. The wind sang in the reeds, much stronger now, bringing a blizzard of eye-stinging snow, which scratched relentlessly at his eyes. As the angler, facing the teeth of the wind, glanced temporarily across the great expanse of water, the severity of the conditions called out to him to hurry, to break his line, to admit defeat and retreat to safety. But no, this great pike was his, this was the fish which he had seen on several occasions before, one whose capture had become a driving ambition.

He returned to his task, to attempt once more to pull the line free, but at that very moment the boat lurched violently under the impact of a great white-crested wave. His balance lost, our hunter plunged head first into the chilling depths.

His frantic struggles snagged the line. The pike felt a sudden release as it slackened, and with freedom regained she swam slowly, warily from the roots, and for one final second the eyes of the hunters met. There was no evil contempt or malice in the cold impersonal stare of the great predator, as she glided gently away.

Our angler broke surface and grabbed the side of his boat but the cold was already taking its toll. His energy drained away and he could find no strength in his arms to draw himself back into the boat. His boots, his clothes grew heavier by the second as they became saturated. Ice-cold water continually sprayed his hands; the bitter north-east wind drove the spray horizontally so that it felt as if it was biting into his very flesh, sapping life from this fingertips,

numbing them. As he gazed desperately around there was no sanctuary, no other angler, no respite, no hope. This lonely bay would be this great hunter's retreat. His grip released, fingers slid from the gunwale and with nails grating the boat's side he sank deep down into clinging mud. As Jack Frost played in the margins death called inexorably.

Index